HOLY CITY ON THE NILE

Omdurman port, circa 1910 (SAD 792/2/174). Reproduced by kind permission of Durham University Library.

Holy City on the Nile

Omdurman during the Mahdīyya, 1885–1898

ROBERT S. KRAMER

Markus Wiener Publishers
Princeton

Cover photograph: Caretaker in the Khalifa's House Museum, Omdurman, 1936.
G. Eric and Edith Matson Photograph Collection, Library of Congress,
Prints & Photographs Division [LC-DIG-matpc-00310].

For information, write to
Markus Wiener Publishers
231 Nassau Street, Princeton, NJ 08542
www.markuswiener.com

Library of Congress Cataloging-in-Publication Data
Kramer, Robert S., 1956-
Holy city on the Nile : Omdurman during the Mahdiyya, 1885-1898 / Robert S. Kramer.
p. cm.
Includes bibliographical references and index.
ISBN 978-1-55876-515-3 (hardcover : alk. paper)
ISBN 978-1-55876-516-0 (pbk. : alk. paper)
1. Omdurman (Sudan)—History—19th century. 2. Omdurman (Sudan)—Politics and government—19th century. 3. Omdurman (Sudan)—Social conditions—19th century. 4. City and town life—Sudan—Omdurman—History—19th century. 5. Omdurman (Sudan)—Religion—19th century. 6. Mahdism—Social aspects—Sudan—Omdurman—History—19th century. 7. Jihad—Social aspects—Sudan—Omdurman—History—19th century. 8. Millennialism—Social aspects—Sudan—Omdurman—History—19th century. 9. Sudan—History—1881-1899.
I. Title.
DT159.9.O43K73 2010
962.6'2—dc22
2010027982

Markus Wiener Publishers books are printed in the United States of America on acid-free paper and meet the guidelines for permanence and durability of the Committee on Production Guidelines for Book Longevity of the Council on Library Resources.

CONTENTS

PREFACE AND ACKNOWLEDGMENTS

This book has had an unusually long gestation. Begun as a doctoral dissertation in 1986 and defended at Northwestern University in 1991, it sat on the shelf for over 15 years while life, for better or worse, intervened. In the interim I taught African and Middle Eastern history to undergraduates, and consequently revised some of my ideas while also learning to express them, I hope, more clearly. Some of my colleagues have felt frustrated waiting for this work to appear in print; I have too. I hope that it was worth the wait. In any case, the subject has never been far from my mind.

So many aspects of the Mahdist period (1881–1898) are important to the study of Sudan and the larger Islamic world: a messianic movement, erupting in a time of tremendous socioeconomic upheaval and millennial excitement, that abruptly inherited a state with all the attendant problems of statecraft; a successful Islamic revolt—the first in modern history—against a Muslim regime of foreign-backed "unbelievers"; a puritanical and absolutist New Order that nonetheless relied on the institutions and personnel of its predecessor; and a society of tremendous ethnic, cultural, and social diversity that ultimately forged the symbols of a nascent national identity. And in the midst of it all, a new city: Omdurman, "the Mahdī's city," a Sudanic town of unprecedented size that served as administrative capital, market center, popular residential site, and place of pilgrimage. All of these things should claim the attention of historians and other scholars; since the events of September 11, 2001, their importance seems to resonate more broadly and urgently.

The creation of Omdurman on the Nile and its rapid growth in size and reputation is one of the most dramatic and significant events of the Mahdīyya. Certainly both supporters and detractors of the Mahdist regime recognized Omdurman's strategic and symbolic importance, and very quickly a rich body of lore developed about it. Despite this, little has been written about it, and the present work is the first known attempt to explain Omdurman within its Sudanese context, drawing on Mahdist state archives, contemporary accounts, and oral sources.

At the heart of this study is an attempt to understand the forces that created Omdurman, the manner in which it was governed, and the social relations that prevailed within it. I have relied on the historical insights of many people, although none so obviously as the late P. M. Holt, whose magisterial history of the period, *The Mahdist State in the Sudan* (1958 and 1970), has been my constant guide (and literally lay on my bedside table in Khartoum). Holt's book is a comprehensive political and administrative history of the Mahdīyya, drawing on the rich and voluminous archives of the Mahdist state. However, as such, its interest in Omdurman is limited to matters of state development, and it is constrained by its sources to regard the city from the perspective of its rulers. This study seeks rather to understand Omdurman from the perspective of its diverse inhabitants, to provide an "internal history" of the Mahdist period. What results, I hope, is insight into the creation of what many Sudanese, but particularly those who self-identified as "Arabs," came to regard as a "holy city."

In the mid-1980s it was still possible to meet people who had lived through the events of the Mahdīyya or immediately thereafter. Two such individuals contributed important recollections to this study: ᶜAbd al-Qādir Sharīf ᶜAbdallāhi (born ca. 1895) and Sharīf ᶜAbd al-Raḥmān al-Nujūmī (born pre-1885). The latter lived in Omdurman throughout its 13 years as Mahdist capital and, due to his family's social standing, was afforded broad access to the important households of the city. Any concerns I had about Sharīf's memory—he was, after all, over 100 years old—were erased soon after meeting him, when he chided me for asking the same questions I had asked five weeks earlier. Over the 14-month period of our interviews his comments were remarkably consistent and detailed, and sometimes whimsical: He confessed once to feeling depressed because all of his friends had become senile ("*kharafū*") and he had not. Lucidity, apparently, has its price.

Many other informants helped me to understand life in Mahdist Omdurman. They were the children, grandchildren, nephews, and in one case a widow of participants in the Mahdīyya. They came from the leading families of the city—the families of the Mahdī, the Khalīfa ᶜAbdallāhi and the junior *khalīfas*, Muḥammad Sharīf and ᶜAlī wad Ḥilū—as well as the families of merchants, migrants, scholars, and soldiers. The vast majority were men, due to the norms of Sudanese society, and I confess to having learned very little firsthand about women's experiences during the Mahdīyya. The majority were also Muslims, although I was able to spend valuable time with the families of former members of the *Masālma* community: those Christians and Jews who were obliged to adopt Islam under Mahdist rule. Most of my informants came from communities that claimed an Arab identity before or during the Mahdīyya, although not all. Most resided in the Khartoum-Omdurman area, although some lived in villages along the White and Blue Niles. Most, but not all, descended from families considered legally free, although several had slave women among their forebears.

Like many researchers, I quickly discovered that patience matters more than enthusiasm: People initially were reluctant to share their information, and it was only after a months-long relationship that they felt able to reveal what they knew. Just as important, it required that length of time for them truly to understand what I was asking, and to recall what they had seen or heard; the final three months of interviews, without a doubt, were the most rewarding. Similarly, it took some time for *me* to understand what I was asking: How does one inquire about the "conditions" of Mahdist Omdurman without eliciting a trite response? Increasingly I found that when I asked people about life in Omdurman, they spoke about their families: who had married whom, from what tribe, where they had originated and where they had settled in the city, what they had done for a living. From this I developed a new understanding of the stresses and opportunities of the period, as well as an appreciation for the powerful and dynamic nature of identity during the Mahdīyya. And although it may seem a cliché, I came to regard Omdurman more as an interconnected group of families and communities, rather than a mere assemblage of zealous *jihādists*.

Ultimately what emerges is a portrait of Sudanese society, and particularly the northern Muslim Sudanese society, absorbing and accelerating the region's ongoing social changes as a result of what I have called "the Omdurman experience." Among the important aspects of that experience were rapid urbanization, the centralization of resources, an emphatic Islamic religious indoctrination, and a more pervasive Arab identity, as the religion and culture of the riverain peoples came to be regarded as normative. Hence this study's title, referring to a widely adopted ideology in a particular place. Moreover the existence of Omdurman as a religious symbol and holy place, and the widely adopted identity of Sudanese as *Anṣār al-Mahdī* (literally, "the Mahdī's Helpers"), encouraged nascent nationalist tendencies, while new marriage alliances led to the formation of a more broadly based elite. These and other aspects of Omdurman's history help to place the Mahdīyya within the larger continuum of Sudanese social change.

There is reluctance among many scholars nowadays to use the word "tribe" in reference to African history, given its racist connotations in earlier Western literature. The preferred alternative, "ethnic group," seems a bit vague, however, particularly when one is discussing (for example) both the Ja^{c}aliyīn tribe and the Nubian ethnic group. I have used the original term, as it is used by many Sudanese colleagues, as the closest approximation of the Arabic term *qabīla*. I trust that readers will perceive no pejorative intent on my part. Also, I have used the term with the understanding that many of Sudan's "tribes" in the eighteenth and nineteenth centuries were dynamic, or at least highly porous, social bodies. I might instead have viewed this chapter of Sudan's history in purely socioeconomic terms, and written of class formation; but that seemed to me to ignore some crucial aspects of Omdurman's history, and moreover to distort the way the Sudanese understood and expressed themselves. Whatever this work's flaws, I hope it will encourage further studies of the city's history.

It has been common for many years to refer to the events of 1896–1898 as the Anglo-Egyptian "Reconquest." I have never understood why. The Sudan had not previously benefited (or suffered) under Anglo-Egyptian, i.e., British, rule. It seems unnecessary and inaccurate to pretend that General Kitchener was restoring some former legitimate order when he defeated the Khalīfa's forces at Kararī. I trust that even Charles Gordon would agree with my referring instead to an Anglo-Egyptian conquest.

The transliteration of Sudanese Arabic is always a problem, and the present study claims no satisfactory solution, nor even consistency. In general, the system adopted by the *Encyclopaedia of Islam* has been followed, although (as is common) "q" has been used for the letter *qāf* and "j" has been used for the letter *jīm*. With regard to familiar place names, the common English spelling has usually been preferred over an exact rendering of the Arabic: hence "Omdurman" instead of *Umm Durmān* (or the colloquial

Umdurmān), "Khartoum" instead of *al-Kharṭūm*, etc. Less well-known place names are literally Arabicized (e.g., *Sinnār* instead of "Sennar"), unless this sharply violates Sudanese rules of pronunciation, in which case consonants are Arabicized but vowels are colloquialized: e.g. "al-Qōz" instead of *al-Qūz*, "Ab Rōf" instead of *Abū Rūf*, "al-Mōrida" instead of *al-Mawrida*, etc. As imperfect as this is, it at least avoids the infelicities of a more regular system. Likewise, the Sudanese pronunciation of names has usually been preferred over a strict Arabic rendering (e.g., ^{c}Abdallāhi instead of ^{c}Abd Allāh), although in this case too I make no claim to consistency. Mahdist titles are rendered as they are written in the historical documents: e.g., *muṣliḥīn al-sūq* instead of the grammatically correct *muṣliḥū al-suq*. Finally, both *wad* (abbrev. "w.") and *ibn* (abbrev. "b.") are used to indicate "the son of," according to Sudanese preferred usage: hence, ^{c}Abd al-Raḥmān w. al-Nujūmī and Ismā^{c}īl b. ^{c}Abd al-Qādir. The "Sudan" indicated throughout the study refers to roughly the territory of the modern Democratic Republic of the Sudan, as opposed to the larger sub-Saharan *bilād al-Sūdān*.

* * * * *

I owe a great debt to many people for their advice and support over the years, most of whom cannot be acknowledged here. My doctoral supervisor, Professor John Hunwick, helped to shape and improve this study, and gave more of his time to it than I could reasonably have expected. The staffs of the Program of African Studies and Africana Library at Northwestern University have helped in innumerable ways over the years, for which I am very grateful. Funding for my research in Sudan was generously provided by a Fulbright-Hays grant from the U.S. Department of Education and a fellowship from the Joint Committee on African Studies of the American Council of Learned Societies and the Social Science Research Council. The staffs of the Sudan Archive at the University of Durham and the Library of the School of Oriental and African Studies, University of London provided much valuable assistance during my visits there in 1987 and 1988. The office of the U.S. Information Service in Khartoum did much to support my research and make my stay in Sudan more comfortable; most particularly, I am grateful for the use of their copying machine, which may have been the only functioning one in Sudan at the time.

Innumerable Sudanist colleagues have inspired and helped me over the years, and none more so than Professor R. S. O'Fahey, who introduced me to Sudan studies in 1983 and has served as both mentor and colleague. His detailed and thoughtful response to my dissertation has served as a study guide as I prepared this book, and saved me from several errors of fact and interpretation. Like so many other students of Sudanese history, I owe him an enormous debt. I must also acknowledge Professor Jay Spaulding, whose scholarship and conference presentations I have always admired, and who has frequently challenged my analysis of events; and Dr. Albrecht Hofheinz, who has been both friend and colleague since our days together in Khartoum, and whose insights have shaped my work in many ways. I would also like to thank Dr. Māzin al-Shaykhlī, formerly of the Faculty of Law, University of Baghdad, for his many years of encouragement and assistance; Mr. Ibrāhīm Ṣāliḥ al-Shāyaʿ of the Kingdom of Saudi Arabia for his help in translating some particularly obscure verses of Mahdist poetry; and Mr. Jay Cook of the St. Norbert College Technical Support Services, whose skill and *baraka* has saved me on innumerable occasions.

To the people of Sudan I owe the greatest debt. Both the late Dr. Muḥammad Ibrāhīm Abū Salīm, *shaykh* of Mahdīyya studies, and Dr. ʿAlī Ṣāliḥ Karrār of the National Records Office (N.R.O.) in Khartoum showed me great hospitality while sharing their abundant knowledge of Sudanese history and guiding me through the vast collection of Mahdist documents at the N.R.O. Professor Sayyid Hurreiz and the late Professor Mohamed Omer Beshir of the Institute of African and Asian Studies at the University of Khartoum provided me with an important affiliation and answered many of my questions concerning Sudanese culture. Of course my research would not have been successful without the able assistance of Nowār al-Shaykh Maḥjūb, the great-granddaughter of the Mahdī, and Aḥmad Ibrāhīm Ab Shōk (now Dr. Aḥmad), who helped me in more ways than they are aware.

Needless to say, I am beholden to my many informants in Sudan. In particular I must mention Sayyid Isḥāq Muḥammad al-Khalīfa Sharīf, Sayyid ʿAlī Yaʿqūb al-Khalīfa Ḥilū, and Sayyid Muḥammad Daʿūd al-Khalīfa, as well as Yūsuf Bedrī, Sharīf ʿAbd al-Raḥmān al-Nujūmī, ʿAbbās Aḥmad Muḥammad Qadaḥ al-Dām, al-Tijānī ʿAmr, ʿAlī Ṣiddīq w. Ūru, ʿUmar Ḥasan al-Ṭayyib Hāshim, Āmina bt. Farajallāh Yūsuf, al-Jīlānī Khidr ʿAbdallāhi, al-Ṭāhir Muḥammad al-Nayl, Zaynab ^{c}Abd al-Qādir Bān Naqā, and Allegra Basyūnī. Those who have done research in Sudan will understand the enormous gratitude and deep affection I feel for these people, who freely shared their knowledge and opened up their homes to me.

Finally, for all they have done for me and all that they mean to me, this work is dedicated to my Three Pleiades: Nancy, Vicky, and Allegra.

ABBREVIATIONS

Al-Āthār al-Kāmila	M. I. Abū Salīm (ed.), *al-Āthār al-Kāmila li'l-Imām al-Mahdī* (Khartoum: 1990–1994), 7 volumes. The collected writings and pronouncements of the Mahdī.
CAIRINT	Archive of the Egyptian Military Intelligence Office at the National Records Office, Khartoum.
Daftar al-Ṣādir	Letter registers of the Mahdī and Khalīfa in the Mahdist archive (MAHDIA 3) at the National Records Office, Khartoum.
E.M.I.	Egyptian Military Intelligence (from 1892, The Department of Military Intelligence), which produced periodical reports on the Sudan from 1885 onwards.
I.R.E.	*Intelligence Report Egypt.* Periodical reports produced by the Egyptian Military Intelligence from 1885 to1898.
MAHDIA	Archive of the Mahdist State at the National Records Office, Khartoum.
N.R.O.	National Records Office, Khartoum.
PMH	P. M. Holt Papers, Library of the School of Oriental and African Studies, University of London.
P.R.O.	Public Records Office, London.
S.A.D.	Sudan Archive, University of Durham.
S.I.R.	*Sudan Intelligence Report 60 (25 May–31 December 1898).* An Intelligence Report prepared by E.M.I. after the Anglo-Egyptian conquest.
S.N.R.	*Sudan Notes and Records.*
S.O.A.S.	School of Oriental and African Studies, University of London.

MAPS OF OMDURMAN

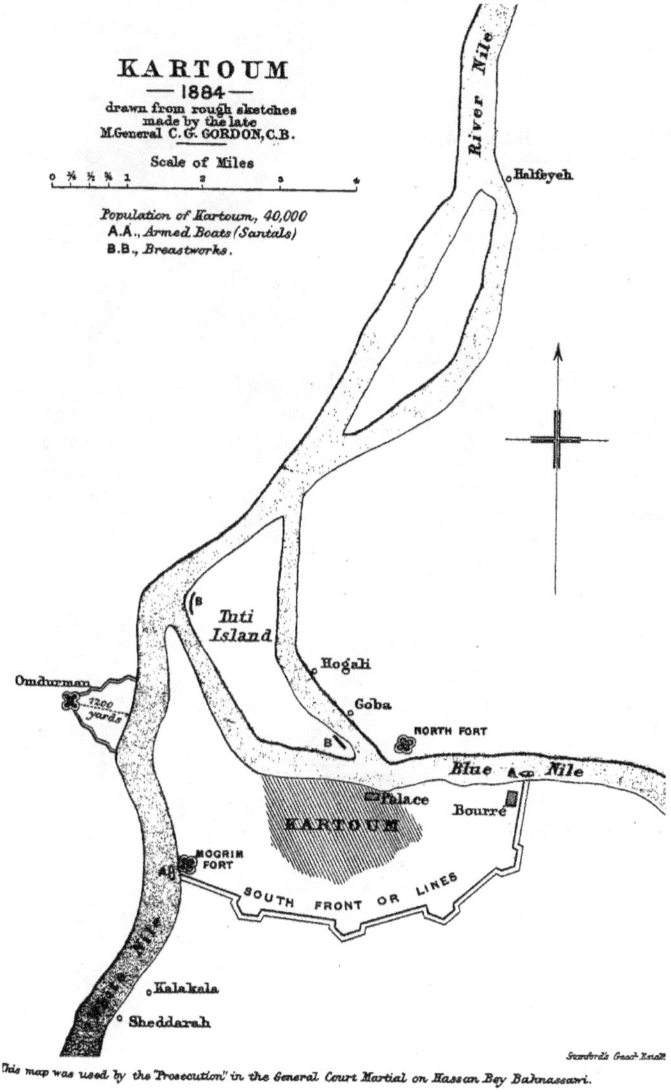

Map 1. Kartoum 1884. A map of Khartoum and its environs. From F. R. Wingate, *Mahdiism and the Egyptian Sudan* (London: 1891, 1968). In the upper left corner is written: "drawn from rough sketches made by the late M.General C.G. Gordon, C.B." (Gordon was the British governor-general of Sudan killed at Khartoum in January 1885.)

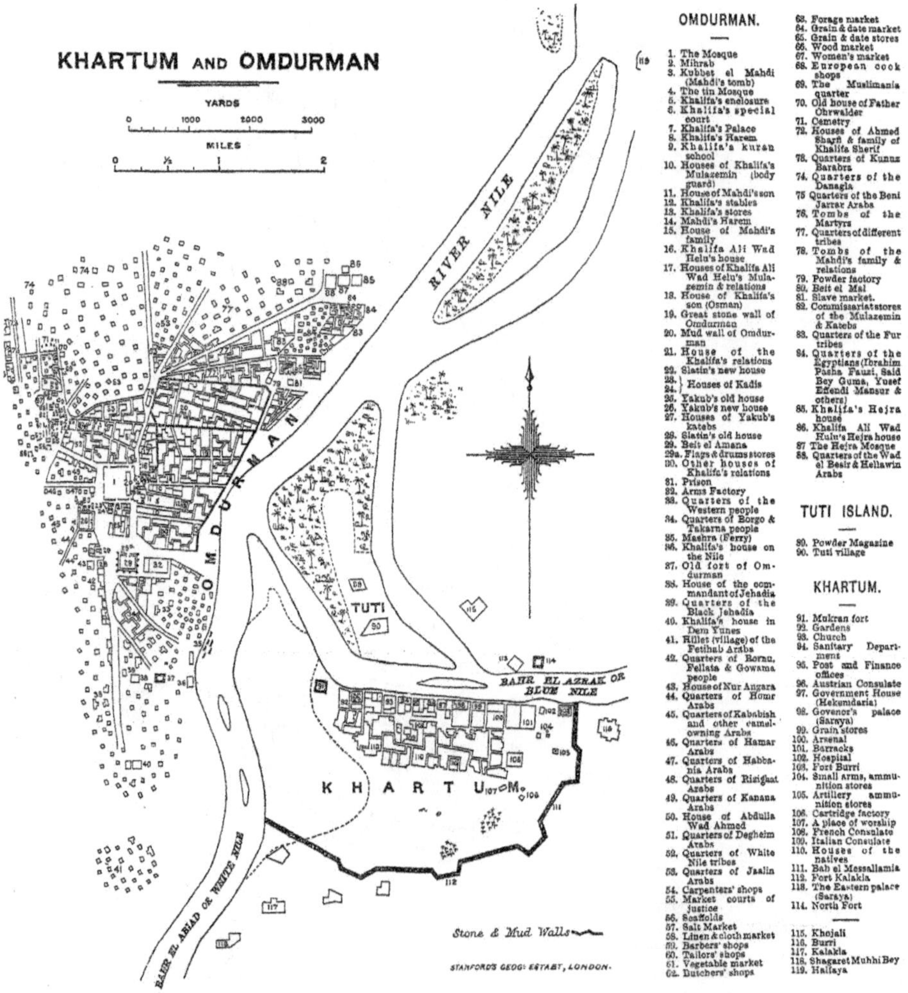
KHARTUM AND OMDURMAN
YARDS
0 1000 2000 3000
MILES
0 ½ 1 2
RIVER NILE
OMDURMAN
TUTI
BAHR EL AZRAK OR BLUE NILE
KHARTUM
BAHR EL ABIAD OR WHITE NILE
Stone & Mud Walls
STANFORD'S GEOG^L ESTAB^T, LONDON.
OMDURMAN.
1. The Mosque
2. Mihrab
3. Kubbet el Mahdi (Mahdi's tomb)
4. The tin Mosque
5. Khalifa's enclosure
6. Khalifa's special court
7. Khalifa's Palace
8. Khalifa's Harem
9. Khalifa's kuran school
10. Houses of Khalifa's Mulazemin (body guard)
11. House of Mahdi's son
12. Khalifa's stables
13. Khalifa's stores
14. Mahdi's Harem
15. House of Mahdi's family
16. Khalifa Ali Wad Helu's house
17. Houses of Khalifa Ali Wad Helu's Mulazemin & relations
18. House of Khalifa's son (Osman)
19. Great stone wall of Omdurman
20. Mud wall of Omdurman
21. House of the Khalifa's relations
22. Slatin's new house
23. 24. } Houses of Kadis
25. Yakub's old house
26. Yakub's new house
27. Houses of Yakub's katebs
28. Slatin's old house
29. Beit el Amana
29a. Flags & drums stores
30. Other houses of Khalifa's relations
31. Prison
32. Arms Factory
33. Quarters of the Western people
34. Quarters of Borgo & Takarna people
35. Mashra (Ferry)
36. Khalifa's house on the Nile
37. Old fort of Omdurman
38. House of the commandant of Jehadia
39. Quarters of the Black Jehadia
40. Khalifa's house in Dem Yunes
41. Hillet (village) of the Fetihab Arabs
42. Quarters of Bornu, Fellata & Gowama people
43. House of Nur Angara
44. Quarters of Homr Arabs
45. Quarters of Kababish and other camel-owning Arabs
46. Quarters of Hamar Arabs
47. Quarters of Habbania Arabs
48. Quarters of Rizighat Arabs
49. Quarters of Kanana Arabs
50. House of Abdulla Wad Ahmed
51. Quarters of Degheim Arabs
52. Quarters of White Nile tribes
53. Quarters of Jaalin Arabs
54. Carpenters' shops
55. Market courts of justice
56. Scaffolds
57. Salt Market
58. Linen & cloth market
59. Barbers' shops
60. Tailors' shops
61. Vegetable market
62. Butchers' shops
63. Forage market
64. Grain & date market
65. Grain & date stores
66. Wood market
67. Women's market
68. European cook shops
69. The Muslimania quarter
70. Old house of Father Ohrwalder
71. Cemetry
72. Houses of Ahmed Sharfi & family of Khalifa Sherif
73. Quarters of Kunuz Barabra
74. Quarters of the Danagla
75 Quarters of the Beni Jarrar Arabs
76. Tombs of the Martyrs
77. Quarters of different tribes
78. Tombs of the Mahdi's family & relations
79. Powder factory
80. Beit el Mal
81. Slave market.
82. Commissariat stores of the Mulazemin & Katebs
83. Quarters of the Fur tribes
84. Quarters of the Egyptians (Ibrahim Pasha Fauzi, Said Bey Guma, Yusef Effendi Mansur & others)
85. Khalifa's Hejra house
86. Khalifa Ali Wad Hulu's Hejra house
87 The Hejra Mosque
88. Quarters of the Wad el Besir & Hellawin Arabs
TUTI ISLAND.
89. Powder Magazine
90. Tuti village
KHARTUM.
91. Mukran fort
92. Gardens
93. Church
94. Sanitary Department
95. Post and Finance offices
96. Austrian Consulate
97. Government House (Hekemdaria)
98. Govenor's palace (Saraya)
99. Grain stores
100. Arsenal
101. Barracks
102. Hospital
103. Fort Burri
104. Small arms, ammunition stores
105. Artillery ammunition stores
106. Cartridge factory
107. A place of worship
108. French Consulate
109. Italian Consulate
110. Houses of the natives
111. Bab el Messallamia
112. Fort Kalakla
113. The Eastern palace (Saraya)
114. North Fort
115. Khojali
116. Burri
117. Kalakla
118. Shagaret Muhhi Bey
119. Halfaya

Map 2. Khartum and Omdurman. From F. R. Wingate/Rudolf C. Slatin, *Fire and Sword in the Sudan*, 2nd ed. (London: 1896). This map is based on information supplied by Slatin to the Egyptian Military Intelligence department. Wingate was the director of Egyptian Military Intelligence from 1889 to 1899.

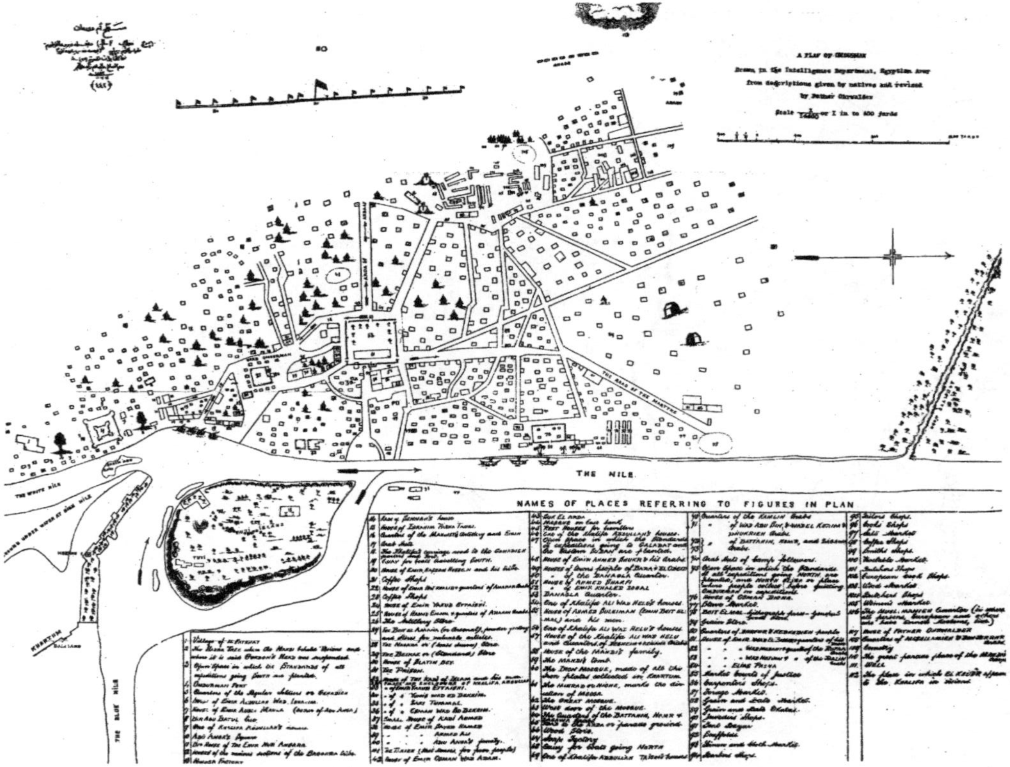

Map 3. A Plan of Omdurman. From F. R. Wingate/Fr. Joseph Ohrwalder, *Ten Years' Captivity in the Mahdi's Camp*, 3rd ed. (London: 1892). In the upper right corner is written: "Drawn in the Intelligence Department, Egyptian Army, from descriptions given by natives and revised by Father Ohrwalder."

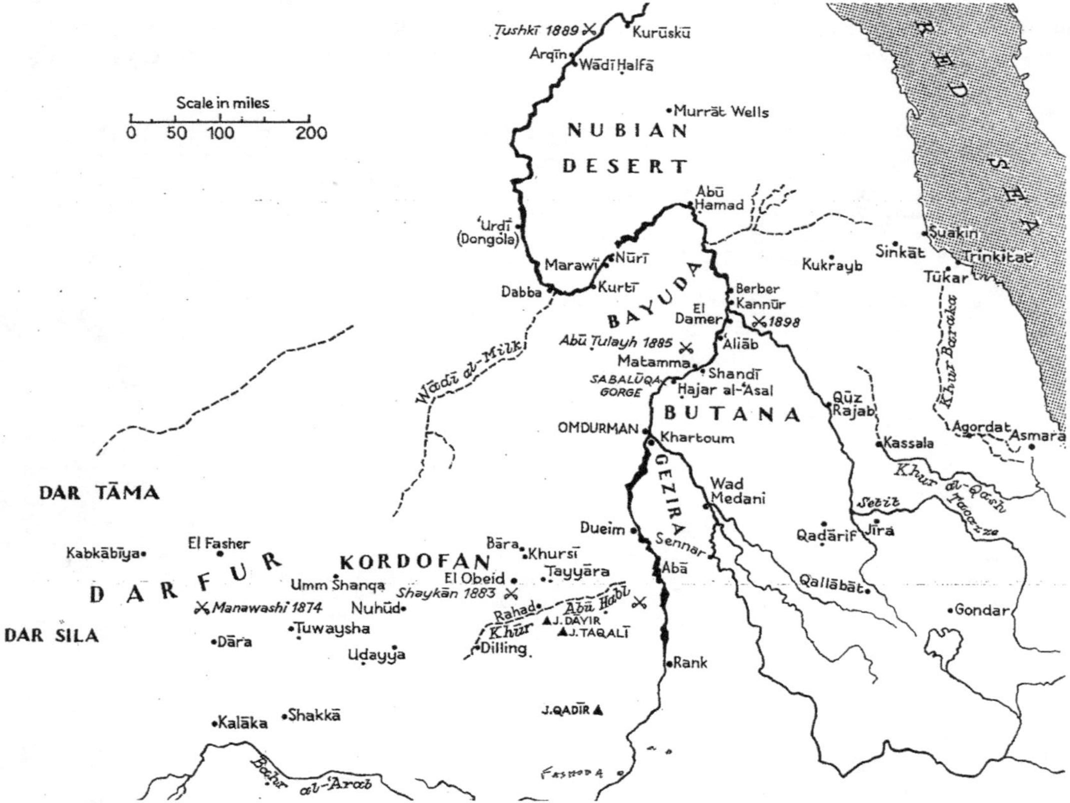

Map 4. Sudan during the Mahdist period. From P. M. Holt, *The Mahdist State in the Sudan*, 2nd ed. (Oxford: Oxford University Press, 1958, 1970). Used with permission of the estate of P. M. Holt.

CHAPTER ONE

Towns in the Sudan

"There is no distinction made in these countries between villages and towns," wrote the Swiss traveler John Lewis Burckhardt of his 1814 visit to the Sudan. "Every inhabited place of any size is called Beled, and a small hamlet Nezle. The word Medineh (city) is never applied to any place in this part of Soudan." Although he was later to describe in some detail the vibrant trade of Shendī and the Red Sea port of Suakin, and although his exposure to the Sudan was somewhat limited, Burckhardt's observation was still valid; for the northern Nilotic Sudan had not long before emerged from an era of what scholars have called "a series of old agrarian states without cities." Certainly the great city of Sōba, capital of the Christian state of Alodia for so many centuries, had long since faded into obscurity. The fifteenth-century Arab historian al-Maqrīzī had described it as having "fine buildings, spacious dwellings, churches with much gold, and gardens," but by the time David Reubeni saw it in 1523 it contained little more than a few huts. For the rest of the Nile valley, it was in the eyes of Burckhardt and other Europeans a monotony of "miserable villages" with nothing that reminded them of a metropolitan area.[1]

Unbeknownst to Burckhardt and others, profound changes were remaking the social and economic environment of the eastern Sudan. The Funj state of Sinnār, successor to the earlier Nubian kingdoms, had arisen in the early sixteenth century between the Blue and White Niles, while far to the west around the Jabal Marra range of Darfur (*Dār Fūr*, "the realm of the Fūr") the Keira state had come to power a century and a half later. Both were controlled by all-powerful dynastic rulers who, with a noble class, monopolized long-distance trade and slave labor while commanding the economy of their respective regions. Beginning in the late seventeenth century, a series of developments unfolded that were to challenge and then change the old order. In Sinnār in particular, the growth of a merchant community with an avowedly Muslim and Arab identity and lucrative trade contacts encouraged the rise of, among other things, an independent Islamic judiciary and coin currencies. The eighteenth century saw the proliferation of "bustling little merchants' towns" throughout the region, the further growth of a merchant class with Islam and capitalism as its guiding lights, and the evaluation of both land and human relationships in monetary terms. By the time of Burckhardt's visit the Funj state was moribund, its royal institutions eroded from within and its power diminished by civil war. Six years later in 1820 the Egyptian viceroy Meḥmet ᶜAlī launched an invasion of the Sudan in search of slaves and gold. An army led by his son Ismāᶜīl entered the city of Sinnār without resistance one year later, and by 1822 the Turco-Egyptian occupation of the Nile territory was complete. Over the next 60 years Sudan's transformation was to accelerate, including the imposition of cash-based taxes, destabilizing population movements, an increased reliance upon slave labor, and the treatment of land as private property. Authority now emanated from the colonial capital of Khartoum, at the confluence of the two Niles and not far from the old city of Sōba. Then, beginning in 1881, a combination of forces made possible the rise to power of Muḥammad Aḥmad al-Mahdī and the creation of a new, and in some ways decidedly old, order.[2]

Long before Burckhardt's arrival however, the Funj realm contained two towns that came to command both regional and international attention. The Sudanese historical account known as *The Funj Chronicle*, compiled from 1504 to 1871, states that after 900 AH (i.e., 910/1504–1505) the Funj "laid out the city of Sinnār. ᶜAmāra Dūnqas laid it out, and he was the first of them. The town of Arbajī was laid out thirty years previously." While both sites were places of trade, there was an important difference between them: Sinnār was made the seat of the ruler's treasury, the place of "royal exchange," but not initially the royal capital until a century had passed. (Only later did it give its name to the kingdom as a whole, "developing by 1700 into a town.") This suggests, according to one scholar, "that the royal institution was already concerned with trade." Most of Sinnār's trading partners were Muslim, and before long the Funj would adopt Islam—and with it, the use of the Arabic language—for both commercial and strategic reasons. As Sinnār grew steadily, Arbajī became an entrepôt of foreign trade conducted by private merchants who "formed a distinct community within the kingdom," enjoying a degree of self-government as well as special status. Among the indigenous Sudanese merchant community, the Beja of the Red Sea region came to dominate—reasserting their earlier, pre-Funj trading dominance—such that by the eighteenth century, "all Sudanese traders who were not Funj were known to their neighbors in Sinnār as *ḥuḍūr*," a variant of the Beja tribal name "Ḥaḍāriba." The difference in function between Sinnār and Arbajī is noteworthy. Interstate trade in the eastern Sudan ordinarily did not occur in the marketplace of the capital: "This difference in physical setting was only one of several institutional usages which distinguished foreign commerce from the regional level of exchange as practiced in the king's city."[3]

Travelers have left valuable descriptions of these towns. The French Jesuit Charles Brévedent, who visited Sudan in 1699, described Arbajī as "large but thinly inhabited, abounding in all provisions." His companion Charles Poncet more expansively wrote of Sinnār: "This city, which contains near a league and a half in compass, is very populous.... They number in it near a hundred thousand souls. The houses are only one story high and are ill built; but the flat roof which covers them is very convenient.... All things are very cheap at Sennar. A camel costs not above seven or eight *livers*, an ox fifty pence, a sheep fifteen, and a hen a penny.... They keep a market every day in the middle of the town where they sell all sorts of provisions and goods. They also have another before the King's palace. 'Tis in this market that they expose their slaves to sale." Unquestionably the most important and comprehensive account of Sinnār belongs to the German Franciscan Theodor Krump, who visited Sudan from 1700 to1702. En route to the capital, Krump stopped at Arbajī, which he called "a fine, attractive place where all the *jallabs* [merchants] cross the river Nile." Furthermore, "in this Funj kingdom there are some large and populous towns, whereas in the kingdom of Nubia there is scarcely more than a few houses standing next to each other along the river." After describing the royal palace complex ("which one could circumambulate in about three-quarters of an hour"), Krump begins his description of the city of Sinnār.

> One should know that in all Africa, as far as the Moorish lands are concerned, Sinnār is close to being the greatest trading city. Caravans are continually arriving from Cairo, Dongola, Nubia, from across the Red Sea, from India, Ethiopia, [Dār] Fūr, Borno, the Fezzan, and other kingdoms. This is a free city, and men of any nationality or faith may live in it without a single hindrance. After Cairo, it is one of the most populous cities. Every day a public market is held in the square in the best possible order, with various merchants and wares that are to be sold. In one place there are trade goods, in another elephant's teeth, in others are camels, horses, donkeys, wood, onions, dates, wheat and *dhurra* [millet] from which they bake bread and with which they also feed cattle. Here are straw, cane for the camels, meat, chickens, wood and similar things, each being bought and sold in its special place. Furthermore, every day at the public market human beings who are slaves—men and women of every age—are sold like cattle.

After a discussion of various subjects (slave sales, the royal succession, tribute from the subordinate ruler of Qarrī, etc.), Krump describes Sinnār's various forms of currency, noting "there is another sort of coinage in the Funj kingdom, and no less in the kingdom of Nubia, and indeed in all of Africa among the Moors. This consists of a piece of cotton cloth twenty-four arms long and two spans wide. The Arabs, in their language, call this *tōb dammūr*." Some seventy years later, the Scottish traveler James Bruce visited Sinnār when it was well into its decline, yet reported that "the town is very populous, containing many good houses after the fashion of the country. They are built of clay, and are mostly of one storey, though the great officers have all houses of two." On his return to Egypt Bruce stayed two days at Arbajī, which he found "a large, pleasant village" with an "abundance of provisions." Eleven years later (1783–1784), Arbajī was razed to the ground by the ᶜAbdallāb ruler Muḥammad al-Amīn. *The Funj Chronicle* eulogized it as "a town full of beautiful buildings, pleasant for cultivation and trade, sophisticated in food and drink. In it were pious men and schools of learning and the Qur'ān. Those who were there tell of its marvels." A similar postmortem account, this of Sinnār, is provided by the American adventurer George English, who accompanied Ismāᶜīl's army into the city in 1821, and observed—amid the ruins—that Sinnnār's mosque "is of brick, is in good preservation; its windows are covered with well-wrought bronze gratings, and the doors are handsomely and curiously carved." English estimated the city to have been "about three miles" in circumference, with many homes of fired or sun-dried brick and rarely more than one story in height. He reiterated: "What struck me most was the workmanship of the doors of the old houses of Sennaar, which are composed of planed and jointed planks, adorned frequently with carved work, and strengthened and studded with very broad-headed nails: the whole inimitable by the present population of Sennaar."[4]

Elsewhere, to the north of Sinnār and Arbajī, were to be found a number of important towns and villages along the Nile. Traditions attribute the political unification of the northern Nilotic Sudan to ᶜAbdallāh Jammāᶜ, a late fifteenth-century Arab leader allied with the Ḥaḍāriba of the Red Sea region. ᶜAbdallāh is said to have made his capital at Qarrī on the Nile, just below the confluence, before conquering the Christian Nubians (the so-called ᶜAnaj) to the south. It was under his rule allegedly that Arbajī was founded as a trading center, marking the southern limit of a unified realm that his descendants—known as the ᶜAbdallāb and bearing the title of *mānjil* (viceroy)—would govern under the Funj kings. Over time Qarrī became an important center of political power, dominating the smaller kingdoms of Nubia to the north. Although it was certainly not a city, it was an important (and presumably wealthy) customs post controlling the caravan trade from Egypt and Suakin into Sinnār. In 1699 Qarrī appeared to Brévedent as "a large village." Krump had little to say about it, other than its surroundings were "like a beautiful garden in which the finest crops and fruit trees had been planted." Bruce estimated that it contained "about 140 houses, none of them above one storey high, neat, well-built, flat-roofed, and all of one height." Perhaps in the late eighteenth century, the ᶜAbdallāb capital shifted south to Ḥalfāya at the Nile confluence, a long-inhabited place with a larger population and an economy based on the weaving of *dammūr* cloth; henceforth it was to be known as Ḥalfāyat al-Mulūk, "Ḥalfāya of the Kings." Krump described it as "a fine large place. The houses are similar in nature to those of Nubia, but somewhat finer—larger, cleaner and also smoother from their coatings of dung." Bruce called it "a large and pleasant town" and estimated there to be "about 300" houses there. In 1821, when the ᶜAbdallāb *shaykh* surrendered to Ismāᶜīl and the Egyptians there, the French traveler Frédéric Cailliaud claimed Ḥalfāya's population had been reduced by warfare from "eight or nine thousand to three or four thousand." Moreover its houses covered an area "not less than four miles in circumference." There were no regular streets, he wrote; the houses were built of clay and "only two or three" had an upper story.[5]

Downriver from Qarrī lay Shendī, an important market town at the junction of caravan routes west to Kordofan and Darfur, south to Sinnār, and north to Egypt. "Shendī," one writer asserted, "was not merely a provincial capital like Dongola or Berber; it was a metropolis of commerce whose connections reached from the shores of Lake Chad to Arabia and India and from Egypt and Europe to Abyssinia. It was the largest town in the eastern Sudan, the entrepôt of trade between Sennar, Kordofan, and Darfur in one direction and Cairo, Mecca, Abyssinia, and India in the others." Bruce was characteristically unimpressed when he visited, calling it merely "a large village, the capital of its district," consisting of "about 250 houses, some of them tolerable dwellings." A little over 40 years later however, Burckhardt had a great deal to say.

> Next to Sennaar and Kobbé (in Darfour), Shendy is the largest town in eastern Soudan, and larger, according to the report of the merchants, than the capitals of Dongola and Kordofan. It consists of several quarters, divided from each other by public places or markets, and it contains altogether from eight hundred to a thousand houses.... Its houses are similar to those of Berber, but it contains a greater number of large buildings and fewer ruins. The houses seldom form any regular street, but are spread over the plain in great disorder. I nowhere saw any walls of burnt bricks. The houses of the chief, and those of his relatives, contain courtyards twenty feet square, enclosed by high walls.... The government of Shendy is much to be preferred to that of Berber: the full authority of the Mek is not thwarted by the influence of powerful families.... His absolute power is owing to the diversity of Arab tribes inhabiting Shendy, none of which is strong enough to cope with his own family and its numerous branches.... The most respectable class of the inhabitants of Shendy are the merchants, amongst whom are great numbers of foreign settlers from Sennaar, Kordofan, Darfour and Dongola: the last are the most numerous, and they occupy an entire quarter of the town.

Burckhardt noted that the ruler (entitled *makk*) united "all branches of authority in his own person," aided by his relatives, "half a dozen police officers, a writer, an Imam, a treasurer, and a body-guard formed principally of slaves." The people of Shendī, he observed, were better dressed with cleaner clothes, and also wealthier, wearing more gold and owning more slaves, than the people of Berber. The trade of Shendī receives the greatest emphasis: "Commerce flourishes at Shendy because the Mek does not extort any taxes from the merchants," and Burckhardt discusses this commerce—the natural resources, agricultural and animal wealth, the market organization and currencies, the numerous imported goods from near and far, the handicrafts and manufactured items, etc.—in great detail. By way of explanation, he writes that "I have extended my remarks upon commerce to so great a length because it is the very life of society in these countries. There is not a single family which is not connected, more or less, with some branch of traffic, either wholesale or retail, and the people of Berber and Shendy appear to be a nation of traders." Otherwise, Burckhardt comments upon "the character of the people" (he was struck by their "drunkenness and debauchery"); the different ethnic and tribal groups represented in Shendī, especially the people of Dongola ("the most acute and intelligent traders of this part of the country") and the Ḥaḍāriba from Suakin ("the richest and most numerous" traders); and the complexities of the Egyptian and Arabian slave trades. Shendī was at its height when Burckhardt visited. Nine years later, in 1823, the town was utterly destroyed by Muḥammad Khusraw, son-in-law of Meḥmet ᶜAlī, to avenge the assassination of Ismāᶜīl by Shendī's ruler, *Makk* Nimr, a year previous. By the time the American traveler Bayard Taylor arrived in 1852, Shendī appeared in shambles—the only "decent dwelling" belonged to a merchant of Dongola—and its only foreign trade was with Arabia by way of Suakin. Taylor guessed (somewhat wildly) the town "probably does not contain more than ten thousand inhabitants."[6]

Downriver from Shendī, before the Nile's confluence with the ᶜAṭbarā, lay the town of al-Dāmir, a place of some economic importance but better known for the Majdhūb (pl. Majādhīb) religious family, whose reputation for sanctity and learning was considerable. During Funj times, al-Dāmir had been "an autonomous community of holy men…the best documented of a great number of similar religious communities, large and small," that stretched along the Nile. Moreover, such communities were exempt from taxes and other state obligations, "nor were royal officials even permitted to enter [them] without permission." Most interesting from the standpoint of governance, al-Dāmir was "a haven for debtors, who could seek asylum, repudiate old obligations and start a new life there. The community kept its own stores of grain, and manipulated food prices to the benefit of the peasants." Burckhardt spent five days there in 1814 and wrote a favorable account of what he called "this little hierarchical state." Al-Dāmir appeared to him as "a large village or town containing about five hundred houses. It is clean and much neater than Berber, having many new buildings and no ruins. The houses are built with some uniformity, in regular streets, and shady trees are met with in several places.... Here are several schools, to which young men repair from Darfour, Sennaar, Kordofan, and other parts of Soudan, in order to acquire a proficiency in the law." Unlike Shendī, al-Dāmir had a mosque when Burckhardt visited: "it rests upon arches built of bricks, and the floor is covered with fine sand. This is the coolest spot in Damer, and much resorted to by strangers to pass a few hours in sleep after the mid-day prayers. Around an open place adjoining the mosque are a number of school rooms. Many *Fakys* [i.e., holy men] have small chapels near their own houses, but the Friday prayers are always performed in the great mosque." Burckhardt noted that agriculture flourished in al-Dāmir to a greater degree than in any other place between Dongola and Shendī, with irrigated fields producing two crops a year. Among their crops he listed *dhurra*, wheat, okra, peppers, "plentiful" cotton, and tobacco. Likewise al-Dāmir was known for its weaving of *dammūr* cloth—it is possible that the cloth acquired its name from the town—and as a place of trade, with caravans passing to Suakin and between Dongola and Shendī. (Al-Dāmir imposed no customs duties, and this helped attract caravans to the town.) Although the Majādhīb were described as men of tremendous piety and austerity, with reputations that kept the nomadic Arabs "in awe of them," Burckhardt was surprised to discover the usual "bouza shops and houses of debauchery" in al-Dāmir that he had encountered elsewhere in Sudan. Apparently even holy men in charge of small hierarchical states had limits to their authority.[7]

Below the Nile's confluence with the ᶜAṭbarā lay the town of Berber, which consisted of four distinct villages, each with its own name. Burckhardt wrote that the dominant population were the Mīrafāb, a tribe within the larger Jaᶜaliyīn group, but that "many strangers" had settled there as well, especially natives of Dongola and ᶜAbābda nomads from the Nubian desert. Each village, he noted, was divided into "about a dozen quarters," with houses divided by large courtyards, "thus forming no where any regular streets." The houses were "tolerably well-built," of mud or sun-baked bricks, consisting of an inner and outer court around which were grouped rooms for the family, for storage and for receiving guests. (Another room was said to be "often occupied by public women.") Somewhat contradictorily, Burckhardt describes the people of Berber as "very handsome," whose complexion varies according to whether their mother is Ethiopian or "from the Negro countries," but then asserts that the Mīrafāb "are careful in maintaining the purity of their race. A free born Meyrefab never marries a slave, whether Abyssinian or black, but always an Arab girl of his own or some neighboring tribe." (Children conceived with concubines apparently were unacknowledged. Likely they were numerous too, since "everyone who can afford it keeps a slave or mistress either in his own or in a separate house.") After an account of the Berber economy, Burckhardt mentions that "almost all the people" engage in trade: "The place has thus become a principal mart for the southern trade, and the more so, as all the caravans from Sennaar and Shendy to Egypt necessarily pass here." Despite Berber's higher prices, some Egyptian merchants were said to prefer it to the cheaper and more considerable trade of Shendī, since they could more quickly conclude their business and return home across the desert.[8]

West of the Nile lay the vast region of Kordofan, home to a large number of ethnic and tribal groups. These included, among the Arabs, the camel herders *(Jammāla)* of the north and cattle herders (*Baqqāra*) of the south, a sedentary population of farmers, plus merchants (the so-called *jallāba*) who had migrated from the riverain Sudan. In the mountainous region of the south lived the Nūba people, ethnically and linguistically distinct from the Arabs. In one part of the Nūba mountains, the independent kingdom of Taqalī, the rulers had adopted Islam and Arabic by the seventeenth century and forged commercial ties with Sinnār. Later, as a result of their marriage alliances with the Funj, the ruling elite of Taqalī came to regard themselves as Funj. Politically, some type of authority was exercised over the nomadic tribes of Kordofan by the ᶜAbdallāb *mānjils* of Qarrī early in the eighteenth century, although for most of that century elements of the Fūr and the Funj vied for control of Kordofan. At stake was the valuable trade in slaves, gum, and gold that passed through the towns of El Obeid and Bāra, which had only recently been established by merchants from the Danāqla and other riverain tribes. In 1782 the Keira sultan Tayrāb finally succeeded in conquering Kordofan, leading to almost 40 years of Fūr rule until Muḥammad Khusraw made it a part of the Turco-Egyptian Sudan in 1821.[9]

The Austrian trader Ignatius Pallme visited Kordofan in 1838–1839 and wrote an account of his stay. El Obeid, like the earlier description of Berber, was said to consist of several villages, each similar in appearance and arrangement to the others. (Pallme did not see the original eighteenth-century town, which was destroyed by Muḥammad Khusraw, but rather a rebuilt town on the original site.) Each "village"—they were not separated to any great extent—comprised a quarter inhabited by a distinct population. He identifies them as "Wady Naghele," consisting of the Danāqla and "foreign merchants" (mostly other riverain Sudanese), who were the original townspeople of El Obeid; "El Orta" ("The Camp," also called "the town of the Turks"), consisting of government buildings, soldiers' barracks, officers' quarters, the arsenal and hospital, as well as the town's market place and only café (shunned by most Sudanese but considered "indispensable to the Turkish officers"); "Wady Soffie," consisting of "the negroes who had immigrated with the Melik Moussalem" (i.e., Musallim, the last Fūr governor of Kordofan); "Takarir," consisting of pilgrims from western Sudanic territories such as Bornu, as well as the home of Muḥammad Abū Madyan, a claimant to the throne of Darfur; "Kongeri" (i.e., Kunjara), emigrants from Darfur; and "Mogghrebeen," a name applied to the irregular cavalry of Muḥammad Khusraw, implying—not always accurately—Moroccan/North African origin. (These, Pallme wrote, "are not provided with barracks and have built their own dwellings.") The total population of El Obeid, exclusive of the military, was estimated to be 12,000 people; a large percentage must have been slaves, as Pallme observed that "slaves are met with in nearly every house." While there were five mosques in El Obeid, the only one built of brick was in the quarter of the Danāqla merchants. The houses were either round *tukls* of wood and straw or mud-built, flat-roofed homes, although in both El Obeid and Bāra it was possible to find "several spacious residences" belonging to the Turks or Danāqla. (Houses at Bāra, where more of the long-distance trade was concentrated, were said to be "more substantially built.") Even the home of the governor was of simple mud construction, although larger and more comfortable than the rest, since ultimately "there was no choice of material." The "Turks" of Pallme's account were, as usual in Sudan, Egyptians, including a cadre of Coptic secretaries, although the governor at the time was an Ottoman Circassian.[10]

The marketplace, located near the government buildings, was divided according to wares. One area was reserved for domestic animals (camels, cows, sheep, etc.) and grain, another for the riverain merchants with imported goods from Cairo, another for water dealers, and yet another for sellers of wood and straw. At either end of the market was an area specific to women merchants, who sold dairy products, lard, fruit, eggs, and tobacco-pipe bowls, which presumably they crafted. Peddlers of old clothing and other items also inhabited the market, selling their goods by auction. Additionally a slave market was conducted daily, consisting of slaves captured from the Nūba and other generally non-Muslim peoples, this being linked to the larger slave market of Cairo. While Pallme's impression of El Obeid was mostly unflattering—"dismal" and "dull" were two of his more common descriptions—he found interesting "the concourse of men from the most distant parts of Africa, even from Timbuctoo, and other negro states as yet totally unknown to Europeans." Likewise he recognized the complexity of things, calling the Danāqla "the most rigid observers of the Mahommedan religion" but also "very fond of brandy."[11]

Beyond Kordofan to the west lay the region of Darfur, ruled by the Keira sultans since the middle of the seventeenth century and only conquered on behalf of the Turco-Egyptian Sudan in 1874. Around 1791–1792, the Sultan ᶜAbd al-Raḥmān had created a permanent capital at al-Fāshir, northeast of the Fūr homeland of Jabal Marra, during a time when "centralizing forces and the Islamizing influences were being rapidly consolidated." One scholar has noted that "Given the position of the sultan, it followed naturally that the physical centre of the Keira sultanate was the *fāshir* or sultan's residence, whose lay-out illustrated succinctly the political and spiritual order within the state." While this *fāshir* was "still basically structured as the residence of a divine king," it was also "to some degree modified by the needs of the new Islamic order." Similar to the arrangement of Sinnār and Arbajī, the commercial center of Darfur was located not in al-Fāshir but in the town of Kobbei to the north, which was the starting point for the famous *Darb al-Arba*ᶜ*īn* ("Forty Days Road") across the desert to Asyūṭ in Egypt. This route carried the long-distance trade of both private merchants and the sultan who, like the ruler of Sinnār, enforced a monopoly on certain goods and collected customs dues.[12]

The British traveler W. G. Browne followed a caravan from Egypt to Kobbei in 1793 and spent three years in Darfur before returning by the same route. He describes Kobbei, which he calls "the chief residence of foreign merchants," as more than two miles long and very narrow, consisting of large, flat-roofed houses adjacent to cultivated plots. On four sides of Kobbei were "dependent villages," one of which he identifies as Ḥillat Ḥasan, named for the *khabīr* (leading merchant or caravan leader) Ḥasan wallad Naṣr and "inhabited altogether" by Danāqla. It is unclear from Browne's account if the other three villages were also tribally or ethnically specific. "Very few houses, perhaps none" were inhabited by Fūr people, since the residents of Kobbei were all merchants and foreigners. Specifically, these were Sudanese "from the river" (Danāqla, Maḥas, and others from as far south as Sinnār) as well as a smaller number of Upper Egyptians, plus "a few Tunisians, natives of Tripoli, and others [who] come and go with the caravans." The merchant community was self-contained, speaking Nubian or Arabic, not Fūr, and "seldom" marrying Fūr women. Twice a week a market was held outside of town that included "provisions of every kind," and Browne counted "four or five" schools to instruct the merchants' sons (plus "children of the indigent") in reading and writing, Qur'ān, and theology. During Browne's stay there was one mosque in Kobbei, plus a *qāḍī* (judge) originally from Sinnār who had trained at al-Azhār in Cairo.[13]

Darfur contained a number of other towns according to Browne, the more important being Suwaynī, a toll station and trade depot that commanded the northern caravan route; Kabkābīya, a large town of diverse inhabitants that was a major station for the western trade; and Rīl, the trade hub on the southeast border region with Kordofan. Otherwise there were several smaller towns (e.g., Kurma, Shōba, Jadīd), inhabited by a mixture of riverain merchants and Fūr or other local people, plus settlements of holy men who had been granted land by the sultan to maintain mosques and Qur'ānic schools. Altogether, perhaps "eight or ten towns" had any considerable population. There were of course many villages in Darfur, although "a few hundred souls form the sum of the largest." Housing styles tended not to vary, being in most cases flat-roofed, clay-built homes, round or square, enclosed with *zarības* (fences of thorn branches). Browne estimated the total population of the region to be around 200,000 people, with Kobbei ("one of their most populous towns") containing around 6,000: "Of these, the greater proportion are slaves."[14]

Just prior to Darfur's conquest, the German explorer Gustav Nachtigal visited it in 1874. His remarks about Kobbei confirm what Browne had written, while clarifying the manner of settlement: The "Children of the River" had immigrated gradually, he wrote, settling in *zarības* according to "tribes and sections of tribes." As their numbers grew and their wealth increased, people built larger homes and took others into their enclosure, such that the occupants "are usually determined according to their original home, but this is by no means always the case." Thus the villages of Kobbei were founded with a riverain tribal admixture (and to Nachtigal's dismay, "scarcely anything that can be called a street.") Subsequently Nachtigal traveled to al-Fāshir, situated in a tree-filled valley, which from above appeared as a series of separate *zarības*, each containing a clay house and "five to ten" straw huts. Fittingly, his party lodged in the *jallāba* village, near the northeast end of town; further north was the village of the Bornu and Kotoko people, from the central Sudanic region. Not surprisingly, the densest settlement of town was around the sultan's *fāshir*: "As is nearly always the case with royal residences in these countries, the town had grown in such a way that the officials most closely associated with the court had settled themselves in separate *zarības* scattered around the king's dwelling, to which in turn were linked up the *zarības* of their underlings." The impression this gave Nachtigal as he approached the palace was of "an enclosed village" of straw huts and clay houses, with "an incredible number of footpaths scattered here and there without any order between the *zarības*." Dismounting before the gate of the palace, Nachtigal removed his shoes before entering, aware of local custom if not the deeper cosmological significance of the sultan's *fāshir*.[15]

The towns of Sudan developed as a result of long-distance trade, and the two most important outlets for Sudanese goods were Egypt and the Red

Sea, whose trading port, Suakin, had arisen perhaps in the eighth century. Controlled by the Beja people, and in particular the Ḥaḍāriba tribe, Suakin's importance as an entrepôt and customs station—but not population center—led to its capture by the Ottoman empire in 1517. Subsequently the Ottoman government was represented by an Agha, who resided on the small island that formed the "town" of Suakin, although actual control of Suakin's affairs (as well as its source of labor and fresh water) remained with the coastal Ḥaḍāriba. Attracting trade from Egypt, Arabia, Ethiopia, Venice, India, and possibly even China, Suakin had more in common with other Red Sea ports than the Sudanic towns to its west. In 1814 Burckhardt compared its buildings to those of Jidda, and counted about 600 houses built of coral, many with two stories, of which two-thirds were in ruins. (The Arabic spoken in Suakin was said to be Ḥijāzī dialect.) However, on the mainland there were "a few houses of stone, built rather in the Soudan than Arabian style, having large courtyards; the other dwellings [of the Beja] are formed of mats, like those of the Nubian Bedouins." The inhabitants of Suakin were described as "a motley race," consisting mainly of the Ḥaḍāriba and other Beja tribes, plus descendants of the sixteenth-century Turkish garrison who had intermarried with the Beja, as well as more recent Turkish arrivals and Arabs from the Ḥijāz region. They were said to have "no other pursuit than that of commerce," and Burckhardt estimated their number at "about eight thousand," of whom 3,000 lived on the island and the remainder on the mainland.[16]

All told, by the time of Burckhardt's arrival there may have been 20 substantial towns in the northern Nilotic Sudan, including the regions of Kordofan and Darfur. These were places of trade and administration, stations along important regional and even transcontinental routes. As already mentioned, it was common in Sudanic states to separate the political and commercial centers: hence Sinnār and Arbajī in the Funj state, al-Fāshir and Kobbei in Darfur, as well as El Obeid and Bāra in Fūr-governed Kordofan, and Nimro and Wāra further west in Wadai. In some cases these towns were also religious communities, places of instruction, mediation and arbitration that attracted students from near and far. Some, such as al-ᶜAylafūn, Abū ᶜUshar, Abū Ḥarāz and Wad Madanī along the Blue Nile, or al-Dāmir along the main Nile, had grown from Ṣūfī *khalwas* into market centers and places of production, and were the clearest indication in the eighteenth and nineteenth centuries of what has been called an emerging "Arab-Islamic consciousness." Ultimately the population of these towns is impossible to determine with a high degree of accuracy. The largest town, Sinnār, was said in 1699 to contain 100,000 people, but this is likely an exaggeration: one scholar has suggested that 10,000 is closer to its normal size! For the other major towns, the figures of 8,000 (Suakin) and 6,000 (Kobbei) are certainly acceptable, and of course Shendī had many thousands of inhabitants as well. Other towns (e.g., Dongola, Khandak, al-Dabba, and Korti along the Nile) were considerably smaller, places of several hundred people, while Sudan's many villages contained, as Browne observed of Darfur, at best "a few hundred souls." In the larger towns, diversity of inhabitants or at least visitors was common, including (for example) western and central Sudanic peoples, Fūr as well as riverain Sudanese, peoples of the upper Blue Nile and Red Sea coast, in addition to smaller numbers of Egyptians, North Africans, Ethiopians, Indians, and Middle Eastern or Mediterranean people. Diversity of architecture however was not common: Excluding Suakin, the towns of Sudan did not differ greatly in appearance, being limited by environment and cultural preference in the choice of home style and building technique. The carved doors of Sinnār are the only notable example of domestic decoration. Additionally, Sudan's larger towns appear to have been hierarchically organized, with ethnic or tribal quarters (or "villages") and a physically distinct royal or administrative quarter, oftentimes guarded by slave soldiers. In many of these towns, particularly along the important trade routes, a daily or biweekly slave market was held, featuring slaves captured from the non-Muslim populations on the periphery of established states. Finally, as virtually every European visitor was to observe, there was no semblance of Western "order" in Sudan's towns, in the sense of zoning, street layout, or public amenities. Many of these things were to change with the arrival of the Turco-Egyptians.[17]

A permanent Turco-Egyptian presence at Khartoum dates to 1822 with the stationing of an administrative officer (*kāshif*) and soldiers there, although the military headquarters at that time was in Wad Madanī. With the appointment of ᶜUthmān Bey Jarkas as commander-in-chief in 1824 and recognition of the site's strategic location, Khartoum gained a mud-brick citadel and later that year was approved as the official headquarters of the provinces of Sinnār and Kordofan. ᶜUthmān's successor, Maḥū Bey Urfalī (1825–1826), began the construction of government buildings (including what was to become the *ḥikimdārīyya* or governor-general's palace) and caravans soon began to arrive at the growing village of mud and straw houses. The most substantial developments came with the long governorship of ᶜAlī Khūrshīd (1826–1838): Brick buildings and a mosque went up, with bricks taken from the nearby ruins of Sōba; a river port and shipyard were founded; residents were encouraged to build more permanent homes, and barracks and storerooms were erected; and importantly, a permanent market was established. A British visitor, Lord Prudhoe, wrote in 1829 that "The bazaar of Khartoom consists of twenty sheds where corn, coffee and black sugar are sold at a high price; and where are retailed a few looking-glasses and glass beads for necklaces and bracelets—ornaments generally worn. Every article of luxury comes from Cairo, and during its journey doubles or trebles its price. Occasional arrivals from India bring preserved ginger, sugar-candy, etc; but these supplies are rare and small in quantity." The administration of the Sudan was meanwhile evolving, and in 1835 ᶜAlī Khūrshīd, now promoted Pasha, was named *ḥikimdār* (governor-general) of "the region of the Sudan," including the provinces of Sinnār, Berber, Dongola, and Kordofan, with Khartoum as its capital. Political stability encouraged economic development, including the growth of Khartoum's merchants, and following earlier practice the government recognized a head merchant (*sirr al-tujjār*) over each of the Turkish, Egyptian, and Sudanese trading communities. Artisans and specialized cultivators began to arrive from Egypt, indigo was introduced and small industries attempted, certain trades flourished (albeit with state monopolies on nearly all export goods), and Khartoum began to take on the appearance of a state capital. A British traveler, A. T. Holroyd, remarked in 1837 that Khartoum "has risen rapidly into importance at the expense of Shendi and Sennar, and is now a place of considerable trade, being convenient as a rendezvous for the slave-caravans from Abyssinia, Sennar and Kordofan." In the decades ahead, the number of visitors from Europe and elsewhere—including missionaries, scientists and naturalists, travelers, explorers, and merchants—increased significantly, especially after the opening of the upper White Nile in 1840–1842 and the subsequent ending of the state monopoly on ivory. Khartoum had become, as one writer put it, a frontier town "perched on the edge of a newly discovered world."[18]

It is clear from the many published accounts that Khartoum continued to develop steadily, both in size and complexity, until the rise of the Mahdī in 1881 and the ensuing political disorder. The Vincentian priest Fr. Luigi Montuori, who arrived in Sudan in 1842 from Ethiopia and established the first Catholic church and school in Khartoum, estimated that "the city has nearly 13,000 inhabitants. With the exception of 200 Copts, a few Catholics, Turks and Algerians, these are Arabs from the neighboring provinces. The city itself sprawls in all directions, and has wide but irregular roads as is customary with the Muslims." Among the city's many facilities he mentioned a military hospital, a government printing press and medical storehouse. Ten years later, when Bayard Taylor arrived in Khartoum, he was immediately struck by the city's "stately" appearance:

> The line of buildings extended for more than a mile along the river, and many of the houses were embowered in gardens of palm, acacia, orange and tamarind trees. The Palace of the Pasha had a certain appearance of dignity, though its walls were only unburnt brick, and his *hareem*, a white, two-story building, looked cool and elegant amid the palms that shaded it.... I could look into a wilderness of orange, date, fig and pomegranate trees, oleanders in bloom and trailing vines. We entered a tolerable street, cleanly swept, and soon came to a coffee house.... The grape season was just over, though I had a few of the last bunches; figs were ripening from day to day, oranges and lemons were in fruit and flower, bananas blooming for another crop, and the pomegranate and *kishteh*, or custard-apple, hung heavy on the branches...

Impressed by the variety of people he met—he mentions Syrian merchants, Egyptian physicians, an "Ethiopian princess," various Europeans, and "almost every tribe between Dar-Fūr and the Red Sea, between Egypt and the Negro kingdoms of the White Nile"—Taylor declared Khartoum to be "the most remarkable—I had almost said the only example of physical progress in Africa, in this century. Where, thirty years ago, there was not even a dwelling, unless it might be the miserable *tokul*, or straw hut of the Ethiopian Fellah, now stands a city of some thirty or forty thousand inhabitants, daily increasing in size and importance, and gradually drawing into its mart the commerce of the immense regions of Central Africa." After further enthusing over the city's two-story brick buildings, its cleanliness and physical beauty (e.g., the gardens of the Pasha and Catholic Mission "shower the fragrance of their orange and mimosa blossoms over the whole town"), Taylor turned his attention to the "native houses," which he found bewildering and dirty, and the slave population, whose houses on the outskirts of town "were constantly springing up like ant-hills." In one remarkable (and all-too-common) passage, he writes:

> Nearly half the population of the place are slaves, brought from the mountains above Fazogl, or from the land of the Dinkas, on the White Nile. One's commiseration of these degraded races is almost overcome by his disgust with their appearance and habits, and I found even the waste plain that stretches towards Sennaar a relief after threading the lanes of the quarters where they live. Notwithstanding the nature of its population, Khartoum is kept commendably neat and clean. It will be a lucky day for Rome and Florence when their streets exhibit no more filth than those of this African city.[19]

Subsequent accounts do not greatly change the impression Taylor has left of the city: a steam yacht is acquired for the governor-general, a stone embankment is built, drainage is improved, etc. As a colonial capital combining the functions of administrative and market center, Khartoum came to rely upon a diverse personnel of Egyptians and other Ottoman subjects (and increasingly, Europeans) to govern a huge state that in 1874 included Darfur. Its population varied and may have reached as high as 50,000 in later years, although most accounts stress that at least half (if not two-thirds) were slaves. The "native" residential quarters were divided according to ethnicity or tribe, and were removed from the administrative area (*mudīrīyya*), Catholic mission, European consulates, Coptic quarter, military barracks, and riverbank. The majority of Khartoum's non-slave residents were riverain Sudanese, especially from the Danāqla, Maḥas, and Jaᶜaliyīn, with a smaller number of traders from Darfur, the Blue Nile, and Red Sea regions. Added to these were merchants of Egyptian, Syrian, Armenian, Greek, Jewish, and other origins, as well as a small European population. The city's slave population was also diverse, including Nūba, southern Nilotics and ethnic groups from southern Darfur and the upper Blue Nile.

To the foreigners who passed through town, progress was marked by the city's growing facilities and amenities, and especially its vigorous marketplace. The Maronite priest Yūsuf Khūrī compared Khartoum's market to that of Cairo, while Fr. Giovanni Beltrame noted in 1853 that in Khartoum "there is everything to be had." The British explorer James Grant was "astonished at the quantity and quality" of goods in Khartoum's market in 1863, including cigars, wine, and "foaming Bass Ale." Even the "Fakee clergymen" earned a good living according to Grant, charging one dollar "at least" for a wedding ceremony. Removed from the cosmopolitan atmosphere that Grant experienced, however, a current was running through northern Sudanese society, charged by massive Sudanese discontent over Turco-Egyptian economic policies and an emerging millennialism, that was soon to dismantle Khartoum, literally brick-by-brick.[20]

CHAPTER TWO

The Creation of a City

When I returned to Rufāᶜa from visiting the Mahdī, I found that my father had been among those summoned to the siege of Khartoum, and had directed me to look after the harvesting of our crops, and to deal with a large quantity of sesame which he had brought from Karkōj. But passion for the Holy War had mastered my mind, and I embarked my mother and my wife and my father's second wife and all the sesame in a boat which I had hired, and sailed to Jirayf, leaving my brother Mūsa Bedrī and the slaves that were with him to work the farm. At Jirayf I disembarked and went to the camp by myself, and when my father saw me he was astonished. 'Why on earth have you come here?' he said. 'In whose care did you leave the farm?' 'In God's care,' I replied. 'The Holy War is more important than farming.'

The Rise of Omdurman

Extremely little is known about the place called Omdurman prior to the nineteenth century. There is archeological evidence for some type of human habitation at the junction of the Blue and White Niles as far back as the Neolithic era, while Sudanese traditions claim that the ᶜAnaj people were the original inhabitants of the west bank of the Nile. The Dinka of the southern Sudan also claim to have lived in that area in ancient times. In fact we know next to nothing about the origin of the site. Even the name is obscure: Some claim that it derives from the presence of two small hills (*durmān*), or that it refers to an ancient queen, *Umm Durmān* ("Mother of Durmān"), but evidence is utterly lacking. A different and equally inscrutable name for the site was "Washal," a usage that survived into the Mahdīyya.[1]

The first settlement at Omdurman for which we have direct evidence is associated with the Maḥasī holy man Shaykh Ḥamad wad Umm Maryam (ca. 1646–1730), who moved there with his followers from nearby Tūtī Island and built a Qur'ān school (*khalwa*). The biographical dictionary known as the *Ṭabaqāt*, compiled from 1753–1805, refers to Omdurman as "his village." While the chronicle indicates that he did not remain there long—his buildings were torched by a rival shaykh—his settlement followed an already well-established pattern of town development, based on the schools and eventually communities surrounding Maḥas religious teachers along the Blue and White Niles.[2]

Omdurman appears on a map for the first time in the travel account of the British explorer W. G. Browne, who visited Darfur in the 1790s, and later on the Williamson map (*Africa*) of 1800 and the John Pinkerton map (*Abyssinia Nubia Etc.*) of 1814. Meanwhile the *The Funj Chronicle* (1504–1871) mentions Omdurman several times. From these sources as well as a number of nineteenth-century travel accounts it is possible to draw a few conclusions about the site. It seems that Omdurman was at best lightly inhabited at the time of the Turco-Egyptian invasion of the Sudan in 1820, and early in the nineteenth century it may have been only intermittently inhabited. In addition to containing a watering site for the herds of local pastoralists, it eventually included some meager cultivation along the riverbank, a small market, and a limekiln for brick-making. More importantly, Omdurman was at the junction of trade routes connecting the Nile confluence to El Obeid and Darfur in the west, Sinnār in the east, and Dongola in the north. Observers mention both Kordofan merchants and a settlement of Jaᶜaliyīn traders there (they may have been one and the same), and a Syrian traveler described it, in contrast to Khartoum, as "the station of the Arabs." Turco-Egyptian officials traveling upriver in the early years of the new regime crossed over to Khartoum from Omdurman, but only after remaining there several days, receiving emissaries and notables, releasing prisoners, sending letters of amnesty, etc. Accompanied as they were by a considerable entourage of soldiers and attendants, this suggests that Omdurman, while not yet a town, was at least a settlement suitable for a large encampment, located at a strategically important site.[3]

With the revolt of the Mahdī well underway in 1883, General William Hicks Pasha was sent to Sudan at the head of a large Egyptian force to put down this threat to Turco-Egyptian authority. Omdurman became the staging site for his ill-advised expedition to Kordofan, which set out in September. Poorly led and ill-disciplined, it was utterly wiped out at Shaykān, near El Obeid, on 5 November 1883. After the massacre of Hicks's army, including its small European officer corps, General Charles G. Gordon arrived in Sudan in 1884, and Omdurman became the site of an important fortress guarding Khartoum's western flank. Gordon mentions in his journal that 240 men were stationed at Omdurman, which was linked to Khartoum by telegraph. While information is scanty, it seems likely that the local Sudanese population also grew in order to serve the various needs of the garrison. On 23 October 1884 the Mahdī arrived at Daym Abū Siᶜd, just south of Omdurman, in support of his siege of Khartoum. From there he issued an invitation to surrender to the commandant of Omdurman, Farajallāh Rāghib Pasha. Surrounded as he was by a far superior force, Farajallāh had no choice but to surrender, which he did on 5 January 1885. This loss, wrote Holt, "was followed by a great decline in the morale of the inhabitants of Khartoum and an increase in desertions to the Mahdī." Three weeks later, on 26 January, Khartoum itself fell to the Mahdists, and with its fall began the rise to prominence of Omdurman.[4]

It is clear from the Mahdī's numerous writings that he had no intention of establishing a new city or capital. His mission was one of universal Islamic reform, and what he required at the time was an open space large enough to assemble his troops for *jihād*. In the months following the fall of Khartoum, the Mahdī remained initially at Daym Abū Siᶜd, while many of his kinsmen and followers took up residence in the homes of the former capital. Later he joined his troops at the burgeoning campsite that was Omdurman, and it was there that he suddenly died and was buried on 22 June 1885. Much about the Mahdist movement changed with the death of its founder, due to subsequent events as well as the character of the man who came to replace him. It suffices to say that the revolution, having succeeded in its initial goal of ridding Sudan of Turco-Egyptian control, settled into the uneasy task of forming a territorial state. The leader of that state, ᶜAbdallāhi al-Taᶜāīshī, commonly known as "the Khalīfa," chose as his capital

Omdurman, which by then was popularly called *Buqᶜat al-Mahdī* (literally, "the Mahdī's place").

Holt has attributed this decision to move the capital across the Nile to the Khalīfa's mistrust of the Mahdī's kinsmen, who were ensconced in Khartoum. Doubtless this was a factor of great political importance, since the Ashrāf (as the Mahdī's relatives were known) openly opposed ᶜAbdallāhi's coming to power.[5] The Mahdī himself had chided his kinsmen for their assumption of privileges and opposed settling in the city of the Turks, as he had earlier opposed settling in El Obeid after its capture. Moreover the Mahdī is said to have quoted to his followers from *Sūrat Ibrāhīm* of the Qur'ān during his final sermon at the Khartoum mosque: "'You lived in the dwellings of those who wronged their souls before you: yet you knew full well how We had dealt with them, and We spoke to you in parables about them.' They plot, but their plots are known to God, even if their plots could move mountains." Certainly the Mahdī was insistent and uncompromising in his rejection of the unbelievers and their domain, which he regarded as spiritually contaminated, and this rigorous ideological posture was often adopted by his successor.[6]

A related consideration in the capital's move may have been Omdurman's proximity to the plain of Kararī, which had long been regarded as the site of an eventual and decisive clash between the Believers and Infidels. There is evidence that both prior to and during the Mahdīyya the Sudanese had anticipated a final battle against the British at that place (as indeed happened in 1898). General Gordon seems to allude to this in a journal entry dated 10 October 1884, writing "It is an odd coincidence, the advance of the Mahdī and of the [British] expeditionary force at the same time, and to the same place (Armageddon)." That Kararī should be the site of an ultimate battle is not be surprising, since it is a large plain north of the Nile's most important crossing-point. At the least, and one cannot discount this belief influencing the Khalīfa's decision to abandon Khartoum.[7]

Other, more practical, concerns certainly lay behind the decision to relocate the capital as well. Khartoum housed the former employees of the Turco-Egyptian regime, whose skills would be essential to the management of a new state, and whose control might be better assured in a safe location outside the former capital. Additionally Omdurman with its sloping sandy terrain was a far healthier place than Khartoum, where the soil's resistance to drainage made it a veritable incubator of disease: a situation that had prompted two Turco-Egyptian governors to consider moving the capital.[8] As previously mentioned, Omdurman lay astride important trade routes, and its natural harbor at al-Mōrida, with direct access up and down the Nile, made it the ideal spot for an entrepôt. Finally, and perhaps most importantly, Omdurman offered the Khalīfa the strategic depth of the western hinterland, inhabited in part by his tribe the Taᶜāīsha, to which he could retreat should his enemies arrive by river. At least toward the end of the Mahdīyya, this aspect of Omdurman's location must have seemed the most important.

On 27 July 1885, some one month after the death of the Mahdī, the Khalīfa ordered the abandonment of Khartoum and settlement of Omdurman in the following proclamation.

> From the Khalīfa ᶜAbdallāhi b. Muḥammad, *Khalīfat al-Ṣiddīq,* to all the people now residing in Khartoum, *awlād al-balad* [i.e., townspeople] and *awlād al-rīf* [i.e., Egyptians], employees and others: May God guide them to that which is right, amen.
>
> My beloved ones, upholding the religion and being concerned with that which enhances it is demanded of every Muslim, and readying one's self for the hereafter is incumbent upon everyone. It is a sign of God's favor and concern for you that you are present during this blessed, happy time and included among His people, so praise God and thank Him for this. This being so, you ought to be in the greatest readiness for whatever you are commanded to do on behalf of the religion.
>
> If you understand what has been said, then know O beloved ones that out of consideration for the interests of the faith and your guidance and the betterment of your religion, we have thought fit that you should move from Khartoum and come to the City of the Mahdī (peace be upon him!), dwelling among us with your children and all that belongs to you. As of today, you must all begin this move. Let no one among you delay, even one employed by the arsenal or dockyard or treasury or wherever. Out of kindness towards you, we have set the date whereby you should complete [your move] for this coming Friday [i.e., four days hence, 31 July]. After Friday, a search will be conducted for you within Khartoum. Anyone found lagging behind will certainly be punished as a deterrent [to others], since he has refused to comply with the order.
>
> This then is serving notice to all Helpers of the Religion in Khar-

> toum, so that whoever has others residing with him from the people of Khartoum who were in it [during the siege]—be they *awlād al-balad* or *rīf* or even relatives—he should be instructed to move [them] and come to the city. It should not be hoped that one can lag behind: The words of him who so hopes will not be accepted, rather a punishment will be meted out to him, if God Most High so wills. Let this [now] be known to you.
>
> We have ordered Ibrāhīm al-Būrdayn to be the overseer of all who are in Khartoum. Anyone found lagging behind after Friday will be reported to ᶜAbd al-Ḥalīm Musāᶜid, and upon his notification that person will be forcibly uprooted. If anyone interferes with the execution of this order, he will be reported to us, that we might punish both the one who delays and the one who interferes. Peace![9]

Invoking his official title as *Khalīfat al-Ṣiddīq* ("Successor of the Caliph Abū Bakr"), ᶜAbdallāhi makes clear that the transfer to Omdurman is not merely a matter of policy or preference but rather a matter of faith: an obligation incumbent upon all believers. Noteworthy is his concern to centralize resources and personnel, emphasizing that both Sudanese townspeople (*awlād al-balad*) and resident Egyptians (*awlād al-rīf*)—and especially former government employees—must heed this order. Relying upon the Mahdī's core supporters as well as more recent adherents, he appoints both Ibrāhīm al-Būrdayn, one of the most influential merchants in Khartoum, as well as ᶜAbd al-Ḥalīm Musāᶜid, a veteran *amīr* (military leader) to execute the order. Ultimately however, practicality won out: with many followers married among or related to the people of Khartoum and the Mahdī's family settled there, the Khalīfa was forced to relent.

For the next year the former capital remained occupied by a variety of people, Sudanese and others. The Mahdī's father-in-law and family patriarch, Aḥmad Sharfī, known as *Jadd al-Ashrāf* ("grandfather of the Ashrāf"), was instructed by the Khalīfa to supervise the city's property and prevent the theft and vandalism of valuable materials. The political influence of the Ashrāf was of course considerable at this time, and the Khalīfa was careful to accord them due respect and deference: Several letters were written to Aḥmad Sharfī informing him of individuals moving to Omdurman and taking wood and other materials from their homes with them.[10]

After the Khalīfa gained ascendancy over his political rivals among the

Ashrāf in 1886, he was in a better position to impose his will on the population of Khartoum, and accordingly in September 1886 he firmly ordered the evacuation of the city. Allegedly ten days were allotted for its complete emptying, which was carried out.[11] From this point on, Omdurman was indisputably the capital of the Mahdist state while Khartoum, picked over for its wood, bricks, and other building materials, lay in near-ruins.

Meanwhile the Khalīfa already had begun to invite Sudanese to Omdurman to pledge an oath of loyalty to him as ruler. Oral summons as well as written invitations were widely disseminated throughout the territory under Mahdist control, instructing individuals as well as entire tribes to be present in "the Mahdi's city" on the feast of ᶜĪd al-Aḍḥā, which that year (AH 1302) fell on 20 September 1885. Many thousands of Sudanese poured into Omdurman in that and subsequent months, and by mid-1886 the city allegedly stretched for more than six kilometers along the Nile.[12]

The appearance of the city at this early stage needs mentioning. Originally Omdurman had been a heavily wooded site, with the exception of a narrow strip along the river that was cultivated by the Jummūᶜīyya Arabs from the village of Fitayḥāb to the south. About a mile west of the river loomed desert. As Sudanese settled Omdurman from 1885 onward they cleared the site of its undergrowth and erected dwellings. These were at first the roughly built huts of wood and dhurra stalks known colloquially as a *tukl*, although later more permanent homes of mud brick were built. Wood eventually became scarce and hence expensive in Omdurman; however, the basic building materials were in abundance and homes tended not to vary considerably in size and style. The Italian prisoner Fr. Rosignoli noted in his memoir that "the homes of the rich are surrounded by walls, the others by mere *zarības*," i.e., barricades of thorny branches. The wealthier residents of Omdurman were also able to employ more mud brick in the construction of their homes. Still, diversity of dwellings was neither a physical possibility nor a value in Mahdist society, and accounts of the city written after the conquest in 1898, although clearly limited, reinforce the image of Omdurman as "miles of mud and straw huts."[13]

Settlement in Omdurman was initially along the river, this being the preferred location for its access to the water. As the population grew, the city began to extend into the interior, although never more than three miles or so. The city's shoreline was distinguished by two natural ports, one in the north end of the city (later the boatyard of *ḥayy* Ab Rōf) and the other in the south (al-Mōrida). This latter port had allegedly been a customs site of the ᶜAbdallāb rulers during the Funj era, and was later the watering spot for the flocks of the Jummūᶜīyya tribe. During the Mahdīyya it served as the main port of Omdurman. The city's initial character was of course military—a gathering spot for the innumerable units of the Mahdī's army—so not surprisingly the northern and southern limits of the city were determined by military considerations. To the north of the city center by about seven miles lay the mobilization site for expeditions going north, known as *al-Ḥujra*. South of Omdurman lay another camp, known as *Ḥujrat al-Quṣayr*, for expeditions going south and west.[14] Additionally, southern expansion was limited by a buffer zone of open space, maintained by the Khalīfa's orders, which segregated his professional soldiers (*jihādīyya*) from the general population. Gordon's old fortress, known as al-Kāra, served as the garrison for these *jihādīyya*.[15]

The center of town fittingly contained the chief symbols of Mahdist society: the Mahdī's grave and the mosque, where all were expected to assemble each Friday for prayer. Nearby were the homes and households of the Mahdī, the Khalīfa ᶜAbdallāhi, the Khalīfa's brother (known as "Amīr Yaᶜqūb"), the subordinate *khalīfas* ᶜAlī wad Ḥilū and Muḥammad Sharīf, and a number of important *amīrs, qāḍīs,* and clerks. During the Mahdī's lifetime the mosque had been simply a large open space, although in late 1885 or early 1886 the Khalīfa built a mud brick wall around it. This may have been meant to adorn the mosque, but it also served to mark space and contain the crowds in the administrative hub of the city: Rosignoli claims that the mosque often held more than 70,000 worshippers. The institutional structure of the city, such as it then existed, was based on the mosque (where the *Sharīᶜa* court met) and a few buildings nearby, such as the treasury (*Bayt al-Māl*). Slightly outside the center of town on the river was the prison, built in 1885 and named for its jailor, al-Sāyir.[16] The city's few main roads reflected its military character: one led north from the mosque to the northern *ḥujra* (eventually named *Darb al-Shuhadā'*, "Road of the Martyrs"), another south to the southern *ḥujra*, and the third west to the army's parade grounds (*Darb al-ᶜArḍa*). Northwest of the mosque lay the Omdurman *sūq*, which during the Mahdīyya was the chief marketplace of the Sudan. Its location was in part a function of the space available, since popular settlement left no room for a market to expand closer to the river. However its position on the edge of town also accorded with the desert-side economy of cattle and camels that flourished at this time.

Townspeople aware of the goings-on would have noted the period of April–May 1886 as a time when the Khalīfa was solidifying his hold on the reins of power. In a series of moves he gained both military and administrative supremacy, stripping his rivals the junior *khalīfas* of their *jihādīyya* soldiers and arms and arresting and replacing an untrustworthy treasury head. The new commissioner of the *Bayt al-Māl*, Ibrāhīm Muḥammad ᶜAdlān, undertook a thorough reorganization of the treasury that included moving it from the crowded city center to along the river north of the prison, where it could more easily inspect and receive incoming goods. At least by 1890, the treasury encompassed a soap factory, pharmacy, telegraph station, percussion caps factory, armory, mint, and lithograph press, in addition to its many storerooms and slave market.[17] Similarly, the judiciary underwent a reorganization and expansion. By 1886 special courts had been established to oversee the particular needs of the marketplace (*Maḥkamat al-Sūq*) and treasury (*Maḥkamat Bayt al-Māl*); these operated in conjunction with the main court (*Maḥkamat al-Islām*) in the mosque. Sometime thereafter, courts also were established to attend to the needs of the *jihādīyya* (*Maḥkamat al-Kāra*) and port (*Maḥkamat al-Mōrida*). As befits a state ruler, the Khalīfa also began construction of his house at this time—eventually the city's only multistory dwelling—using bricks and wooden fittings taken from Khartoum and built under the guidance of a captive Italian engineer.[18]

The years 1888–1890 (AH 1306–1307) saw the completion of the great period of emigration to Omdurman, which brought vast changes in the appearance of the capital. In the city as in the rest of the Sudan, however, 1306—referred to as *sanna sitta*, "the year six"—has another, ominous importance, for it was in this year that a great famine struck, decimating the Sudanese population.

The causes of this famine were both natural and man-made. Almost no rain had fallen the previous year, and as a result the Nile flood of 1306 was low and the harvest of 1306 / late 1888 meager. Meanwhile there were three large armies stationed in the north at Dongola, in the east at al-Qallābāt, and in the west in Darfur, steadily consuming the state's and the countryside's supplies of grain. Then, in early 1306, the Ta^cāīsha and other western pastoralists (the so-called "Baqqāra") began their long-delayed emigration to Omdurman. Met by Mahdist officials at Shabasha on the White Nile, they were transported by steamer to the city and settled in a vacant southern sector.[19] The Khalīfa had committed the treasury to providing for these tribes until they were settled—he had little choice in the matter—and quickly they consumed the state's immediate grain supply, which allegedly had been 500,000 *ardebs* (approximately 2.5 million bushels). As supplies in the agricultural Jazīra region also dwindled, prices rose and merchants began to look desperately for sources of grain.

Since the Khalīfa was obliged to support his armed forces in Omdurman, but also was unwilling to bankrupt the state, he later ordered that they be sold grain at preferential rates.[20] Eventually in 1307 / 1889–1890 it became necessary to move about 8,000 of the Ta^cāīsha and their families to Fashoda on the upper White Nile, where grain supplies were plentiful and they would cease to be a burden on the capital's reserves. By this time however, millet had risen from six *riyāls* per *ardeb* (approximately five bushels) to forty *riyāls*, and as much as three hundred *riyāls* in the vicinity of Kassala.

The effects of the famine on the population of Omdurman are vividly described in the memoirs of the period. No manner of horror seems to have been spared the Sudanese who, in extreme cases, were forced to resort to cannibalism to save their own lives. Many thousands flocked to the capital from places such as Berber, Kassala, al-Qallābāt, and Karkōj. "They were attracted by the hope of being able to break their fast," recalled the Italian Rosignoli. "Instead, they merely increased the number of corpses to be found on the street." Thousands more settled in areas around the capital, resisted by the local people but hoping to get grain as it was brought into the city. Rosignoli recalls a saying that was "on everyone's lips," that "He who did not die during the famine of 1889 will never die."[21]

The combination of the famine and settlement of the western tribes shifted the political and social balance of Omdurman in the Khalīfa's favor. The southern half of the city was now his strategic reserve: In it he settled the Baqqāra tribes (his own Ta^cāīsha, plus the Rizayqāt, Ḥabbānīyya, Misīrīyya, and Ḥumr) as well as other peoples of western origin (including the Fūr, Berti, and "Fellāta," i.e., Fulānī), most of whom were deeply loyal to him. Their presence provided a buffer between the professional soldiers of al-Kāra and the Khalīfa's political enemies from the riverain Sudanese, who mostly felt antipathy towards the western people. In this sector the Khalīfa also built a weapons and supply depot (*Bayt al-Amāna*) in 1888, which contained the state's guns, powder, army standards, and official drums. Finally, the route west to Kordofan and Darfur lay in this southern sector: Should escape have been necessary, the Khalīfa's security would have been insured by his access to the depot and the presence of his tribesmen and *jihādīyya*.

Omdurman now contained a huge collection of tribal and ethnic groups. Rosignoli called it "a real museum of human types," and added that besides the various Sudanese peoples it included "Egyptians, Indians, Arabs from Mecca, Syrians, Greeks, Italians, Turks, Ethiopians, and finally cannibals from Niam-Niam [Zande] and Mangbetu."[22] Bordering the westerners in the southern sector and extending into the center of town north of the mosque were the followers of Khalīfa ᶜAlī wad Ḥilū, who were White Nile Arabs from the Kināna and Dighaym tribes. Settled in the north and northwest sectors were northern riverain Sudanese, merchants and craftsmen among them, including the followers of Khalīfa Muḥammad Sharīf. These were comprised of Danāqla, Kunūz, and other Arabized Nubians, as well as Rikābīyya, Rubāṭāb, and other branches of the Jaᶜaliyīn Arabs. Close by the *sūq* lived the community known as the *Masālma*, former Christians and Jews who converted to Islam during the Mahdist uprising and mainly engaged in trade. Finally, near the treasury along the river lived many of the Egyptian former employees of the Turco-Egyptian regime who now served the Mahdist state. Omdurman had grown to about five miles in length—it eventually may have reached six miles—and the increased size and population had prompted structural changes.

In 1888 the Khalīfa oversaw the reorganization of the *sūq*, reassigning stalls to the vendors so as to concentrate each type of merchant in a specific area and increase competition. Intended to benefit the consumer, it was also a means for the treasury to assert its control over the marketplace and increase revenues from rental plots. In an act of great symbolic importance, the Khalīfa also ordered the construction of the Mahdī's tomb. Inaugurating the project himself with great fanfare, he allotted shares of the labor to the entire population of the city, tribe by tribe and district by district, promising that all workers would gain entry to heaven. Many Sudanese undertook this task with great enthusiasm, anxious to receive the Mahdī's *baraka*, and the tomb (hereafter known as *al-Qubba*) immediately became the preeminent religious and ideological symbol of Omdurman, unifying the Anṣār even as it validated the Khalīfa's regime. In a related move, the Khalīfa had the mud brick walls of the mosque replaced with red brick taken from Khartoum, further emphasizing the permanence and power of the Mahdīyya to its followers.[23]

The years 1889–1891 were a critical period for the Mahdist state. Chief among several military setbacks was the disastrous defeat inflicted upon the Anṣār by an Anglo-Egyptian force at Ṭūshkī near the Egyptian border in August 1889, which claimed the life of one of the Khalīfa's most capable *amīrs*, ᶜAbd al-Raḥmān al-Nujūmī. This period also saw the deaths of the *amīrs* Ḥamdān Abu ᶜAnja and ᶜUthmān Ādam, as well as the outbreak of tensions between Arab Anṣār and the Beja on the eastern front. These setbacks had their effect on the population of Omdurman. After Ṭūshkī in particular, the Mahdist enthusiasm of many of the Jaᶜaliyīn began to wane, owing largely to a popular perception that the Khalīfa had deliberately sent al-Nujūmī, a Jaᶜalī, to his death.[24] Of greater significance was the discontent of the Ashrāf with the Khalīfa's rule: In origin a political antagonism, it was exacerbated by the Khalīfa's economic policies that disadvantaged many riverain Sudanese merchants and boatmen, including members of the Mahdī's family. On 23 November 1891 the discontent erupted into open revolt in the capital. Led by the kinsmen of the Mahdī and Khalīfa Muḥammad Sharīf, it had the backing of many aggrieved Danāqla traders in Omdurman and the Jazīra. The two days of the revolt were described by Rosignoli as "a period of general panic," during which people remained in their homes while order broke down and "Arabs from outside" the city robbed and pillaged. Eventually, each neighborhood organized its own local security arrangements; with the breakdown of order, "it seemed as if the reign of the Khalīfa had come to an end." On 25 November the Khalīfa was able to effect a formal reconciliation with the Ashrāf, vowing to restore the honors and pensions due them as the family of the Mahdī. However at the Rajabīyya festival of 1309 (26 February 1892), a great council of notables was convened and issued a condemnation of Muḥammad Sharīf, which was followed by his arrest on 2 March. Meanwhile, many supporters of the Ashrāf, including the former treasury head Aḥmad Sulaymān, were exiled to Fashoda on the White Nile and put to death, while Danāqla in the Jazīra were rounded up and stripped of a third of their goods. The former Mahdist Bābikr Bedrī describes in his memoirs the pathos of their abasement, forcibly marched to Omdurman "with slave forks on their necks." The resistance of the Ashrāf and their backers thus completely broken, the Khalīfa was now able to rule as a fully autocratic sovereign. Reflective of this was the addition of a second floor to his house, completed some time in 1891, which allowed him to monitor activities in the mosque and center of town. The only two-storied house in Omdurman, its symbolic significance was not lost on the Sudanese.[25]

Following his rise to unquestioned ascendancy, the Khalīfa embarked on his largest public-works project in Omdurman, the construction of a great stone wall enclosing the central administrative quarter of the capital. Relying largely on "volunteer" labor from Omdurman and the Jazīra, the project commenced in the dry season of 1310 (early 1893) and was completed in 1895. Extending north 800 yards from the Mahdī's tomb, then east 1500 yards to the Nile, the wall ran 1600 yards along the river before turning inward again towards the city center. (Either by design or circumstance, its western side was never completed; however, as a defensive barrier, the desert-side section would have been the least essential.) Contained within the wall were the homes of the Khalīfa, his brother Amīr Yaᶜqūb, the Mahdī's household, the homes of the *khalīfas* ᶜAlī wad Ḥilū and Muḥammad Sharīf, the *Qubba*, *Bayt al-Amāna*, and a small market. Insulated from his subjects in a compound that resembled the enclosed royal quarters of the Funj and Fūr sultans, the Khalīfa now rarely ventured out among his people, sending others to officiate at the Friday military parades and, occasionally, the daily prayers. If the wall provided the Khalīfa with a measure of distance from his subjects, it increasingly also assumed a defensive significance. After the Mahdist defeat at Agordat in Ethiopia on 21 December 1893, a separate mud brick enclosure was added to contain the Khalīfa's new bodyguard, the *mulāzimīn*, drawn from both the *jihādīyya* and loyal Taᶜāīsha and other Arabs.[26]

The years 1892–1895 witnessed a number of internal developments in Omdurman, mainly of an administrative and economic nature. Among these were the Khalīfa's frequent dismissal and appointment of treasury and judiciary heads—a destabilizing practice fueled by his growing mistrust and insecurity—and a currency crisis linked to debasement and counterfeiting in 1894.[27] Increasingly, however, events were of a military nature, as external forces combined to topple the Mahdist state.

Rosignoli mentions that after the Italian victory at Agordat, "fear and panic was everywhere." Just eight months later, on 17 July 1894, the Italians occupied Kassala and Omdurman "took on the appearance of an armed camp." Weapons and ammunition were distributed to the Anṣār and the Khalīfa's bodyguard was increased. Additionally the Khalīfa ordered that the roads of Omdurman be widened, probably to facilitate the passage of troops through the city. Of great significance, Muḥammad Sharīf was released from prison and the Ashrāf recalled from exile, as the Khalīfa sought the much-needed support of the Mahdī's clan and their riverain followers. As an added security measure, the Khalīfa ordered shut all prepared food shops and cafés in the city, presumably to curtail idle talk of the Italian victories, and imposed a modified curfew on the town after dark.[28]

Rosignoli's account of the atmosphere at this time finds corroboration in the memoirs of Bābikr Bedrī, who lists the fall of Kassala as among the three events that "shook the faith of true believers."[29] Meanwhile, popular and official opinion in Britain had finally rallied in support of an invasion of the Sudan, with the justification of liberating the Sudanese from their tyrannical government, stopping the slave trade, and to a lesser extent avenging the death of General Gordon. The Anglo-Egyptian invasion of Sudan began in 1896, and from this point on, Omdurman and the Mahdist state were preoccupied with defensive measures.

On 29 March 1896 the Khalīfa instructed his agent in the Jazīra, Aḥmad al-Sunnī, to send all Baqqāra and *jihādīyya* to Omdurman, as a general conscription began. Shortly thereafter, the army of the *amīr* Maḥmūd Aḥmad returned from Kordofan and Darfur and joined the concentration of troops at the capital. Problems of overcrowding and food scarcity immediately resumed in the city, and as he was forced to do years earlier, the Khalīfa ordered all available grain sent to the capital to feed his troops. This, according to Bābikr Bedrī, was responsible for the defection of the Jazīra people and "the reversal of their faith." It was also responsible for the initial breakdown of the infrastructure of Omdurman.

After capturing Dongola on 23 September 1896, the Anglo-Egyptian army began construction of a desert railway to Abū Ḥamad on the Nile to supply its troops, and the destruction of the Mahdist state proceeded apace. Any chance of Sudanese solidarity in the face of this invasion disappeared on 2 July 1897, when Baqqāra troops of Maḥmūd Aḥmad massacred the Jaᶜaliyīn at Matamma on the Nile for their disloyalty to the Khalīfa and subsequently ravaged the countryside. Meanwhile, the shortage of grain in Omdurman hampered the Khalīfa's ability to supply his soldiers, and as Maḥmūd Aḥmad vacillated in Matamma, the morale of his troops plummeted and thousands deserted back to the capital.[30] The Anglo-Egyptian railway finally reached Abū Ḥamad on 4 October 1897; six months later, Maḥmūd Aḥmad's army was destroyed at the river ᶜAṭbarā.

In Omdurman the Khalīfa had ordered the construction of numerous fortresses along the Nile in 1897, and additional ones were built after ᶜAṭbarā in Khartoum, Tūtī Island, and on the east bank of the Nile. The mood in the capital was extremely somber. Bābikr Bedrī recalls that "men were preparing their souls for death, and daily the news of terrifying happenings deafened one's ears. You could not join any gathering where you were not asked for news, and even if you invented it people would believe it and spread it, though they... knew for certain that you had invented it."[31] The end of the Mahdist state finally came on 2 September 1898, when the Anṣār resolutely but futilely attacked the guns of General H. H. Kitchener's army at Kararī, incurring perhaps 11,000 casualties. Omdurman was subjected to a steady bombardment from British gunboats and howitzers during the course of the battle, with most of the fire being directed at the center of the city, particularly the *Qubba.* Although the Khalīfa escaped the battle and remained a fugitive until being hunted down and killed at Umm Dibaykarāt in Kordofan on 23 November 1899, Omdurman was captured immediately after the fighting. An Anglo-Egyptian military administration under the immediate command of Colonel John Maxwell was promptly established in the city, and for some time Omdurman remained the seat of the new government and its chief dockyard. Gradually, various governmental departments were transferred back to Khartoum. With the establishment of the municipality of Khartoum in 1901, the administrative and political capital of Sudan returned to its former site. Omdurman, though still the popular capital and central market, was left to decay, most of its inhabitants returning to their former homes or settling to cultivate in the Jazīra or along the two Niles.

The Peopling of the City

From the earliest days of the revolt, the concept of *hijra* ("flight" or "emigration") was central to the Mahdī's teaching and served an important role in mobilizing the Faithful. The Mahdī's manifestation on 29 June 1881 was announced in letters to the Sudanese urging them to renounce the world, embrace the ascetic path, and make the *hijra* to him at Abā Island. This call followed the practice of seeking refuge with a holy man in the face of oppression, known in both the Nilotic Sudan and the earlier western Sudanic *jihād* movements. More importantly, it evoked the experience of the original Muslim community under the Prophet Muḥammad. Holt has noted that the Mahdī and his followers "were deliberately re-enacting in their own persons the sufferings and the triumphs of the early days of Islam and their consciousness of playing a part in this great drama was an inspiration to them."[32] After the Mahdī's first victory over government troops (12 August) and subsequent flight to Jabal Qadīr in Kordofan, the call to join him went out to individuals and tribes throughout the Sudan, and *hijra* became linked with the waging of *jihād* against the infidels. Those Sudanese who flocked to the Mahdī—called Anṣār ("Helpers") after the followers of the Prophet—were also both *muhājirūn* (emigrants) and *mujāhidūn* (soldiers on behalf of the faith): that is, their flight offered them not only protection from oppression and immunity from taxes, but also fulfilled an important religious obligation. Until the end of his life, the Mahdī continued to express his intentions in terms of *hijra* with its concomitant sense of *jihād*. As one scholar has put it, this was less a manipulation of Islamic tradition than a creative development of the concept, based on the Mahdī's faith and experience.[33]

The Mahdī's successor also emphasized the need for *hijra*, although there were important differences between the two, owing to the circumstances of their rules as well as their intended policies. In the main, the Khalīfa utilized the concept of *hijra* to carry out a broad and detailed program for the mobilization and relocation of many of the Sudanese people. This was in turn linked to his urban policy, which promoted the spiritual and economic primacy of Omdurman, encouraged the notion of Mahdist exclusivity and the avoidance of unbelievers, and de-emphasized the religious duty of pilgrimage to Mecca. Naturally, it also bolstered the Khalīfa's authority in times of stress, such as when he was facing serious resistance from the Ashrāf.

The Khalīfa's avowed purpose, of course, was the continuation of the Mahdī's call to wage *jihād* both within and without the Sudan. As in the Mahdī's time, the call to *jihād* was articulated in terms of a *hijra* to the main body of believers. (Thus Omdurman was styled "Dār al-Hijra" on certain Mahdist coins.) Practicality, however, required that this policy be tempered to fit circumstances. So while the pastoralist Baqqāra were expected to devote themselves entirely to *jihād*, the farmers of both the Jazīra region and Kordofan were often released from campaign when the coming rains signaled the start of cultivation. Likewise, the village of Qiṭayna on the White Nile, important enough in grain production and transport to be labeled "the throat of Omdurman," was limited in its *jihād* obligation to the siege of Khartoum and other skirmishes of the revolt. Villagers recall that "*Hijra* was for the westerners and the people whom the Khalīfa didn't trust." Bābikr Bedrī likewise describes the ways that farmers (and in his own case, merchants) were able to reconcile the obligation of *jihād* with the needs of their livelihood. And at least in some cases, it was possible for Jazīra people to pay an indemnity to the *Bayt al-Māl* to escape the obligation of *hijra*.[34]

Certainly not all Anṣār were required to resettle in Omdurman. Some members of important religious families were left to their pious pursuits, while others, such as the religious leaders of El Obeid, were made to settle in the new city. Several of the pastoralist tribes of the Jazīra were forced to settle in Omdurman in 1886, but after convincing the Khalīfa of their loyalty, they were sent home, where they "rendered [their lands] prosperous." The very vastness of the Khalīfa's intentions demanded flexibility. In sum, the policy of *hijra* might serve any of the following objectives: the mobilization of troops, centralization of resources, punishment of miscreants, supervision of unruly tribes and suspect individuals, indoctrination of local authorities, settlement of disputes, protection of vulnerable members of society, and the integration of communities or rewarding of followers through the distribution of unmarried women from the *ghanīma* ("spoils of war"). All of these objectives served, to varying degrees, in the creation of Omdurman.[35]

The Khalīfa's first call for *hijra* to Omdurman went out less than a month after the death of the Mahdī. Emphasized was the need for Sudanese to make (or renew) their oath of allegiance (*bayᶜa*) to him, to visit the grave of the Mahdī, to confer about "matters of the faith," and to join the *jihād* underway. The date set for arrival in Omdurman was the festival of ᶜĪd al-Aḍḥā (20 September 1885). Over the next two months several hundred letters were sent to regions as far-flung as the Egyptian borderland in the north and Bornu in the central Sudanic region. The appeals to emigrate were directed to specific tribes, ethnic groups, clans, and individuals, and constitute a detailed list of the powerful and influential of that time. Among the individuals invited (or more accurately, instructed) to renew their oath were several Mahdist *amīrs* absent from the capital, many of whom were leaders of the riverain Sudanese. A great many tribal *shaykhs* were invited to Omdurman (e.g., Ilyās ᶜAlī Kannūna of the Ghudīyyāt, ᶜAbdallāh ᶜAwaḍ al-Karīm Abū Sinn of the Shukrīyya, and Ṣāliḥ Faḍlallāh Sālim of the Kabābīsh), but also entire tribes, and most especially the pastoralists of marginal or wavering loyalty to the Mahdīyya. Explicitly stated in many of these summonses was the Khalīfa's offer to settle tribal disputes on the occasion of the ᶜĪd.[36]

No less explicit was the Khalīfa's desire to remove to the capital all of the riverain traders settled in Kordofan and Darfur, thereby enhancing the state's control over economic resources while also insuring his own security in the west. In a telling example, the Khalīfa wrote to members of the Jawāmaᶜa tribe on 10 August urging them to make the *hijra* and instructing them to bring to Omdurman "the *awlād al-balad* who are among you in the region." After naming specific individuals who are sought, he adds "Do not leave a single one behind...[bring] all of them, including their women and children and all that they possess. Whoever resists is to be taken with might and iron."[37]

The summons of 1302 was answered by thousands of loyal Anṣār, who understood that refusal of *jihād* constituted disobedience to God and robbed their prayers and fasting of all efficacy. However by early 1303 / late 1885 many tribes still had not emigrated, and the Khalīfa resorted to more direct methods. Perhaps as an example to others, Shaykh ᶜAsākir Abū Kalām of the Jimiᶜāb was imprisoned in Omdurman, while 7,000 of his tribesmen were rounded up and sent either to the capital or the siege at Sinnār. Additionally Jimiᶜāb cattle were seized as a penalty for the tribe's defiance.

Ultimately the Khalīfa could not compel all tribes to come immediately to Omdurman, and as with the evacuation of Khartoum, he was forced to be patient. In 1304/October 1886–September 1887, a new series of letters were issued. Directed mainly to the Arab tribes of Kordofan and Darfur, these letters outlined in greater detail the penalties for disobedience and named an individual, often a *shaykh* of that tribe, responsible for bringing in the group. A representative letter from this period is the summons to the Banū Jarrār of Kordofan, dated 1 March, cited here in full.

> In the name of God (etc.)... From the servant of his Lord, the Khalīfa of the Mahdī (peace be upon him), the Khalīfa ᶜAbdallāhi b. Muḥammad, *Khalīfat al-Ṣiddīq,* to his beloved ones in God, all of the Banū Jarrār, great and small. May God befriend them, Amen.
>
> My beloved ones, I have continuously mentioned to you the virtue and reward of emigration [to Omdurman] and the wickedness and punishment of relying upon this world. Since the passing of the world and the imminence of its end is not hidden from you, that which is with God is better and more lasting. The Imām al-Mahdī (peace be upon him) has come to lead the worshippers to God, and to take them away from the terrors [of Judgment Day] and keep them from straying. Inasmuch as you are honored by seeing him and paying allegiance to him, what is this longing for [your] homelands and material comforts and [concern for] lineage? Is there not a lesson in [the fate of] the wealth of your fathers and grandfathers? Do you not know that death is coming to you and will take you by your necks as it took them? If you know this, will you not heed [the call] for the bliss of eternity and prepare yourselves to meet God Most High?
>
> In short, O beloved ones, out of our concern for you regarding the punishment of God and our desire that you should have bliss, we have dispatched to you the bearer of this [letter], the beloved one, your governor Muḥammad Nūbāwī. Upon his arrival to you, it is necessary that you set forth with him to this place, emigrating in the path of God Most High with all of your children and goods and dwellings and all that pertains to you, and that you do not leave behind even the least attachment. Do not yearn thereafter for [your] homeland. Know and be certain that whoever lags behind has brought evil and ruin and sin upon himself, while all who come (if God Most High wills) shall see nothing but honor and a goodly end, and shall become one of the Com-

> panions of the Mahdī (peace be upon him). Prepare for your happiness and success. May God bless you. Peace.[38]

About the same time that this letter was sent, the Mahdist chief judge at Omdurman ruled that the goods of all tribes resisting emigration were liable to seizure and sale by the government, with the proceeds left in trust for the tribe at the *Bayt al-Māl*. Some combination of the Khalifa's threats and use of force eventually prevailed in the west. On 16 April the *amīr* Ḥamdān Abū ᶜAnja arrived at Omdurman with a huge army consisting mainly of western tribesmen and *jihādīyya* from the Nūba mountains of Kordofan. Among these were the subjects of the Muslim state of Taqalī, whose wavering loyalty led to their forced emigration and the death of their ruler. By late 1887, the bulk of the Kordofan tribes had settled in Omdurman, although a section of each was left under the command of a local *amīr*, presumably to watch over a portion of the tribal herds.[39]

The *hijra* of the western tribes was an enormously difficult undertaking, requiring the cooperation and resources of the state. The Mahdī had recognized this, and he called upon his officials in the provinces to assist the tribes in their emigration to him. The Khalīfa likewise gave special attention to the needs of the westerners during the *hijra* of 1302: The *amīr* Muḥammad ᶜUthmān Khālid was instructed on 14 August to gather together the various sections of the Jawāmaᶜa tribe and issue them with clothes, provisions, transport camels and expense money for their trip to Omdurman. Similarly, western emigrants and *jihādīyya* engaged in fighting in the Jazīra region were provisioned and transported to Omdurman at state expense for the ᶜĪd celebration, with the state's share of the war booty (the *khums* or "fifth") used for this purpose. Indeed throughout the main years of emigration, the state's steamers were busily engaged in transporting westerners down the Nile from Shabasha or al-Duwaym to the capital. At least during the emigration of 1304 (and presumably at other times as well), grain was sent from Omdurman to Kordofan to sustain the emigrants along their way.[40]

Not all emigrants to the capital were as well treated as the western Baqqāra. Some eastern pastoralists (e.g., the Rufāᶜa al-Hōy) and farmers of the Jazīra region who were obliged to make the *hijra* because of their questionable loyalty had to pay their own expenses. Certainly the Anṣār who came willingly from the Jazīra came at their own expense: Ibrāhīm al-Būrdayn, who helped supervise the move from Khartoum to Omdurman in 1885–1886, recalled people of the Jazīra crowded on the east bank of the Blue Nile waiting for the government steamers, which for a fee of 60 dollars per load would transport them across the river. (A further 20 dollars was needed to hire camel transport from the town of Masallamīyya to Omdurman).[41] It is tempting to see in this the Khalīfa's favoritism towards the Baqqāra, although in fact their needs were substantial, given the much greater distance and difficulty of their journey. Additionally, travel across Kordofan was dangerous: In 1887 the Khalīfa ordered the decapitation of highway robbers, and throughout the period he and his brother Yaᶜqūb wrote hundreds of letters of safe-conduct, and employed detachments of *jihādīyya*, to bring emigrants safely to the capital.[42] Most westerners who made the *hijra* were expected to devote themselves entirely to *jihād*, breaking all bonds with their homelands. Hence the name "Emigrant" (*muhājir*) came to apply specifically to them, while Jazīra people and others engaged in seasonal fighting, even those who resettled in Omdurman, considered themselves rather as warriors (*mujāhidūn*) and maintained ties with their villages and lands.

That the Mahdī and Khalīfa expected the western Arabs to bring all their possessions with them on the *hijra* is quite clear, although less clear are the expectations of the westerners themselves. For example, the Baqqāra who joined the Mahdī in 1884 are said to have taken "a large proportion of their cattle" with them, and Gordon wrote that the Mahdī had 15,000 head of cattle with him, but this gives no indication what share of the Baqqāra cattle were brought. The Khalīfa's letters of 1885–1887 stress that the emigrants are to leave "nothing behind," and the *amīr* Yūnus al-Dikaym was dispatched on occasion to receive Baqqāra cattle and baggage, that they might travel more easily to the capital. It seems likely, however, that the Khalīfa's policy towards the cattle shifted in the wake of events, particularly the famine of 1306 / 1888–1889. Certainly the Khalīfa was aware—or would have been made aware by his brother, Amīr Yaᶜqūb—of the limitations of Omdurman's grazing area, as well as the deleterious effects of Baqqāra cattle on cultivable Jazīra land. Nor could the Khalīfa have intended to totally denude Kordofan and Darfur of their human and animal resources. It is revealing to note letters as late as 1313 / 1896, addressed to the Khalīfa, which specify that Ḥumr, Rizayqāt and White Nile Arabs are preparing to come to Omdurman and are leaving behind herders to tend their cattle.[43]

After the completion of the great period of *hijra* in 1890, Anṣār continued to emigrate to Omdurman for the purpose of *jihād*. Letters written to the Khalīfa inform him of the arrival of 1,819 *mujāhidūn* in 1892, of 1,101 *mujāhidūn* with their families ("from the deserts") in 1893, etc. As the Anglo-Egyptian invading army approached in 1897, the Khalīfa renewed his call for *hijra*, insisting that "it is not worthy" for the Anṣār to live anywhere other than Omdurman, instructing them to come with all of their families and belongings.[44] By this time, however, the force of the Khalīfa's summons had diminished, and during the final two years of the Mahdīyya the call to *hijra* went largely unanswered.

The policy of *hijra* often served purposes other than the waging of *jihād*. Unmarried women and widows in the provinces were brought to the capital to be settled among members of their tribal or ethnic community, a measure intended to protect vulnerable members of society and maintain the moral order. Alternatively, they could be distributed to the Khalīfa's followers as concubines or wives. The fate of such women depended upon their legal status: whether or not they were considered "spoils of war" (e.g., members of a rebellious community) and hence property of the state. Women captured in the course of *jihād*, either within or without the Sudan, were usually given to the Anṣār elite and favorites of the Khalīfa, as in the 95 women of the Rufāᶜa Ab Rōf in 1887 and the 35 women of the Misīrīyya in 1893. There were, however, limits to this practice. The Jaᶜalī women captured at Matamma in 1897 were initially declared *ghanīma* and intended as concubines for the Baqqāra; however, the Khalīfa reversed this decision and released them to their kinsmen when the Jaᶜaliyīn of Omdurman threatened civil unrest.[45]

Some Sudanese were called to Omdurman to teach in its schools, as in the 131 religious leaders (*fuqarā'*) of El Obeid who emigrated in 1886. Former employees of the Turco-Egyptian regime were always sought after for their skills and relocated to the capital. There was also a seasonal population that came to the city to do business. Bābikr Bedrī writes that "Some of my cousins, from both my father's and my mother's side, used to come to Omdurman every winter, and remain there trading until the middle of

August. During the whole of this time they were my guests." Additionally, on an annual basis the Khalīfa required his *amīrs* and regional officials in Omdurman at ᶜĪd al-Aḍḥā to report on the affairs of their provinces. Finally, criminals and offenders of various sorts frequently were brought to the capital for punishment or rehabilitation (or, as it was usually phrased, "in the interests of the faith").[46] All played a role in the peopling of the city, although Omdurman was predominantly a result of the emigration for *jihād*.

Given the frequently unsettled conditions of the time, it is not surprising that pilgrimage to Mecca was disrupted. The official interpretation of British and Egyptian authorities was that "pilgrimage to Mecca is not permitted." A more nuanced view, acknowledging both Mahdist policy and the popular will, is the statement of Egyptian prisoner Ibrāhīm Fawzī that the Mahdī had declared *hijra* and *jihād* to be better than pilgrimage, and that according to popular belief, *hijra* was equal to seventy pilgrimages. Certainly the honorific title "al-Ḥājj" continued to be used during the Mahdīyya, and there is evidence that at least some Sudanese made pilgrimage to Mecca at this time. Those Anṣār who made the *hijra* to Omdurman for the purpose of fulfilling their *ḥajj* commitment were joined by an intermittent stream of pilgrims from the western and central Sudanic regions, who arrived in the city throughout the 1890s following a centuries-old pilgrimage route. In some cases they appear to have continued on to Mecca; others remained in Omdurman as a distinct community among the Anṣār.[47]

The rise of Omdurman through the policy of *hijra* naturally affected other towns of the Sudan. Khartoum was abandoned outright, although it was not quite the "city of the dead" that Holt has characterized: Its gardens continued to provide revenue for the Ashrāf and some of the Taᶜāīsha, and its dockyard and arsenal continued to function throughout the Mahdīyya. Some Anṣār found Khartoum a comfortable place to rest for a day or two while traveling and, contrary to Anglo-Egyptian reports, there remained standing some houses within the old capital limits: The German prisoner Charles Neufeld was housed there in 1896 in a two-story dwelling. Of course, most of the people of Khartoum moved to Omdurman, however some apparently were allowed to settle in the neighboring villages of Būrrī al-Maḥas, Būrrī al-Daraysa, Manjara, al-Qōz, and Jirayf.[48]

Many of the larger towns did not fare well. Ibrāhīm al-Būrdayn reported to Egyptian Military Intelligence that the Khalīfa had given orders for the destruction of five towns in the Jazīra region: Masallamīyya, Rufā^ca, Wad Madani, Abū Ḥarāz, and Kāmlīn. Likewise he mentions the destruction of "all the towns and villages" between Karkōj and Khartoum (i.e., along the length of the Blue Nile), and "all the cities" of the district of Berber, from Artūlī to Ḥajar al-^cAsal to Omdurman. The evidence for such broad destruction does not exist: Bābikr Bedrī visited and conducted business in the markets of Kāmlīn, Wad Madani, and Sinnār during the Mahdīyya and says nothing about their destruction. It is important to add that many of the towns and villages in the riverain region were already deserted and devastated prior to the Mahdīyya, as a consequence of harsh Turco-Egyptian policies and the emigration of men to the west. Certainly a total demolishing of the Jazīra and northern towns did not occur: Sir William Garstin, in his *Report on the Soudan* of 1899, mentions that although Sōba and Masallamīyya are "in ruins," Kāmlīn and Rufā^ca are fairly prosperous, while Wad Madani "appears to be the most prosperous town in the whole Soudan, not even excepting Omdurman." With regard to the Berber district, Garstin notes that Shendī and al-Matamma are "practically deserted" and "in ruins" (he is writing only two years after the Ja^caliyīn massacre); and the Wad Ḥabashi-Ḥajar al-^cAsal region shows some signs of former cultivation, although Garstin deems it probable that cultivation there ceased prior to 1884.[49]

Most likely—and similar to other aspects of his administration—the Khalīfa's policy with regard to towns was influenced by a variety of conditions and circumstances. It is clear the Khalīfa was determined to make Omdurman the economic as well as administrative center of Sudan, and to this end he suppressed other market towns and redirected their commerce to the capital. This was particularly apparent in the Jazīra, although in the north the Khalīfa was forced to recognize the importance of the markets of Berber and al-Dāmir. Meanwhile Abū Ḥarāz on the Blue Nile was the home of Shaykh Ḥamad al-Nīl of the ^cArakīyīn, an opponent of the Khalīfa: Obliteration of Ḥamad al-Nīl's influence was linked to the destruction of his town. Similarly, Sinnār posed a danger as a population center and potential base for the Khalīfa's enemies among the *awlād al-balad*. Immediately after Sinnār was taken, the Khalīfa exhorted his followers to destroy the town, bring its wood and other materials with them, and settle in Omdurman. In his *Proclamation of the Hair* in 1885, he intoned: "Most emphatic and confirmed is the warning against dwelling in Sinnār." As for the western region, El Obeid was largely depopulated during the Mahdīyya because its people were required in the capital, many of them being merchants and former government employees. The city was not destroyed, nor was it completely abandoned: in fact, Mahdist court documents from 1890–1892 mention the need for additional legal officials in El Obeid, Bāra, and al-Fāshir.[50]

As wood became increasingly scarce and expensive in Omdurman, Sudanese found an incentive to strip the doors, windows, and other fittings from their homes elsewhere and bring them to the capital for sale. This at least partially accounts for the ravaged condition of the countryside so commented upon by the British in 1898. Otherwise the fate of Sudan's towns seems to have varied considerably, depending upon the Khalīfa's perceived needs and a host of changeable conditions.

If the Mahdist policy of *hijra* was the principal means of populating the capital, Omdurman's allure as a holy place reflects an important popular role in the growth of the city. Throughout the Mahdīyya, untold numbers of Sudanese flocked to Omdurman, often traveling great distances, to visit family members and partake of the *baraka*, the tangible holiness, emanating from the Mahdī's tomb, the mosque, and the presence of the Mahdī's and Khalīfa's families. For the most part, visits to Omdurman coincided with two important dates: the Rajabīyya festival (on the 27th of Rajab) and the feast of ᶜĪd al-Aḍḥā (on the 10th of Dhū'l-Ḥijja), although visits also coincided with the Prophet's birthday, the *mawlid al-nabī* (on the 5th of Rabīᶜ al-Awwali) and ᶜĪd al-Fiṭr at the end of the month of Ramaḍān. Such visitors were a transient rather than permanent population, although some remained in the city for extended periods. Hundreds of their letters exist, requesting permission from the Khalīfa to travel to Omdurman. Whether written by the senders themselves and fixed with a seal or written by a scribe, these letters cross ethnic, tribal, and regional lines and cover the entire period of the Mahdīyya. The language of many letters suggests that visiting Omdurman was equivalent to making the pilgrimage: Omdurman is given a name commonly reserved for the Prophet's city, *al-Madīna al-Munawwara* ("The Radiant City"). In other cases, the visit to Omdurman and the Mahdī's tomb is equated with the traditional visitation (*ziyāra*) of a saint's tomb.[51]

Emigrants en route to the city were often carefully observed by Mahdist officials, who sent word of both their condition and comportment to the Khalīfa and Amīr Yaᶜqūb. Great importance—both symbolic and practical—was attached by these officials to the entry into Omdurman, and emigrants were urged to clean themselves thoroughly and don fresh clothes before treading on the soil of the Mahdī's city; when necessary, the state supplied emigrants with new clothing. Some Sudanese wrote to the Khalīfa and Yaᶜqūb when they neared the city, informing them of their imminent arrival and preparations to enter "in an agreeable condition." An extreme degree of reverence was shown by the poet Muḥammad wad Sūrkattī, who removed his shoes before entering the city out of respect for the Mahdī's remains.[52]

The most frequently used name for Omdurman, both in official correspondence and common speech, was *Buqᶜat al-Mahdī* (the Mahdī's "place" or "spot"), *al-Buqᶜa* having been the designation of all of the Mahdī's camps from Abā Island to El Obeid, Rahad, and Omdurman. However, the other names by which the city was popularly known reveal the high regard in which it was held. The poets of the Mahdīyya constructed from "Umm Durmān" the names *Umm Durr* ("Mother of Pearls"), *Amān* ("[Place of] Safety") and *Umm Durr Amān*, and these names enjoyed wide circulation both during and after the Mahdīyya. One poem of the period, *Qaṣīdat Umm Durmān* by Aḥmad wad Saᶜd, began: "Buqᶜat Umm Durmān, refuge of the fearful, none reject it, save the wretched.... Her people are ever enwrapped in kindness, a place where the starving become fattened." Among the hundreds of letters written to the Khalīfa from various Anṣār, we find other designations for the city: *al-Buqᶜa al-Ṭāhira* ("The Pure Place"), *al-Buqᶜa al-Mubaraka* ("The Blessed Place"), *al-Buqᶜa al-Dā'ima* ("The Lasting Place"), *ᶜĀṣimat al-Islām* ("The Capital of Islam"), *Markaz al-Falāḥ* ("The Center of Prosperity"), and *Markaz al-Irshād* (The Center of Guidance). Of truly startling significance, however, are the following three names: *al-Buqᶜa al-Musharrafa* ("The Noble Place"), a designation typically applied to the Kaᶜba in Mecca; *al-Madīna* (or *al-Buqᶜa*) *al-Munawwara* ("The Radiant City/Place"), a name typically applied to Medina; and *al-Ḥaram al-Sharīf* ("The Noble Sanctuary," used in reference to the Mahdī's tomb), which refers to a sacred space in general but is most commonly applied to either the mosque of the Kaᶜba or the Temple Mount in

Jerusalem. Such designations were not, and could not be, imposed upon the Sudanese by the Khalīfa, and indicate the tremendous reverence of the Anṣār towards the city. An additional name found in the Mahdist correspondence, *Dā'irat al-Kawn*, is a Ṣūfī term meaning "The Center of Being," with the further identification of the Mahdī (or Khalīfa) as *Ra's Dā'irat al-Kawn*, "Head of the Center of Being."[53]

Rarely was the name Omdurman used by Sudanese at this time, and when it was, it was usually in conjunction with such modifiers such as *al-Musharrafa*, *al-Ṭāhira*, *al-Mubaraka*, etc. Even the Italian prisoner Guiseppe Cuzzi, in a secret letter to Egyptian Military Intelligence in 1888, signs it "Buqᶜa, near Omdurman." *Umm Durmān* was adopted as a proper name, however, by some Anṣār. In the recorded instances at least, they are members of the *jihādīyya* (and hence of slave origin), suggesting that the name was intended to elevate the status of its bearer.[54]

The spiritual center of Omdurman, and by extension the Mahdist Sudan, was the Mahdī's tomb in the center of town. "*Al-Qubba*," as it was popularly known, was the repository of his *baraka* and occupied an important place in both the poetry of the Mahdist period and the hearts and minds of the Sudanese. Located adjacent to the mosque, east of the *miḥrāb* and hence directly before the Anṣār as they prayed, it loomed over the city and reflected the sun in its whitewashed dome. Fittingly, it was the most visible feature of the city from a distance, serving as a beacon to approaching emigrants and pilgrims. In the tradition of *ziyāra* to a saint's tomb, visitors approached the *Qubba* with a mixture of reverence and awe, often seeking the Mahdī's blessings for improved fortunes, restored health, or protection from calamity. The Egyptian Military Intelligence at times minimized the significance of the tomb, stating in a report of 1891 that "pilgrimages from a distance to the Mahdi's tomb have entirely ceased, and now the women of Omdurman are almost the sole visitors, except at the Bairam festival [ᶜĪd al-Aḍḥā], when all people attend." Whether or not this is correct—and it is questionable whether the report's informant could distinguish an Omdurman resident from a visitor—the report does confirm that Sudanese continued to come to the city for the annual ᶜĪd festival and visited the tomb at this time. The tremendous popular devotion toward the *Qubba* is in any case beyond doubt: The revolt of the Ashrāf against the Khalīfa in 1891 significantly took place in and around the tomb, making obvious their connection to the Mahdī's *baraka* and their claim to privilege; the Mahdī's sons usually received visiting pilgrims at the *Qubba*; while Bābikr Bedrī records that his mother exclaimed upon her death bed, "How I pine for sweet rest in the shadow of the dome!" In the bombardment of the city before the battle of Kararī, British ships trained their guns on the *Qubba* as the symbolic heart of the Mahdīyya. Sudanese had gathered there expecting to find protection with the Mahdī's *baraka*, and a British correspondent after the battle counted 102 dead lying before the tomb.[55]

Considerable devotion was also directed toward the Khalīfa's mosque, which was regarded by the Anṣār to be the fourth great holy place in the world, after the mosques of Mecca, Medina, and Jerusalem. As with the Mahdī's tomb, poetry was composed and recited in praise of *al-Masjid al-Rābi*ᶜ, and well into the 1980s a survivor of the Mahdīyya recalled that he was born "in the vicinity of the Fourth Mosque." An additional (and renewable) source of *baraka* for many Anṣār was the family of the Mahdī, including his wives and children, as well as the Khalīfa ᶜAbdallāhi and his family. Pilgrimages to Omdurman included visits to their homes, or if this was impossible, to the central quarter of town where their *baraka* was concentrated. The Khalīfa especially, as the chosen successor to the Mahdī, was believed by many Anṣār to have the power to intercede with God and direct their prayers to success: a belief with precedent in both Ṣūfī tradition and Sudanic practice. Numerous letters of a highly devotional nature were written to the Khalīfa. It is tempting to dismiss these as mere flattery, except for a common theme—the Khalīfa's power of healing—that suggests widespread popular belief. Thus one Aḥmad Dāyy al-Nūr writes asking the Khalīfa for water from his ablution bottle in order to cure himself from fever; in expectation of his request being granted, he also has sent a messenger to carry the water back to him. Others seek permission to visit Omdurman, since "there is no cure for illness other than you," "a visit to al-Buqᶜa is the cure," an ill brother's cure will be to "view your beautiful face," etc.[56]

Just as devotion to Omdurman outlived the Mahdīyya, so did devotion to the Khalīfa outlive him: The British Inspector at Kosti reported to the Governor of Kordofan in 1918 that "the last time I visited the Khalīfa's tomb [at Umm Dibaykarāt] I found a number of people visiting it and evidence that it was very much frequented." While the popularity of the Khalīfa's administration had dwindled by the end of the Mahdīyya, the dramatic sacrifice of the Sudanese at Ķararī underlines the Khalīfa's continued personal popularity, Or, as in the case of Bābikr Bedrī, even Anṣār who had lost their enthusiasm for *jihād* seem to have maintained a high regard for "the noble" Khalīfa.[57]

The Population of Omdurman

For a nineteenth-century Sudanic African town, Omdurman was an astonishingly huge and diverse place, yet its exact population—like that of the Sudan as a whole—is impossible to determine. Despite abundant quantifiable data in the Mahdist archive, there is no information that covers a broad enough area or extensive enough time period. Surviving records mainly concern troop strengths or treasury revenues and expenditures, and they are of uneven quality and difficult to use in any but the most specific contexts. While estimates of both the Sudanese and Omdurman populations are contained in the various memoirs and intelligence reports, these are, according to Holt, "the roughest of rough guesses." Certainly no census of Omdurman or the Sudan was prepared during the Mahdīyya, and in his annual report of 1904, the British consul in Cairo Lord Cromer claimed that even a rough estimate of the population would be "out of the question."[58] All of this notwithstanding, it is possible, using population estimates and Mahdist documents, to determine at least the average minimum population of Omdurman from 1885 to 1898, while drawing attention to the core population of the city.

When Khartoum was captured by the Mahdī in 1885, there were approximately 30,000 people in the city.[59] There is no agreement on the number of casualties incurred among its soldiers and civilians—claims of as high as 35,000 were made—but the Egyptian Military Intelligence soberly estimated "at least 4,000" killed. Shortly thereafter the Khalīfa's call to *hijra* went out and many thousands of Sudanese poured into Omdurman. But how many thousands, and how many remained in the city? The historian and Egyptian Military Intelligence officer Naᶜūm Shuqayr heard that in late 1885 there were as many as a million people in Omdurman. Rosignoli estimated that the population in 1888 had been 120,000 to130,000 people, while by 1894 there had been approximately 150,000 in the city, "and there may be many more." Ohrwalder also estimated the population at 150,000, although the E.M.I. *General Military Report* for 1890 stated the Omdurman population to be "in ordinary times" 15,000 to 20,000. Finally, the *General Report* for 1895, based on the testimony of the recently escaped Austrian prisoner Rudolf Slatin, gave a figure of "upwards of 400,000."[60] Alongside these figures are several estimates of troop strength in Omdurman, prepared by the E.M.I. and spanning the period 1890–1898. These would be expected to be more reliable than general population estimates, given the specific nature of the subject and the British War Office's obvious interest in its enemy's numbers. At least aspects of these troop estimates may be checked against Mahdist records to calculate the population of the city.

As a rule, the population of Omdurman fluctuated tremendously. Most free, male, adult Anṣār were considered soldiers, *mujāhidūn*, and were away on campaign at irregular intervals. Additionally, some number of wives and slave women usually accompanied them to provide support services. Excluded from military service were certain administrators, members of the Muslim-convert (*Masālma*) community, and the immediate relatives of the Mahdist elite, although some members of all of these groups are known to have participated in *jihād* at times. So for example, anywhere between 18,000 and 100,000 Sudanese—for such are the estimates given!—entered the city with the army of Abū ᶜAnja in April 1887; and during the 1888–1890 Baqqāra immigration, the size of the Taᶜāīsha tribe alone is said to have been approximately 60,000. Meanwhile, two huge expeditions, those of Yūnus al-Dikaym and ᶜAbd al-Raḥmān al-Nujūmī, left Omdurman between 1887 and 1888, and an untold number of the Baqqāra were resettled at a later date in the Jazīra. In addition to *jihād* and *hijra*, the city's population also responded to the needs of agriculture: It has already been mentioned that many people returned to Kordofan and the Jazīra to cultivate each winter, while the *General Military Report* for 1895 more specifically mentions that seventy-five percent of the population left Omdurman to cultivate after the rains. Finally, the famine of 1306 / 1888–1889 obviously had an effect on the population. ᶜAlī al-Mahdī recalled that 8,000 Taᶜāīsha with their families were transported to Fashoda to relieve the state of the burden of feeding them. As to the deaths attributable to the famine, Ibrāhīm Fawzī claimed them to be not less than seventy-five percent, while Ohrwalder gives a figure of sixty percent: Both are speaking of the Sudanese population as a whole, however, and both are guessing. A more specific statement is Slatin's, that "the majority of those who died belonged rather to the moving population than to the actual inhabitants of the town." These latter had been able to store some grain, "and the different tribes invariably assisted each other."[61] Certainly many thousands died in Omdurman during the famine, but many thousands also came to the capital in search of food. The precise effect of the famine on the city's population is therefore unknowable.

Another important fact is that women (or more accurately, women and children) constituted the largest portion of Omdurman's population at any one time. The German prisoner Neufeld even claimed that by November 1888 Omdurman had been almost depleted of its male population due to military needs. Virtually all relevant intelligence reports and many accounts of the Anglo-Egyptian conquest make the observation that women preponderate, and furthermore note that women outnumber men by about three-to-one. This seems a reasonable ratio. A Mahdist document listing the members of the Rikābīyya tribe in Omdurman in 1306 / 1888 records the names of 168 family members and 54 *mujāhidūn*, for an almost exact three-to-one ratio. Naturally the size of a family and number of wives would have varied according to wealth and circumstances: A list of soldiers coming to Omdurman from the desert hinterland in 1893 mentions only 1,101 family members for 1,005 *mujāhidūn*; while the party of *amīr* Musāᶜid Qaydūm included 25 family members and six Anṣār. It is possible that the former were coming to the capital purely on behalf of *jihād* (i.e., leaving some family members behind), while the latter came with the intention of resettling in the city. The Shukrīyya who emigrated involuntarily in 1888 included 5,800 family members and 2,023 *mujāhidūn*, again close to a three-to-one ratio. Considering Mahdist policies that encouraged multiple marriages, and the frequent absence of men on campaign, it is not difficult to accept the premise of a three-to-one ratio of women (or women and children) to men; in fact this ratio is almost certainly too low. Interestingly, a 1921 unofficial census of Omdurman reveals the same three-to-one ratio.[62]

Do these estimates of "family members" in the Mahdist documents include slaves as well as free women and children? Likely they do not: At least the party of Musāᶜid Qaydūm was said to contain, in addition to the family members, five *adamīyyāt* (slave girls) and 17 *khādimāt* (female servants). This is significant, as some studies suggest that Omdurman's population was roughly half slaves. Ohrwalder commented that "Omdurman is full of slaves; even in the poorest houses one female slave at least will be found," a statement that mimics eighteenth- and nineteenth-century travel accounts of the Sudan. Again, this figure may be low: Khartoum's population in 1883 was said to be anywhere from one-half to three-quarters slaves, while Bayard Taylor in the 1850s had estimated its population to be half slaves.[63]

The E.M.I. prepared four estimates of troop strength in Omdurman for the period 1889–1890. These can be examined for insight into the population of the city based on the three-to-one ratio, with the caveat that this represents the absolute minimum figure since it is, one, exclusive of non-combatants and two, probably exclusive of slaves. The estimates are contained in the testimonies of Maḥmūd Effendi ᶜAbdallāh and ᶜAbdallāh Effendi Muḥammad, former officers of the Turco-Egyptian regime who escaped from Omdurman; a June 1890 report of Egyptian Military Intelligence; and the *General Military Report* for 1890. Maḥmūd Effendi mentions 12,000 soldiers "of all types" in Omdurman, ᶜAbdallāh Effendi gives a figure of 20,000 soldiers "of all types," the June 1890 report claims 25,500 soldiers "of all types," and the *General Report* claims only 8,500 soldiers. Based on the three-to-one ratio, these would yield minimum population estimates of, respectively, 48,000, 80,000, 102,000, and 34,000. Given that these reports all address the same period, their inconsistency is puzzling. The *General Report* is certainly too low: Elsewhere it gives the population of Omdurman as 15,000 to 20,000, which is less than the three-to-one ratio would suggest. The estimates of the two effendis and the June 1890 report are likely also low, even if they are counting only those Anṣār committed full-time to the *jihād*: This was a period of conciliation and retrenchment for the Mahdīyya, and there is no reason to suppose that Omdurman would have been stripped of its male population. It is of course possible that the city's population had dropped dramatically as a result of the 1306 famine, although Slatin's account suggests the contrary. More importantly, these estimates do not reflect what must have been an enormous demographic increase following the *hijra* of the Baqqāra tribes. A more convincing estimate is contained in the *General Military Report* for 1891, which gives a figure of 49,000 soldiers in the capital, for a total of at least

196,000 persons. This resembles the Rosignoli and Ohrwalder estimates of the population, although again it is a minimum figure: Rosignoli estimated that the mosque could hold more than 70,000 worshippers; similarly, the Mahdist poet Aḥmad wad Saᶜd wrote that in Ramaḍān of 1303 (1886), "70,000 prayer mats prayed behind the Khalīfa, night after night." Since these worshippers would have been males, at the three-to-one ratio this would indicate at times a population in excess of 250,000.[64]

The later estimate in the *General Report* for 1895 of "upwards of 400,000" in Omdurman appears at first unusually large. This figure may reflect a concentration of troops in the capital following Mahdist losses at Agordat (21 December 1893) and Kassala (17 July 1894). Additionally, the report counts 61,600 soldiers in the city, which at the accepted ratio would indicate a population of 246,400. Doubling this number to include the proposed fifty percent population of slaves would suggest a total of 492,800, although again, it is unclear if such a doubling is warranted.

Following the conquest of 1898, E.M.I. prepared a *Sudan Intelligence Report* based on captured Mahdist material that estimated 52,000 Anṣār were present at the final battle of Kararī. At the three-to-one ratio, this would suggest an Omdurman population at the end of the Mahdīyya of at least 208,000. By way of comparison, the Sudanese historian (and former Anṣārī) Muḥammad ᶜAbd al-Raḥīm claimed that after Kararī, only twenty-five percent of Omdurman's population remained, the rest having fled or died. Meanwhile, a 1901 census and a 1906 survey—both of questionable accuracy—estimated the city's population at, respectively, 50,000 and 60,000: If these reflect the twenty-five percent left after Kararī, the 1898 population would have been at least 200-240,000. A similar figure is given by the Egyptian physician Dr. Ḥasan Zakī, who spent the Mahdīyya in Omdurman: Charged with inoculating people during a smallpox outbreak in 1885, he claims to have limited the mortality rate to five percent. Meanwhile, he states that the Treasury distributed 12,000 shrouds for the dead, which again suggests a population of 240,000.[65]

This figure of roughly one-quarter million, whether or not it is inclusive of slaves, represents an extremely large average population for its time and place: in fact, it is unprecedented in Sudanic history. Joining the women and children, free and enslaved, as a core population would have been the *jihādīyya* garrisoned in al-Kāra (and after 1894, also serving in the

Khalīfa's *mulāzimīn* force). Mahdist records as well as E.M.I. intelligence reports suggest an average of 3,000 (al-Kāra only) and 8,000 (al-Kāra and *mulāzimīn*) in Omdurman.[66] With the three-to-one ratio, this would indicate a population of *jihādīyya* and their families of 12,000 persons (pre-1894) and 32,000 (1894-), although certainly not all *jihādīyya* had families.

Administrators and other employees of the state constituted another part of the city's core population. The *Sudan Intelligence Report* of 1898 lists 234 such persons, including officials of the treasuries, courts, and arsenal, as well as clerks and artisans. The three-to-one ratio would increase their numbers to at least 936 persons. Overlapping to some degree with these were the former Turco-Egyptian officials, officers, soldiers, and their dependents, who at the time of the conquest numbered some 8,676 persons; and the Muslim-convert community, which numbered approximately 199 persons before the battle of Kararī.[67]

Finally we must consider the households of the Mahdist elite, which formed an important component of the core population. The structure of this group is discussed elsewhere, although for present purposes they can be considered as the spouses and children of the Mahdī and his brothers, and of the Khalīfa ᶜAbdallāhi and his brothers and sisters; the Ḥāmid Muḥammad household, which included the family of Khalīfa Sharīf; the Aḥmad Sharfī household of the Dongola Ashrāf; and finally the spouses and children of Khalīfa ᶜAlī and his brothers and sisters. Available data suggest that these households contained, at the very minimum, 353 women and children, exclusive of slaves and most concubines. A large number of *amīrs* were also considered a part of the household of the Khalīfa ᶜAbdallāhi, and the addition of their women and children significantly increases the size of this category.

Taken collectively, the core population of *jihādīyya*, administrators and state employees, Muslim-converts, former Turco-Egyptian employees, and the Mahdist elite totals perhaps 42,000 persons, or about seventeen percent of an estimated average minimum population of 250,000. Added to this core population was the far larger number of Anṣār women and children, soldiers coming from or going to *jihād*, and visiting merchants and pilgrims. The governance of such a huge and diverse population, densely settled under difficult conditions—and further, living in a time of messianic fervor—raises important questions about what the Khalīfa instructed, what the Anṣār believed, and how they lived their lives.

CHAPTER THREE

Governing the Mahdī's City

When on the day of the fall of Khartoum the order about taking possession of the houses reached us, Muḥammad Muṣṭafā and I took the house of a man called Muḥammad ᶜAlī Bey Wuṣūṣ, who I think was a merchant from Aswān. There was no one in it, but we found there currants and wheat flour and clarified butter and dried meat and sacks of millet. I did not touch any of this food, because I was fasting; but even if I had not been fasting I could not have eaten any of it, as my companions did, until permission came from Walad al-Nujūmī on behalf of the Mahdī allowing us to eat any food that we found. This permission did not reach us till Tuesday morning, when we baked small unleavened loaves from the flour, and ate them with oil, although there was butter and honey there, because we wanted to be ascetic.

Authorities and Structures

While many of the Anṣār were devoted and enthusiastic supporters, the Khalīfa still faced conditions in Omdurman that were hardly conducive to stable governance, and these were compounded by his political insecurity and frequent dismissal of administrators. On a more fundamental level, there was the question of how exactly a leader is to encourage mundane order in a millennial society: Why dispose of trash properly when *al-Mahdī al-Muntaẓar*—the divinely guided Expected One—has appeared and the End of Days is imminent? Moreover, what models and standards of urban governance should be retained from a Turco-Egyptian regime that was regarded as irredeemably corrupt? Is "urban governance" even a goal in a state defined by *jihād* and shaped by *hijra*, in a city that is just a *buq*^{c}*a*, a "spot," on the path to universal and correct Islam?

The view of the Khalīfa ^{c}Abdallāhi presented in European accounts of the nineteenth century was, needless to say, harshly critical, due in no small part to the efforts of F. R. Wingate, the director of Egyptian Military Intelligence from 1889 and the author/editor of the three most popular and influential English-language books on the Mahdist period. Until the publication of P. M. Holt's *The Mahdist State* in 1958, this view largely prevailed: namely, the Khalīfa as malevolent dictator, who controlled all aspects of life in Sudan on behalf of his own interests and those of his tribe, the Ta^{c}āīsha. Holt challenged this view and revealed the degree to which the Khalīfa was a prisoner of his circumstances. An additional point is that while the Khalīfa was the supreme political and religious authority in the Sudan, his power had its limits. For example, like all Sudanese he was forced to defer to his relations in family matters, even being barred from divorcing his first wife by his brother and others. Like all rulers, he was at the mercy of his advisors and staff, who sometimes misinformed and misspent to their own advantage. He may have been deeply suspicious of his opponents, yet he was unable to trace the whereabouts of three Khatmīyya leaders in Omdurman in 1887 and had to commission someone to come to the city in search of them. Certainly he was at times constrained in his actions by popular will: For example, he was forced to revoke his order to treat the women of Matamma as war booty in 1897 after the Ja^{c}aliyīn of Omdurman reacted with outrage. As a companion of Bābikr Bedrī asked rhetorically, "Could [the Khalīfa] do that without setting all Omdurman ablaze?"[1]

In light of this, it is interesting to read a description of the Khalīfa given by the former prisoner Charles Neufeld in 1898 to the war correspondent Bennett Burleigh. Unaware of the criticisms against him for his failure to flee Omdurman, Neufeld spoke without the need to curry favor that characterizes his later memoir, and provides what may be the most objective European account of the Mahdist ruler. Neufeld told Burleigh that the Khalifa

> was not at all a bad sort of man, nor an exceptionally cruel Arab taskmaster, and certainly not a monster. The Khalifa, he said, had often come and chatted with him. Abdullah had vowed to him that if he were

> able to have his own way he would make a close friend of him, and have him always near his person. The Khalifa asserted he liked white men, admired their knowledge and ability, and would, were he permitted, have many of them in Khartoum. As everybody knew, he befriended the Greeks, because he could do that with safety, for the natives were not so jealous of them as of other white men. The Taaisha were, he declared, absurdly suspicious of his intercourse with Neufeld, and were always bringing him tales to try and get him to kill all the white men without exception. His countrymen's jealous, narrow fanaticism annoyed him, but what, he asked, could he do, for he was very much in their power and unable to afford to fly in their faces? Abdullah often spoke thus, according to Neufeld, and as the latter also said, frequently that leader of the fanatical dervishes exhibited keen interest in acquiring information about Europe and its people. He hoped to make peace someday with the outside world, and be allowed thereafter to rule the Soudan.[2]

The fact that the Khalīfa was at times constrained in his actions is important: Omdurman, like other Sudanic towns, lacked the formal municipal organizations that tend to characterize towns in the West, and hence much depended on the authority of the state ruler. Given the limits of that authority, the question is raised: What combination of personal leadership, state institutions, social and economic structures, and popular will combined to organize, to even make possible, daily life in Mahdist Omdurman? Additionally, what role did Mahdist belief play? These questions are all the more pressing given the revolutionary climate, with its religious excitement and frequent upheaval, of the Khalīfa's 13-year reign.

Omdurman was given precise definition as an administrative and geographic unit by Mahdist authorities. Although provincial boundaries tended to shift with changing political conditions, 16 separate provinces (*ᶜimālāt*) were identified by the Egyptian Military Intelligence after the conquest. Of these, three constituted the region of "Greater Omdurman": al-Sharq (the eastern district), from ᶜAylafūn to Ḥajar al-ᶜAsal, under the *ᶜāmil* Abū Bakr Muḥammad al-Amīn; al-Gharb (the western district), from Khūr Shambāt to Ḥajar al-ᶜAsal, under the *ᶜāmil* Aḥmad Nāṣir al-Makk; and Umm Durmān, the capital itself, from Abū Siᶜd in the south to Khūr Shambāt in the north, at least nominally under the direct supervision of the

Khalīfa. As Holt has pointed out, these interior provinces were more fiscal areas than administrative units, with the *ᶜāmil* in essence a chief tax collector. In Omdurman at least, tax revenue was paid directly to the central Treasury.[3]

As a region, Omdurman was chiefly important for being the mobilization site and command center of the Mahdist state, which was preeminently a military state, created and defined by *jihād.* With the exception of the *jihādīyya* and *mulāzimīn* garrisons, its army was composed of Anṣār volunteers. Indeed, ᶜIsmat Ḥasan Zulfō wrote that at Kararī, "all of the men were soldiers, and a man was a combatant before he was anything else." Nor were administrators exempt: *Qāḍīs* were obliged to dress in the military garb of the Anṣār and carry a sword, and *Qāḍī al-Islām* Aḥmad ᶜAlī commanded his own unit under the largest division, the Black Standard. Fittingly then, the state's principal form of organization was military, with the Khalīfa as commander-in-chief. Thus an examination of the city's administration begins with reference to the Mahdist military command structure, since, as the son of one Anṣārī recalled, there was no "official face" to governance in Omdurman, rather "urban organization was tantamount to military organization."[4]

At the top of the chain of command was the Khalīfa, who as supreme commander was ultimately responsible for all matters of strategy and planning. Directly below him, however, was the actual chief executive of the Mahdist state and army, his brother Amīr Yaᶜqūb, whose importance cannot be overstated. As the director of the general command and administrative structure, Yaᶜqūb supervised all matters related to defense and daily operations. Since all important matters of state were inherently "military," all administrative officials and commanders reported directly to him. Yūsuf Mikhā'īl plainly stated that Yaᶜqūb "managed the affairs of the state and was responsible for everything," while Bābikr Bedrī recalled that he was both widely popular and indispensable.[5]

In his capacity as commanding general (*al-qā'id al-ᶜāmm*) of the army, Yaᶜqūb oversaw the divisions of the Green Standard of the Khalīfa ᶜAlī wad Ḥilū, consisting of tribal levies of the White Nile Arabs, principally the Dighaym, Kināna, and Laḥāwīyīn; the Red Standard of the Khalīfa Muḥammad Sharīf, consisting mainly of the Danāqla; the *mulāzimīn* commanded by the Khalīfa's son ᶜUthmān Shaykh al-Dīn, which by the time of Kararī was the largest and elite force of the Mahdīyya; the *jihādīyya* commanded by the Khalīfa's cousin Ibrāhīm al-Khalīl Aḥmad, garrisoned in al-Kāra; the artillery units in the fortresses of the capital; and the various provincial forces scattered throughout the Sudan. Additionally, Yaᶜqūb personally commanded the Black Standard, originally the largest force in the Mahdist army, which consisted of levies from 52 tribes at Kararī.[6] Finally, in his capacity as chief executive, Yaᶜqūb supervised the affairs of the central institutions of state. These included the *Bayt al-Māl*, which provided wages and grain for the standing army and operated a storehouse for troops at al-Mōrida; the *Bayt al-Amāna*, which stored all armaments and munitions; the camel post (*Hajjānat al-bōsta*), which was concerned mainly with military correspondence; and the munitions workshop (*Warshat al-jabkhāna*), which produced ammunition.

Amīr Yaᶜqūb's command of the Black Standard is of greatest interest to the story of Omdurman, since after the Khalīfa Sharīf's Red Standard was disbanded and absorbed into the Black Standard in 1886, it became the main force for volunteers. Hence all men of Omdurman who were not regular soldiers of the *jihādīyya* nor attached to the *mulāzimīn*, regardless of tribe, belonged to the Black Standard.

The organizational structure of the Black Standard resembled that of other Mahdist forces: The commander directly oversaw the four divisions (*rub*ᶜ) of his army, led by their respective *amīrs*. Each *rub*ᶜ was further divided into a number of standards (*rāyas*) distinguished by tribe or sub-tribe, the sizes of which varied according to the ability of their *amīr* to mobilize them (or in some cases, according to the number of soldiers assigned them by the Khalīfa or Yaᶜqūb). The soldiers in a *rāya* might be cavalry, foot soldiers (i.e., sword and spear men), or *jihādīyya*, and were divided into groups of one hundred, each led by a *ra's mī'a* (literally, "head of a hundred"). These one hundred were further divided into groups of twenty-five led by a *muqaddam*.

This military command structure in most instances derived from the already-existing social hierarchies. Its significance for Omdurman's administration is apparent: Each *amīr* was held directly accountable to Yaᶜqūb for the well-being of his soldiers, who as a tribe, sub-tribe, ethnic group, or clan tended to settle together in a specific part of the city. (The use of the term *farīq* highlights this: Originally pertaining to a band of soldiers or a kinship group, it acquired a spatial sense in Omdurman where it came to mean "neighborhood.") In the absence of most municipal officials or authorities who had functioned under the Turco-Egyptian regime (e.g., the *ᶜumdas* and *nāẓirs*), the *ra's mī'as* and *muqaddams* became responsible for the daily affairs of their people. Specifically, they were required to submit written lists of their troops to the *Bayt al-Māl* in order to facilitate the disbursement of grain and division of booty. To coordinate and record payments of money and grain, each *rāya* was ordered by Yaᶜqūb to employ a clerk—the Black Standard had more than 25—and some of these (as in the case of Yūsuf Mikhā'īl) were drawn from the Egyptian Coptic population. Illustrating the Khalīfa's reliance on a traditional and military hierarchy is his letter to ᶜAlī Jādallāh, son of the *shaykh* of the Kawāhla, in 1887. ᶜAlī's father had left on behalf of the *jihād*, leaving the Kawāhla of Omdurman without a leader to advocate on their behalf. The Khalīfa wrote that "our intention is that you stay with us in *al-Buqᶜa*, that you might be at the head of your people there and inform us [as to their condition.] For without your presence among them, they can get no rest."[7]

Such a form of organization existed from the earliest days of the Mahdīyya, and is apparent also in the case of non-Sudanese who had no basis for communal or "tribal" authority. In 1882, the Syrian Christian Jūrjī Istāmbūlī—renamed "Muḥammad Saᶜīd al-Muslimānī" by the Mahdi—was given responsibility over "the Christians" of Kordofan. After the capture of El Obeid, *amīrs* of the Greeks and Egyptians also were chosen. The Khalīfa allegedly remarked to Sayyid Bey Jumaᶜa at this time that "you are an Egyptian, and everyone likes his own compatriots best." Memoirs of the period make reference to the *amīrs* and *muqaddams* of the Muslim-convert (*Masālma*) community of Omdurman; for instance, Dimitri Kokorembas (renamed ᶜAbdallāhi) served as *amīr* of the Greeks. These appear to have been elected by members of their own community: Yūsuf Mikhā'īl writes that after the battle of Ṭūshkī in 1889, the Khalīfa ordered all "alien groups" to have an *amīr*, "and that each tribe should be on its own and run its own affairs without meddling with other tribes."[8]

The responsibilities of the various *amīrs* in Omdurman extended beyond looking after the material needs of their people. Of equal importance, they were expected to help mediate disputes that did not require the attention of the courts, as well as explain and enforce the rulings of the Mahdī and

Khalīfa contained in the published *manshūrāt* or proclaimed in the Friday sermons at the mosque. This was specifically stipulated by the Mahdī with regard to the seclusion and veiling of women. Generally stated, the *amīrs* were responsible for the comfort and comportment of their people, and among the Muslim-converts, for their whereabouts as well. Even a trip to the dockyard or gardens of Khartoum required the permission of an *amīr*, and as the European accounts make clear, flight from Omdurman was taken at the expense of those left behind, who had to answer to Mahdist authorities. Finally, the *amīrs* were responsible to the *Bayt al-Māl* for the collection of tax revenues as well as disbursement of state aid. Rosignoli recalled that during the building of the *Qubba* and city wall, "the Bayt al-Mal obliged each Emir to pay a fixed amount and he was responsible for collecting the sum from whomever he could among his dependents."[9]

The military form of organization seems to have sufficed in Omdurman for most of the period, until the approach of the Anglo-Egyptian army in 1898 when it became necessary to delegate more authority on behalf of the defense of the city. Apparently a Taᶜāīshī *amīr* named Yaᶜqūb Abū Zaynab, a relative and confidante of the Khalīfa, was made responsible for maintaining order in the city as a whole, a position akin to formal civil authority but also an extraordinary and short-lived measure.[10]

The Khalīfa's recognition of earlier forms of authority was, like other aspects of his rule, more pragmatic and flexible than contemporary accounts admit. Certainly there were instances when he, like the Mahdī before him, appointed his own followers in the place of disaffected or unreliable tribal or community *shaykhs*: His letter to the Banū Jarrār of 1304/1887, warning them against pride of descent and appointing Muḥammad Nūbāwī as their *ᶜāmil*, has been cited already, and other examples could be mentioned. Likewise, however, a preponderance of evidence suggests that the Khalīfa recognized earlier authority wherever possible. In addition to the case of the Kawāhla, the Khalifa appointed an *ᶜāmil* of the Ḥamda in conformity with their wishes and a *muqaddam* of al-Kawwa "according to the desire of the people of al-Kawwa"; Nāṣir Ibrāhīm al-Makk, *nāẓir* of his tribe during Turco-Egyptian rule and descended from the Funj era *makk*, was made *amīr* of the Jummūᶜīyya during the Mahdist period; Muḥammad ᶜAlī Aḥmad Kamtūr was allowed to withdraw the Kamātīr tribe from their assigned *rāya* and join another one led by a close kinsman; and among the

Dār Ḥāmid there is a clear continuity in tribal leadership from the Turco-Egyptian period through the Mahdīyya. The list of *amīrs* of the *rāyas* and quarters of Omdurman reinforces this point: Muḥammad Ṣāliḥ Sūwār al-Dhahab, a notable among the Danāqla of El Obeid, was asked to choose one of his sons to serve as *amīr* over his following; al-Fakī Makkāwī Aḥmad ᶜAbd al-Raḥīm, a leader of the Rikābīyya of Kordofan and *khalīfa* of the Khatmīyya Ṣūfī sect, commanded his own *rāya*; ᶜAbdallāh al-Shaykh Ḥamad al-Nīl, eldest son and *khalīfa* of his father, served as *amīr* of the ᶜArakīyīn after joining the Mahdī at Rahad; Ibrāhīm Mukhayyir, son of the *shaykh* of the Zayyādīyya of Darfur, served his people as *amīr*; etc. Finally, one sociological study of the Mahdist elite finds that almost half of the "top Mahdist leaders," broadly defined, were traditional tribal and religious authorities. Given this study's narrow base of evidence, the actual percentage was likely much higher.[11]

Among the influential people of Omdurman, both administrators and *amīrs*, were many with ties to the Ṣūfī orders, and to some extent this form of authority also provided structure to the city. The Ṣūfī *ṭarīqas* were regarded as superseded of course by the appearance of the Mahdī, who abolished them as well as the use of the term *darāwīsh* ("dervishes"). At the same time, much of the ideology and organizational strength of the Mahdīyya had its origins in Sufism.[12] Consequently, while the public devotional activities of the orders largely ceased during this period, the respect commanded by the Ṣūfī *shaykhs* remained intact through their incorporation into the "higher spiritual calling" of the Mahdīyya.

The situation of the Mīrghanīs in Mahdist Omdurman is particularly interesting in this regard. One of Sudan's preeminent "holy families," the Mīrghanīs were the founders and leaders of the Khatmīyya Ṣūfī *ṭarīqa* from the early nineteenth century, had formed an alliance with the Turco-Egyptian authorities and opposed the Mahdī from the beginning. Meanwhile, at least five members of the family, including Aḥmad ibn Muḥammad ᶜUthmān al-Mīghanī II, lived in Omdurman until its fall. Accorded a measure of respect by the Khalīfa (Rosignoli wrote that they were "not ill-treated") and supported by the *Bayt al-Māl*, they were nonetheless kept under careful supervision and required to pray the five daily prayers at the mosque. It hardly seems possible that they were active supporters of the Mahdīyya, although they were suspected of Mahdist sympathies by the Egyptian Military Intelligence, perhaps for their reluctance (or more likely, inability) to flee the city. Regardless, their influence among the Anṣār, especially in the mediation of disputes, was untarnished, as Bābikr Bedrī makes abundantly clear. Ohrwalder adds that *Sharīfa* Nafīsa (a granddaughter of Muḥammad ᶜUthmān I) was among "the most influential people in Omdurman."[13]

Not surprisingly, association with the Khatmīyya influenced the social relations and settlement patterns of some Anṣār and helped organize their life in the capital. This is noticeable in the case of four extended families originally from El Obeid and Bāra in Kordofan, who settled alongside one another and formed a number of *rāyas*: the families of ᶜArabī and Makkāwī Aḥmad ᶜAbd al-Raḥīm (of the Rikābīyya); Muḥammad Ṣāliḥ Sūwār al-Dhahab (of the Danāqla); Muḥammad Ṣāliḥ wad Ūru (of the Maḥas); and Muḥammad al-Makkī Ismāᶜīl al-Walī (of the Bidayrīyya). A similar pattern may be discerned with former adherents of the Tijānīyya *ṭarīqa*, such as the Hāshimāb extended family who faithfully served the administration as secretaries to the Khalīfa, teachers of the Khalīfa's and Yaᶜqūb's children, and as *amīr*. While the only overtly "civic" service provided by these individuals was the rest houses they made available to visiting members of their former orders—a not insignificant service in a city as crowded as Omdurman—their influence and social contacts smoothed the way in a variety of matters, helping to facilitate an orderly transition to urban life. Likewise, family and tribal ties were extremely important in mediating problems in Omdurman, and constituted a fundamental level of "governance." Bābikr Bedrī, for example, describes well-placed Jaᶜaliyīn interceding with both the treasury head and the Khalīfa to solve the problems of their fellow tribesmen. On his own behalf, Bābikr made use of his Rubāṭāb connections to settle debts, obtain employment as a clerk, fix a troubled marriage, etc.[14]

A structure with a more obvious connection to the governance of the city was the organization of merchants in the market. The position of chief merchant (*sirr al-tujjār*) had existed in Sudan before the coming of the Turco-Egyptians, who retained it as a means of facilitating relations with the local merchant communities. Each community had its own organization with a chief merchant: Khartoum, as previously mentioned, had three chief merchants during the Turco-Egyptian period, one each for the Turkish, Egyptian and Sudanese merchant communities. A similar situation prevailed in El Obeid.[15]

It is unclear whether this position existed in the early months of Mahdist Omdurman, but probably not in a formal sense, given the confusion of the time. Certainly it was the Khalīfa's intention to appeal to merchants individually, as fellow Anṣār, in coordinating the activities of the market. In a letter dated 22 August 1885, addressed to "his beloved in God, especially the merchants and those who frequent the markets," the Khalīfa ordered them to accept all types of currency, foreign and local, without attempting to devalue its worth. At issue was the money minted by the *Bayt al-Māl*, which the merchants were reluctant to accept at face value. Eventually the Khalīfa was required to create a special institution to treat market matters, the *muṣliḥīn al-sūq* ("market regulators"), discussed below. At some point, however, necessity compelled the formal recognition of a chief merchant—perhaps by 1889, when one is known to have existed in Tōkar. Bābikr Bedrī mentions one Muḥammad Ibrāhīm Zarrūq, styled *rā'is al-umanā'*, who served as representative of the trading community to the Khalīfa. Assisted by ten deputies, Muḥammad Ibrāhīm organized a meeting of the merchants with the Khalīfa when the value of Mahdist currency was again a problem; and in 1892 he was a signatory to the Khalīfa's order confiscating private boats for the use of the *Bayt al-Māl*. It is doubtful that Muḥammad Ibrāhīm exercised the far-ranging authority vested in the *sirr al-tujjār* of earlier times, since many of those responsibilities were assumed by the market regulators. However, as chief merchant, he provided a means of mediation in disputes between the government and merchants and assisted the Khalīfa in the promotion, if not the enforcement, of economic policies.[16]

Another position retained from earlier time was the port director (*rā'is al-baḥr*), which existed at least as far back as the Turco-Egyptian period. This official was originally responsible for the mooring of ships and safety of property in port and, like the chief merchant, had some of his responsibilities subsumed by the Mahdist government (in this case, by the *Bayt al-Māl*). Not surprisingly, all four of the individuals remembered as having held this position during the Mahdīyya came from prominent riverain trading families. One, Faḍl al-Sīd wad Tātāy, was identified by Egyptian Military Intelligence in 1890 as a "governor of the market," reflecting both the convergence of port and market affairs and the social closeness of the individuals involved in these forms of commerce. Faḍl al-Sīd is later reported to be commissioner of boats for the Privy Treasury (*Amīn Marākib Bayt*

Māl al-Fay'). Whether he held this last position for any length of time is unknown, although again it reinforces the idea that the Khalīfa's administration developed from, and co-opted, traditional social and economic authorities to help organize life in the capital.[17]

The Khalīfa, Yaᶜqūb and the Anṣār

At the center of Mahdist administration was the Khalīfa ᶜAbdallāhi, whom Holt called "not only the ultimate authority in the administrative system but its prime mover." All authority emanated from him, although he was not the sole source of legislation in the state. In numerous letters to his subordinates in the provinces, the Khalīfa urged them to base all legal and administrative judgments on *al-Kitāb wa'l-Sunna wa Manshūrāt al-Mahdī*, linking the Mahdī's published teachings with Qur'ān and prophetic practice. The Mahdī's oral teachings (*majālis*) are also known to have been a source of law, while customary practice likely continued outside the attention of the provincial courts. In the capital, however, the Khalīfa's authority carried significantly more weight. Slatin claimed that justice in Omdurman was rendered according to the *Sharīᶜa*, *Manshūrāt* (of the Mahdī) and the wishes of the Khalīfa (*al-ishārāt*). The *General Report on the Egyptian Soudan* of 1895 more bluntly asserted that "a semblance of just government, administered in accordance with the Moslem law, is kept up by the Kadis," but the only true source of law is the will of the Khalīfa. Holt argued that the Khalīfa's insistence on absolute authority was an indication of the inherent weakness of his rule, which required his involvement in all spheres of administration. Certainly both the Khalīfa and Amīr Yaᶜqūb were involved in a wide variety of matters, both large and (seemingly) small, in the capital and in the provinces. Amid the staggering volume of official correspondence conducted by the Khalīfa, Yaᶜqūb and various Anṣār, we note letters concerning such things as family squabbles, dockyard problems, slave ownership, the division of booty, the scarcity of paper, funding for laundry soap for the *mulāzimīn* soldiers, illness, and "a quarrel between two women."[18]

A number of personal secretaries—perhaps eight—served the Khalīfa and Yaᶜqūb, who met daily with the chief officials of the treasury, courts, and market and were in frequent contact with various department heads. A larger cadre of officials also served them in their capacities as overseers of the military and institutions of state, but there was never a central apparatus concerned specifically with Omdurman. Unlike the governance of state, the administration of the city generated virtually no letters, directives, or registers: It was in fact conducted orally, through meetings with the *shaykhs* of the quarters and other local notables, and directly, through the Khalīfa's weekly sermons at the mosque. Ohrwalder recalled the mosque being a place of instruction and indoctrination: "Formerly, every important emir and fiki had his own rukuba, in which he prayed with his own people; but the Khalifa put a stop to this." This policy of an obligatory Friday collective prayer enforced the unity of the Anṣār in a weekly act of great symbolism, and additionally provided the Khalīfa with a regular opportunity to address the people on a variety of subjects, including such pedestrian (but important) matters as the need to keep their neighborhoods clean and streets unobstructed. Of course the military chain of command served as another means of disseminating the Khalīfa's edicts and instructions. Further, Ohrwalder makes reference to "town criers," who spread the news of the Khalīfa's wishes throughout the city. Since no such office is known to have formally existed, these individuals may have been either market regulators or members of the *mulāzimīn*, exhorting people, for example, to turn out for the weekly military parade.[19]

In similar fashion, the Khalīfa received information about affairs in the city's quarters and marketplace through the military chain of command, the *shaykhs* of the quarters and market officials. For instance, Yūsuf Mikhā'īl recalled that the clerks of the *rāyas* often served as messengers between their *amīrs* and the Khalīfa and Yaᶜqub. Additionally, accounts of the period refer to a widespread system of spies who kept the Khalīfa informed of rumors circulating in town. Allegedly these spies also monitored and reported on peoples' behavior, turning in the names of offenders against Mahdist policy to the Khalifa's secretaries. According to Shuqayr, an individual named al-Ḥājj Zubayr al-Jaᶜalī conveyed the Khalifa's messages to his *amīrs* and passed on to the Khalīfa news and gossip and the reports of spies. Such a practice had been known since the Mahdī's days in Kordofan. Originally concerned with identifying and punishing petty criminals and the users of tobacco and alcohol, it was, according to the European prisoners of the regime, abused as a means of personal gain and revenge. It is probably a mistake, however, to assume anything like a "system" of spying in Omdurman: A survivor of the period explained instead that the Anṣār were zealous to enact the moral and ethical teachings of the Mahdī and Khalīfa, and that the principle of collective responsibility—the need for the Anṣār to police their own ranks—naturally led to individuals informing on those whom they regarded as aberrant or dangerous.[20]

Despite their involvement in the myriad affairs of state, both the Khalīfa and Yaᶜqūb were accessible to the Anṣār to a surprising degree, even after the central quarter had been partially enclosed and the *mulāzimīn* unit formed. Shuqayr states that if anyone had a complaint to raise, he could bring it to the Khalīfa in the mosque, crying "O Khalīfat al-Mahdī, I have been wronged!" The Khalīfa would immediately attend to the complaint and pass judgment on the case. Yūsuf Mikhā'īl's account further reflects both the Khalīfa's accessibility and the military chain of command: Someone might approach the Khalīfa and request permission to build a new home; if the Khalīfa approved, he would instruct Amīr Yaᶜqūb to execute the order; he in turn would instruct a clerk of the Black Standard to pass the order onto the appropriate *amīr*. More so than the Mahdī, the Khalīfa convened councils of law and state to formulate his policy. At least twice yearly, on ᶜĪd al-Aḍḥā and the Rajabīyya festival, the Khalīfa met with a collection of notables that included state officials and *amīrs*, tribal leaders, and "the survivors of the Mahdī's chief companions." The records of two extraordinary state councils from 1892 survive, rendering judgment on the Khalīfa Sharīf after the revolt of the Ashrāf and approving the confiscation of boats for the *Bayt al-Māl*. These records are interesting for their signatories, who represent most of the tribal groups of the northern Sudan. If these councils were, as Holt has suggested, merely a "rubber stamp" for the Khalīfa, they indicate the degree to which he felt public affirmation to be necessary. Less formal advisory councils (*majālis al-shūra*) also seem to have been held on an irregular basis with local merchants and tribal and religious *shaykhs* to discuss matters strictly related to the communities of Omdurman. Mūsa Basyūnī, a prominent Jewish merchant from the Muslim-convert community, recalled his participation in a ten-member advisory council known as "The Eminent Ten" (*al-ᶜashara al-kirām*) that met periodically with the Khalīfa to discuss the affairs of the *Masālma* and trade.

(It is unclear if this was identical to the aforementioned merchants' council led by Muḥammad Ibrāhīm Zarrūq.) The Amīr Yaᶜqūb, as the state's chief executive and the Khalīfa's chief advisor, was ever-present at these councils and meetings.[21]

The population of Omdurman, for its part, evinced a high degree of enthusiasm for the policies of the Khalīfa, although naturally not all residents and not all the time. This is most apparent in the various acts of voluntary labor that he called them to perform. Rosignoli relates that the *Qubba* was built "by the entire population of Omdurman," with a share of the work "allotted to each district." The Khalīfa personally inaugurated the project, going down to the river to carry water and materials to the building site. Promised entry to paradise in return for their efforts, the Anṣār worked "on God's business" (*fī shān Allāh*), sustained by a quantity of grain supplied by the *Bayt al-Māl*. Likewise the people of Omdurman built portions of the city wall, the Mahdi's home, and a smaller mosque for the families of the Mahdī and Khalīfa (known as the "Iron Mosque" for its metal roof), as well as the homes of the two junior *khalīfas* and several *amīrs*. Rosignoli adds that the "population was highly enthusiastic," especially the Baqqāra "and other fanatics," and that women and children worked alongside the men.[22]

Among the residents of the city less enthusiastic about voluntary labor were the *Masālma* and many of the captive Egyptians, who of course were in Omdurman against their will. Regarding these projects as forced labor, they paid their respective *amīrs* to release them from duty whenever possible. Nor was everyone's labor freely given: The masons who designed the *Qubba* and wall, formerly in the employ of the Turco-Egyptian government, constituted skilled labor and demanded and received pay for their efforts. The element of self-sacrifice inherent in the experience of most Sudanese however is worth emphasizing, since, for all his authority, the Khalīfa could not have dictated the building of the city nor ruled the state effectively without the active participation of his followers.[23]

On a more regular basis, the people of Omdurman were held responsible for their own districts. Slatin recalls a *fakī* opposed to the Mahdīyya who preached against its "innovations" and was promptly arrested and hanged. Thereafter, "several hundred houses, surrounding the abode of the murdered man, were confiscated; their inmates arrested, bound and carried off to prison; but through the intervention of [Ibrāhīm Muḥammad] Adlan [the

Amīn Bayt al-Māl] they were subsequently liberated. The Khalifa now issued a proclamation to the effect that all the inhabitants of the city were responsible for the actions of their neighbors."[24] While this incident seemed a despotic abuse of power to Slatin, it would have appeared differently to the Anṣār, who might have reasoned thusly: "Opposition to the Mahdī and his Khalīfa is tantamount to opposing the will of God; sedition is a serious crime, punishable by death; and the people of the city are compelled to take responsibility for their neighbors, who in most cases are their near or distant kinsmen." If this call to social cohesion, a fixture of both the Mahdī's and Khalīfa's teaching, was not uniformly embraced, in the dynamic context of Omdurman society it was deemed necessary to the orderly functioning of daily affairs.

Institutions and Omdurman Society

The two chief institutions of the Mahdist state, the *Bayt al-Māl* and *Maḥkamat al-Islām*, played an important role in the governing of Omdurman, although delineating that role is difficult given the absence of a clear distinction between their functions on the state and city levels. With regard to the *Bayt al-Māl*, the largest and most important institution, it is possible to describe those aspects of its operations that more directly affected Omdurman: Most obviously, the Treasury fed and clothed a large percentage of the Anṣār, before, during, and even after their emigration. Unfortunately there are few surviving records of revenues and expenditures relating specifically to the city as such. Surviving records from the Mahdist court meanwhile are similarly unhelpful, although the workings of the market court are of obvious importance. Of interest here, however, are the points of convergence between the operations of these institutions and the development of Mahdist society in Omdurman, most noticeable in the management of the affairs of the marketplace. For an appreciation of this we must briefly review the basic structure of administration, of which the market organization formed a small part.

The supreme organ of administration in the Mahdist state was the *Bayt al-Māl*, which combined the functions of treasury and storehouse and was ultimately responsible for the material well-being of the Anṣār. Its staff encompassed most employees of the government, including many of the *qāḍīs* as well as clerks, central administrative workers (e.g., the camel post), artisans, and weapons manufacturers, in addition to the actual treasury employees. Under the supervision of its chief officer, the *Amīn*, were the workers of the soap factory, pharmacy, a hospital, telegraph stations, percussion caps factory, armory, mint, and lithograph press. Additionally, the *Bayt al-Māl* conducted the sole slave market in Omdurman. In a purely economic sense, it was responsible for revenues and expenditures; policies of land ownership, manufacturing, foreign trade, agriculture, and taxes; the supervision of economic practices; and the implementation of economic policies.

Hindering the treasury's ability to manage the economy, however, was the political tension between the Khalīfa and his riverain opponents. Holt writes that the Khalīfa was obliged to rely on the experience and specialized skills of the *awlād al-balad* in administrative matters: "Hence the commissionership of the Treasury had a frustrated development, since the office was held by men coming from those groups that the Khalīfa was least able to trust." In the 13 years of the Khalīfa's reign, seven men held the title of *Amīn*, and the office changed hands eight times. Only one of these was a Taᶜāīshī, Muḥammad al-Zākī ᶜUthmān, who jointly ran the *Bayt al-Māl* with a riverain colleague for several months in 1890. The others were Aḥmad Sulaymān (1882–1886), a Maḥasī; Ibrāhīm Muḥammad ᶜAdlān (1886–1890), of the Khawālda from the Jazīra region; al-ᶜAwaḍ al-Marḍī (1890, 1893/1894–1897, 1898), a riverain of unknown tribal origin; al-Nūr Ibrāhīm Jirayfāwī (1890–1893/1894), of mixed Maḥasī-Wadai origin; Ibrāhīm Ramaḍān (1897), called "al-Aswānī" and either a Nubian or *muwallad*; and Aḥmad Yāsīn al-Nīl (1898), whose name indicates he is a riverain Sudanese.[25]

By the end of the Mahdist period a number of separate treasuries existed, having developed as an elaboration of the state bureaucracy. Foremost among them was the Public Treasury, or *Bayt Māl ᶜUmūm al-Muslimīn*, which was the highest fiscal office in the state, concerned with taxes (*zakāt*, *fiṭr*, *ᶜushr*, gum, and boat taxes), export goods, and merchants' debts. A second treasury was the *Bayt Māl al-Mulāzimīn*, in existence by 1890, which was wholly concerned with the support of the Khalifa's bodyguard. The *mulāzimīn* were central to the security of the Khalifa's rule, and hence they received greater attention in the form of supervision and sustenance than any other force of Anṣār. A third treasury was the personal treasury of the Khalīfa, also in existence by 1890, which supported his large household and retinue. Called *Bayt Māl Khums wā'l-Fay'* (or *Bayt Māl Khums al-Khalīfa*), this drew upon the revenues of the domain-lands (*fay'*) and the Khalīfa's portion (a *khums* or "fifth") of all booty, as well as taxes on ivory, ostrich feathers, ferries, gum, and imported goods. Additionally, three smaller treasuries existed at times in Omdurman, although the extent of their fiscal independence is unclear. The treasury of the military workshop and dockyard (*Warshat al-Ḥarbīyya wa'l-Tarsāna*) paid such military expenses as maintenance of the steamships and the manufacture of gunpowder. The *Bayt Māl al-Jihādīyya* supported of the troops of al-Kāra, although at least a portion of its revenues was later allocated to the *mulāzimīn*. Finally, the treasury of the market police (*Ḍabṭīyat al-Sūq*) collected shop taxes as well as fines imposed upon smokers, drinkers, and gamblers in support of the market police, a state-run guest house at the marketplace, and other such public expenses as the construction of the city wall. The administrative and clerical staffs of these treasuries numbered fewer than one hundred, of whom approximately sixty-three served the public treasury, nine the market treasury, seven the *mulāzimīn*, and four each the military and personal treasuries. Many if not most of these had previously served the Turco-Egyptian government in the same capacity as they served the Mahdīyya, the Egyptian Copts and riverain Sudanese being particularly prominent. Among some positions, such as the telegraph operators, all were former Turco-Egyptian employees. Additionally, some hundreds of *jihādīyya,* artisans and others were also employed by the *Bayt al-Māl.*[26]

The Mahdist courts exhibit a similarly high degree of specialization. The High Court at the mosque, known as *Maḥkamat al-Islām*, heard all serious criminal cases and served as the court of appeal for cases tried in the provincial courts. Headed by the *Qāḍī al-Islām*, this court consisted of approximately twenty judges, any one of whom could try a case and render judgment according to the Qur'ān, *Sunna,* and *Manshūrāt* of the Mahdī. In matters where the Mahdī's teachings were insufficient, judgment was postponed until after the weekly judicial deliberative council (*yawm al-shūra*), at which the assembled judges would discuss the cases and render opinion according to the Mālikī legal rite. The judgments of this court were final, and its sentences were carried out immediately.

The judges of the High Court included at times both riverain Sudanese, particularly Jaᶜaliyīn, and several westerners. Regarding the latter, Slatin said, "They are not permitted to give judgment, and merely give their votes to their higher colleagues." Doubtless the westerners did defer to those who had a greater knowledge of Sharīᶜa, many of whom came from prominent learned families and had previously served as judges under the Turco-Egyptian regime. At the same time, the presence of westerners on the court indicates the Khalīfa's concern for greater social integration, as well as the more obvious political necessity of sharing power with his western backers.[27]

In addition to the High Court were a number of smaller courts in Omdurman. A court at the *Bayt al-Māl* heard cases involving officers of the treasury, such as cases brought by or against the *Amīn* concerning matters of inheritance or taxation, as well as cases concerning booty, ownership of slaves, and personal status. The treasury *qāḍīs* also served to authorize the sale and purchase of slaves. In existence since 1886, this court consisted of one judge (*nā'ib al-shārᶜ*), a claims officer, and two clerks at the time of the Anglo-Egyptian conquest.[28] Two small courts apparently also served the needs of the *mulāzimīn* and *jihādīyya*, although little is known of their operations. The former, probably established after the enclosure of the bodyguards' area in 1894, consisted of a Taᶜāīshī judge who mediated disputes between the *mulāzimīn* and the townspeople. Judging from the account of Bābikr Bedrī, such a court was certainly needed, as the *mulāzimīn*—emboldened by their special status—were known to engage in extortion and other forms of harassment-for-profit. The latter consisted of two judges who worked alongside the *amīr* of the *jihādīyya* at al-Kāra. Their cases involved matters of marriage, property, and debt among the *jihādīyya*, who, unlike other segments of the Anṣār, had no ready family or tribal structure to mediate disputes. As in all matters related to the military, these cases were of direct interest to the Amīr Yaᶜqūb, who supervised the workings of these courts.[29]

A small court also existed for some period of time at al-Mōrida, consisting of a judge, a superintendent (*amīn al-maḥkama*), and a clerk, to hear cases related to the operations of the port involving boat owners, merchants, and port employees. As was the case with all courts, however, important matters were also brought directly to the attention of the Khalīfa at the mosque or to Amīr Yaᶜqūb. For example, when the Ashrāf patriarch Aḥmad

Sharfī sought to challenge the state's requisitioning of private boats in 1892, he wrote directly to Ya^cqūb instead of taking his claim before the Mōrida court.

The court at the marketplace (*Maḥkamat al-Sūq*) represents the most deliberate attempt at public administration by Mahdist officials. Operating in conjunction with the aforementioned market police, it helped maintain order in the city's only truly "public" space. Regrettably, very few of the records it kept have survived. The immediate precedent for a market court is found in the reign of the Mahdī, who assigned to a market judge the responsibility for the separation of the sexes in public places. As with other Mahdist institutions, however, the development of this office only came about with the accession of the Khalīfa ᶜAbdallāhi. In late 1886, simultaneous to the reorganization of the *Bayt al-Māl*, the Khalīfa ordered the reorganization of the market. Houses in the market area were torn down, new sites were allocated to merchants according to their particular wares, and a court and small jail were constructed in the center of the marketplace. The Khalīfa thereby not only increased competition among merchants, but also facilitated the state's greater control over market affairs. Credit for the reorganization and supervision of the market is given by Ohrwalder to the Khalīfa ᶜAlī wad Ḥilū, but in this he is clearly mistaken: From the beginning of the ᶜAbdallāhi's reign until approximately 1895, supreme responsibility for the market was vested in a former police supervisor and commander of irregular troops under the Turco-Egyptian regime. Born in Berber of Jaᶜalī and ᶜAbbādī parents, Muḥammad Wahbī wad Ḥusayn Adāy held various titles, including *ṣāḥib al-sūq*, *shaykh al-sūq*, *amīr al-shurṭa*, *ḥākim al-sūq,* and *ma'mūr maḥkamat al-sūq*, which collectively speak to his broad responsibility as police chief, market supervisor, tax collector, and judge—an office that closely resembles the "market and morals police" embodied in the classical Islamic *muḥtasib*. Accompanied by a force of about 25 police, known as *muṣliḥīn al-sūq* ("market regulators"), he patrolled the marketplace inspecting meat, vegetables, and other foodstuffs; supervised the regularity of sales, prices, weights and measures, payments to workers, and matters of currency; enacted the judgments of the *Qāḍī al-Islām*; enforced the separation of the sexes and safeguarded public morality (e.g., preventing public prostitution); guarded against the smuggling of goods (including also slaves and camels) to the enemy; attended to problems of traffic and crowding in the streets; discouraged forms of antisocial behavior prohibited by the Mahdī and Khalīfa (e.g., verbal and physical abuse, public urination and defecation); enforced the proper disposal of garbage, including animal carcasses; and urged the regular attendance at prayers in the mosque. To facilitate the carrying out of these tasks, Muḥammad Wahbī divided the marketplace into quarters, over each of which he placed a subordinate officer known as *shaykh al-ḥāra*. Responsible in a general sense for the safety of the people, he was commanded to overtake Ohrwalder and return him to Omdurman after the latter's escape in 1892.[30]

Some distinction between the duties of the market court and the *muṣliḥīn al-sūq* did exist, although it was often an unclear one, most especially because Muḥammad Wahbī Ḥusayn acted as both judge and policeman. Slatin's statement that the "Mehekemet es Suk (market police) are charged with maintaining order in the town" perfectly expresses this ambiguity. In an ideal sense, the *muṣliḥīn al-sūq* acted to supervise correct behavior and the upholding of law in the market, while the market court passed judgment upon offenders. The personnel of these two offices did not overlap, although they acted in concert. A letter of 1890 from the *Qāḍī al-Islām* to the *muṣliḥīn al-sūq* indicates that these market regulators might also be used to investigate claims of injustice brought against the market judges themselves.[31]

The size of the market court probably varied throughout the Mahdīyya. By the time of the conquest, it consisted of five judges (an *amīn* and four assistants), a clerk, and a contingent of *jihādīyya*. Its jurisdiction included cases prosecuted by the market regulators, involving moral offenses (most commonly, the use of tobacco and alcohol), fraud, debt, master-slave disputes, etc. Additionally, cases submitted before the *Maḥkamat al-Islām* might be referred back to the market court for judgment if they were not of a serious nature, such as the support of orphans or settlement of an estate. For this reason, most of the cases adjudicated in Omdurman were brought eventually before the market court.[32]

The *muṣliḥīn al-sūq* for their part treated the broad range of matters that were the concern of Muḥammad Wahbī. Taken as a whole, their charge was nothing less than the implementation of Mahdist teachings on an ideal society in the city's public space. Their effectiveness is not reflected in the few surviving documents of their office, although their flaws are. In a letter to three of the *muṣliḥīn*, the Khalīfa writes that he has relieved one of their colleagues of his duties, in order to abolish a source of corruption; in another letter, he reprimands one of them for favoring certain butchers in the market and preventing others from slaughtering their animals. The Khalīfa was emphatic in his definition of their duties: They were to concern themselves with the affairs of the *sūq* only, such as matters of buying and selling, and not overstep their bounds by dealing with matters of booty and claims unrelated to the *sūq*. Memoirs of the period make clear that the *muṣliḥīn* were certainly zealous in the execution of their duties: One survivor of the period, a merchant, recalled being stripped of all his goods three times for the offense of drinking alcohol.[33] If such zeal did not entirely change peoples' habits, it at least enforced a public conformity to Mahdist norms, which in the short 13 years of the Khalīfa's reign is perhaps all that could have been hoped for.

Muṣliḥīn al-sūq were also appointed in other towns of the Sudan, such as Dongola, Rufāᶜa, al-Qaḍārif, Sinja, and al-Masallamīyya. Little is known of their duties, although it is likely that they acted more as assistants to the provincial *ᶜāmil* than as actual market regulators: A letter from the Khalīfa to the *muṣliḥ* ᶜAlī Shashūb in al-Masallamīyya entrusts him only to collect taxes and send them back to Omdurman. In Wad Madani, where a formal office of *muḥtasib* was created at the special request of the townspeople in 1885, the Khalīfa wrote to Aḥmad al-Rayyiḥ Dushayn that he must cooperate with the local *ᶜāmil* "as one hand, and not enter into any affair without first consulting with him."[34] Doubtless the Khalīfa was keen to control authority outside the capital, while the unique conditions in Omdurman required a larger and more assertive market presence.

Issues of Health and Safety

European writers tended to stress the unsanitary conditions in their descriptions of Omdurman: Slatin called it "a great stench-pit" abounding in filth, refuse and disease; Ohrwalder was more restrained, commenting that the city "at the present time is by no means a particularly clean or sanitary town." The Principal Medical Officer of the Egyptian army claimed that upon occupation, Omdurman was "quite unfit for human habitation" due to numerous cesspits, stagnant pools of water and "other nuisances." E. G. Sarsfield-Hall, governor of Khartoum Province from 1929 to 1936, wrote at least four lengthy reports stressing the squalid nature of Omdurman, which he claimed developed without regard for "sanitation or any other public consideration." ("The New Khartoum," capital of the Anglo-Egyptian administration, naturally compared quite favorably.) Lost in these condemnations is the fact that, judging from the available memoirs and oral accounts, Omdurman did not appear to be an unusually dirty place to the Sudanese living there; indeed, its importance as "The Mahdī's city" probably precluded any such consideration. Moreover, there are explanations for the city's appearance in late 1898 that the European writers wholly ignored, including the stress of a huge military mobilization and the Anglo-Egyptian army's shelling of the city during the battle. Omdurman at least was not alone in receiving such criticisms: Sir Samuel Baker wrote of Khartoum during the Turco-Egyptian period that "a more miserable, filthy and unhealthy spot can hardly be imagined."[35]

Western impressions aside, it is clear that health conditions were precarious for much of the Mahdīyya. Times of great military concentration in the capital, such as during the *hijras* of 1885–1886 and 1888–1890, the arrival of Abū ᶜAnja's army in 1887, and the final mobilization from 1896 to 1898, contributed especially to the problem of overcrowding and led to a breakdown of sanitary arrangements, scarcity of food, and frequently the spread of disease. A particularly virulent outbreak of smallpox struck in 1885 after the fall of Khartoum and again in 1889 after the great famine, and cerebrospinal meningitis was widespread after the Anglo-Egyptian conquest in 1898. Typhus was allegedly endemic throughout the period. The result in terms of mortality rates can only be guessed at: Ohrwalder estimated that by 1891, almost half the total number of Muslim converts had died from hunger, disease, or other hardships. This statement must be considered alongside Slatin's assertion that it was the "the moving population" rather than "the different tribes" (i.e., Sudanese residents of Omdurman) who suffered most during the 1888–1889 famine. Certainly the Muslim converts and itinerant Sudanese were the most vulnerable population, lacking those forms of support—familial and tribal—available to Sudanese residents of the city, and they would be expected to die at higher rates. At the same time, many Sudanese in Omdurman also died from a variety of causes throughout the period, and the collected accounts suggest a high toll exacted on the city's population across the board.[36]

The people of Omdurman were naturally not oblivious to health problems and gave greater attention to medical issues than the standard accounts of the period acknowledge. In an unpublished report from 1907 on "native remedies" during the Mahdīyya, Senior Medical Inspector J. B. Christopherson identified four types of Sudanese medical practitioners: the *baṣīr* (bone setter), *ḥallāq* (barber-surgeon), *fakīr* (amulet maker), and *dāya* (midwife). Christopherson admitted that despite their ignorance of modern medicine, "they still possess, with their alert observation and varied pharmacopoeia, a not inconsiderable armament of effective medical knowledge." These practitioners took care of normal medical needs during the Mahdīyya. However, when smallpox broke out in 1885, the Mahdī ordered that a search be made for qualified doctors to administer vaccinations to his family and the people of Omdurman. As previously mentioned, Ḥasan Zakī, the Egyptian physician in Omdurman, recalled that he and others vaccinated "at a rate of 1,000 a day ... until all were vaccinated.... Mortality from smallpox was reduced to five percent." The *Bayt al-Māl* was meanwhile ordered to issue shrouds for the dead: "I have been informed by Ahmad Sulayman, the Mahdi's treasurer, that 12,000 shrouds were issued in Omdurman alone, and many were inhumed in their clothes without anybody going [to] the trouble of shrouding them."[37]

For his part, the Khalīfa ᶜAbdallāhi wrote letters to the tribes and villages of Kordofan in April of 1885, ordering all those who had not yet suffered from smallpox to be inoculated. Following the death of the Mahdī, the Khalīfa turned over the medical stores in the *Bayt al-Māl* to the care of Dr. Ḥasan Zakī, under the condition that he treat the poor people of Omdurman for free. In essence, a public hospital was created at the *Bayt al-Māl*, and consequently, people "flocked to us in great numbers, and we used to dress wounds, etc. for 200 or 300 daily." Aḥmad Sharfī, the patriarch of the Ashrāf, recalled that "the Khalīfa issued an order that whoever was wounded or had fever, etc. was to go to Ḥasan Effendi Zakī" at the *Bayt al-Māl*.[38]

Sanitary problems certainly abounded in Omdurman, again due to the frequent problem of overcrowding. As new emigrants entered the city, sites were excavated to make mud bricks for home building. The resulting trenches in the ground were allowed to fill with water to serve as drinking troughs for the animals, and these eventually became the "stagnant pools" commented upon later by the British. No institutional apparatus existed to attend to the city's sanitation problems, apart from the office of Muḥammad Wahbī Ḥusayn and his *muṣliḥīn al-sūq* in the marketplace. Rather, the Khalīfa chose to address the Anṣār directly on this issue in his weekly sermon at the mosque, requiring them to assume responsibility for their respective quarters. For example, the people had initially buried their dead in the residential districts of the city, which were already densely settled; during the famine of 1306, the Khalīfa ordered that the dead be buried outside the city's limits to the northwest. People were also made responsible for burying those corpses found near their homes. Failure to comply with this order resulted in the confiscation of the offender's property—a measure that Slatin admitted "had some effect." Likewise, Ohrwalder recalled that the Khalīfa once noticed sewage in the center of town and complained of it at the mosque. As a result, everyone was made "directly responsible" for the cleanliness of his own dwelling and vicinity, "and this order had a most excellent effect; it was further enforced by the presence of horsemen, who took good care to see that the instructions were carefully carried out." Anyone caught defiling a place was forced to carry "the impurity" from the public street to an "appointed place," apparently to the great mirth of passers-by.[39]

The identity of the "horsemen" mentioned by Ohrwalder is unknown, although it may simply have been Anṣār of the local quarter, since responsibility for the common good was not only a legal requirement in Omdurman, but also a matter of Mahdist faith. Naturally, the *shaykh* of each quarter had a personal interest in ensuring compliance. In the market area—the quarter Ohrwalder knew best, where most of the Muslim converts lived—the *muṣliḥīn al-sūq* would have provided an additional measure of enforcement.

A similar situation existed with regard to personal safety in the city. Western accounts tended to exaggerate the dangers in Omdurman (e.g., "There is practically no system of preserving public security") and criticized what few safety arrangements they admitted to as evidence of Mahdist misgovernment. Some of these arrangements, such as security patrols of *jihādīyya* throughout the city, were a continuation of Turco-Egyptian practice. Different communities of the city certainly had different experiences of safety, as they did of public health: A prominent Jaᶜalī family in Omdurman recalled that there was "great personal security" during the Mahdīyya, while a family of Fulānī origin—West African emigrants who arrived during the Mahdīyya—remembered that "there was no peace or safety for property." There is little reason to doubt the European accounts that the Muslim-convert community as a whole enjoyed the least security, although again, individual *Masālma* families also prospered within the limits permitted by the Mahdist state.[40]

As with health arrangements, there was no institutionalized public security apparatus, no permanent citywide police force, in Omdurman. In times of stress, the different quarters supplied their own watchmen at night, as Rosignoli noted during the Ashrāf revolt of 1891. Otherwise, immediate responsibility for personal and public safety lay with the *amīrs* of the various *rāyas*, the *shaykhs* of the different quarters, tribal and family elders, etc. who, as mentioned above, mediated disputes, executed the orders of the Khalīfa and courts, and answered to the Khalīfa and Yaᶜqūb for the misconduct of their people. As in other administrative matters, the *amīrs* carried out their responsibilities through their *ra's mī'as* and *muqaddams*. Security in the marketplace was of course the duty of Muḥammad Wahbī Ḥusayn and his *muṣliḥīn al-sūq*, who on occasion patrolled other districts of the city at night with a force of *jihādīyya*. When conditions required it, the Khalīfa or Yaᶜqūb announced an evening curfew, although even in calm times people found on the streets at night were often stopped by this force and questioned. Ultimately, security in the city was the direct responsibility of all Anṣār: The Mahdī had ruled that one who fails to expose a crime is deserving of the same punishment as the criminal, and this ruling was enforced by the Khalīfa. For example, when Slatin escaped Omdurman in 1895, Ḥasan Sharaf Abū Kudōk, a *shaykh* of the Berti of Darfur, was imprisoned for knowing of the escape and failing to report it. As one survivor of the period recalled, "all of the people were police."[41]

CHAPTER FOUR

The Mahdist Social Order and Omdurman

I was sitting in my shop when there passed by no other but ᶜAlī Ḥamad, the owner of the she-donkey which I had sold in Balānā, as I have told you.... ᶜAlī Ḥamad's eyes were roving over the shop and staring at the goods, till he said, 'Whose is this shop?' 'Mine,' I said. 'Is all this your property?' 'Yes.' 'I take refuge in God, who gives and takes away! Have you turned Christian, Bābikr? Can a Companion of the Mahdī own the likes of this without breaking his oath?'

Towards an Ideal Society

The Mahdī's sudden death in 1885 left unfulfilled his dream of universal conquest and the regeneration of the Islamic world. The legacy of his various teachings however, contained in his printed proclamations, letters, and sermons as well as his remembered speech, served as a powerful force for social change among the Anṣār of Omdurman and elsewhere. While the Mahdī created no comprehensive plan for society, no major theoretical work explaining what a "restored" Islamic society would look like, he expounded on a number of important issues that shaped his followers' understanding of morality, ethics, propriety, and belief. Under the rule of the Khalīfa ᶜAbdallāhi, an attempt was made to apply these teachings to the daily life of the Sudanese and so transform them into the ideal Islamic society envisioned by the Mahdī.

At the basis of the Mahdī's thought was the conviction that the universal practice of Islam had been degraded through centuries of oppression and evil accretions, and that Muslims needed to return to the social order that had prevailed under the Prophet's community at Medina. The path to such a return lay in a number of practices: recitation of the Qur'ān and the Mahdī's own book of devotions, the *Rātib*; regular attendance at the Friday communal prayer; the waging of *jihād* externally (against God's enemies) and internally (against one's base desires); and complete obedience to the Mahdī's commandments and prohibitions. An oath of loyalty sworn by every follower expressed the commitment to this mission: "We swear by God and by His Messenger, and we swear by you, to uphold the unity of God and not associate anyone with Him; to not steal, not commit adultery, not make false accusations and not disobey you in your lawful commands. We swear by you to renounce this world, to be content with that which is with God and the Hereafter, and to not flee from *jihād*."[1] The intention of this oath, and of the Khalīfa's later policies of *hijra* and *jihād*, was that each individual be the unit for creating a new society. Great reliance was thus placed on individual initiative and responsibility in the ordering of daily affairs in the capital, as indeed elsewhere in the Sudan.

Among the values that the Mahdī espoused were simplicity and self-denial, social justice and integration, political consultation, the upholding of religious precepts and the abolition of innovations and excesses, and the subordination of traditional social rank to Mahdist loyalty. The specific teachings that expressed these values were contained in his writings and sermons from 1881 to 1885 and naturally developed in response to changing conditions in the Sudan. In certain cases later teachings abrogated or modified his earlier views. Nonetheless, the Mahdī's intentions were clear and consistent with regard to the essential issues of prayer, unity, status, public interest, and morality.

Representative of the Mahdī's teachings are two proclamations, quoted below in part. The first is undated and addressed simply to "all the beloved of God." Like other early works, it sometimes allows for a measure of discretion in the punishments meted out, and it begins with a lengthy diatribe against the Turks and a description of the Mahdī's investiture by the Prophet Muhammad (omitted here).[2]

...The Master of Existence [Prophet Muḥammad] instructed me that [the bride price for] marrying a widow or divorced woman is five *riyāls*, and for a virgin ten *riyāls*, to ease [the affairs of] his community. Whoever lowers the dower beyond that is closer to me than the white of the eye to its pupil, so beware of increasing it.

Forbid your women from wailing and lamenting and spending extravagantly [at funerals]. As for the means of [paying] the diggers [of the grave] and the bearers of the coffin, it is necessarily at the expense of the deceased if he had any wealth, and if not, at the expense of the *Bayt Māl al-Muslimīn*. She who weeps or blackens her door or laments or mourns for anyone other than her husband is to be punished by beating and reprimanding, appropriate to the circumstances, until her repentance is apparent.

I have forbidden to you the evil tobacco. Whoever among you smokes it is to be punished until he repents or dies.

The *jihād* is a religious duty. Whoever is absent from it is a rebel against God and His messenger: His prayers will not be accepted, nor his fasting nor his alms, in fact all that he does will be in vain. He who leaves without a clear excuse is judged accordingly.

As for the scholar who follows me as Mahdī, he is like the prophet who has been sent [by God], and the common man who follows me has the rank of *Shaykh* ᶜAbd al-Qādir al-Jīlānī, while the scholar who opposes me is like Pharaoh, and the common man who opposes me is like Haman.

Whoever among you has stolen something, either great or small, cut off his hand, so that on the Day of Judgment he will be resurrected without a hand and be beaten down like a slave in this world.

Likewise an adulterer is to be stoned to death if he has been married before, and if he has never engaged in lawful sexual relations, he is to be lashed. As for the woman, if she has consorted with a strange man whom it is feared might take advantage of her, they are both to be punished assiduously according to the judge's discretion: For if a young man and woman get together, the devil will be their guide.

He who ceases to pray or neglects it must necessarily be killed according to the divinely stipulated punishment [i.e., as specified in the Qur'ān].

As for whoever among you assails his brother, speaking against his honor or property, he is not of me and I am not of him. And if you claim to be my followers and yet do not act accordingly, then you are hypocrites, according to the word of Him Most High: "They utter with their mouths a thing that is not in their hearts" [Qur'ān 3:167]. So if you do not love one another as brothers from different fathers, then you are not my followers.

Whoever conceals a theft that he has witnessed, or the drinking of alcohol or committing of adultery, out of pity [for the offenders], is [to be judged] like the one who committed [the offense].

Let God not bless those of sound body who are absent from *jihād*. If you have taken as an excuse [your] cattle or sheep or camels or farming to leave the *jihād*, God will bring disgrace upon you and not ease up on it.

Leave the comforts and delusions of civilization,[3] for the death of souls is their life.

Wear the patched *jibba* and dress your women in tattered garments.

Do not be a neighbor to one who has left *jihād* or done some reprehensible thing forbidden by Qur'ān or *Sunna*. Seek help against him, and seize his person and property as booty for the Muslim soldiers if he thought doing such things was lawful; if [he did not insist they were lawful], punish him.

Do not refuse [people] the land for it cannot be owned, being the possession of the *Bayt Māl al-Muslimīn*.

If someone on *jihād* requests hospitality from you, then give him shelter, and if he seeks help from you, then give him help.

As for those of high standing whom you have taken as patrons, if they forbid you from following us then they are unbelievers. Do not listen to a word they say, since they have gone astray and lead others astray: in fact they are the worst people of the Hell fire. The nobleman [*Sharīf*] derives no benefit from his nobility, nor the scholar from his learning, nor the saint from his sainthood, except by following me, and the sum of what is good is to be found in submitting [to me].

The judgment of women is that she who turns against her husband is to be confined in a shelter or dark house until she relents or God Most High causes her to die, as [is the case] with an adulteress. As for she who holds herself back from her husband, her property becomes booty for him; and if he seeks to appease her, his property then becomes booty for the Muslims. If they do this, do not visit them when they take ill, do not accompany their funeral bier, and do not support them in times of misfortune.

The second proclamation, judging by its language, was composed sometime before May 1883, and is addressed to "all *shaykhs* of the religion, *amīrs*, judicial deputies (*nuwwāb*), subordinate officers (*maqādīm*) and followers."[4]

> ...Wage *jihād* on behalf of God, and know that a sword unsheathed on behalf of God is preferable to seventy years' worship. Settling for the dregs of the she-camel [i.e., her milk] while on *jihād* is preferable to seventy years' worship.
>
> Incumbent on women is *jihād* on behalf of God. She who has passed the child-bearing years and is no longer desired by men, let her wage *jihād* with her hands and feet. As for the young women, let them wage *jihād* against their natural desires, and remain within their homes and not adorn themselves in the pagan manner, nor venture out save for a lawful reason. [Let them] not speak in public, nor let men hear their voices except from behind a veil. [Let them] perform their prayers, obey their husbands and cover themselves up with their garments.
>
> She who allows her head to be uncovered, even for the blink of an eye, let her be beaten with twenty-seven lashes; and she who speaks in a loud voice be beaten with twenty-seven lashes.
>
> He who utters obscenities, let him be beaten with eighty lashes; and he who addresses a fellow believer as dog, or pig, or Jew, or pimp, or dissolute, or thief, or fornicator, or traitor, or cursed one, or unbeliever, or Christian, or homosexual be beaten with eighty lashes and imprisoned for seven days.
>
> As for he who speaks with a marriageable woman, to whom he is not engaged or without legitimate reason, let him be beaten with twenty-seven lashes.
>
> He who smokes is to be beaten with eighty lashes and the tobacco burnt if it is on his person; similarly punished are those who keep it in their mouths, or use it as snuff or spit it. As for one who buys it or sells it, even if he does not use it, let him be beaten with twenty-seven lashes.
>
> He who drinks alcohol, even a tiny sip, is to be beaten with eighty lashes and imprisoned for seven days. As for his neighbor, if he has no power to stop [the drinker], he is to inform the local *amīr*; if he does not inform him, [the neighbor also] is to be beaten with eighty lashes and imprisoned for seven days. Whoever aids a drinker of alcohol, even [by giving him] a mouthful of water or a vessel [to use], is to be similarly punished and imprisoned for seven days.

He who wages *jihād* against his natural desires out of obedience to God is truly more powerful than he who wages *jihād* with a spear. For natural desires are more powerful than an unbeliever: With the unbeliever, you fight him and slay him and then you are free of him; while natural desires are an enemy in the form of a dear friend, the killing of whom is difficult and the way of whom is tiresome.

He who intentionally ceases to pray is a rebel against God and His messenger, and some say he is an unbeliever and should be killed. As for his neighbor, if he has no power [to influence him], he is to inform the local *amīr*; if he does not inform him, he is to be beaten with eighty lashes and imprisoned for seven days, and it is said his property becomes booty [for the Muslims].

As for a girl of five years' age, if her family does not cover her [properly] they are to be beaten but not imprisoned.

As for he who knows of his slave girl being with a man to whom she is not married [or engaged], and keeps quiet [even] for a day and does not say anything, some say he should be killed or imprisoned or his property be taken as booty.

Many more examples of the Mahdī's rulings could be cited here, and much could be said about their legal basis in Islamic jurisprudence.[5] However it is only necessary for the present purpose to highlight the main themes of his teaching, which, applied by the Khalīfa, came to be regarded as the law of Omdurman.

Predominant among all other issues, throughout the Mahdī's writings and sermons, is the need for unrelenting *jihād*: the struggle on behalf of the faith to create a moral society and defend the lands of Islam from oppressive and corrupting influences. And indeed, in a Sudan saturated with Ṣūfī influences and customary practices, in a region constantly traversed by migrants and merchants from west and east, in a time when the practices of not only Turco-Egyptian rule but also the Darfur and Sinnār sultanates remained within living memory, any attempt to implement a social order based upon a rigid interpretation of Qur'ān and *Sunna* would require constant struggle. In the Mahdī's view, the obligation towards *jihād* transcended all other requirements, and neither livelihood nor gender released one from the commitment, since *jihād* is a "religious duty" and one who shrinks from it is "a rebel against God." Post-menopausal women are even ordered to wage physical *jihād* "with her hands and feet," although this was not necessarily tantamount to hoisting a spear, while younger women are left to wage the more difficult form of struggle against their "natural desires." Quite clearly, *jihād* is "preferable" to prayer, and helping those engaged in it may be seen as a form of struggle as well. It is revealing that the penalty imposed for avoiding or fleeing *jihād* varied over the course of the revolt, from loss of property to imprisonment to death, and the Mahdī probably found it necessary to allow some degree of flexibility in this matter, given the varied circumstances of the time.

Complementing the Mahdī's teaching on *jihād* is his insistence upon the simplicity of his followers, whom he instructs to dress plainly, avoid ostentation and beware the seductive allure of modern comforts. In other writings, the Mahdī adds that "the rich man must not own more than one slave woman to serve his family and another one to serve him," and each man should limit himself to one slave boy "to run behind his mule." As with his teaching on *jihād*, the Mahdī was uncompromising in this matter, not even sparing his family. Bābikr Bedrī recalls that at the first Friday service after the fall of Khartoum, the Mahdī preached that "Aḥmad Sulaymān [*Amīn Bayt al-Māl*] has distracted the Ashrāf with riches. Say after me three times, 'We ask the protection of God that we be not like them.'" (Bābikr adds that "He spoke this as a serious judgment, and not lightly in jest.") This emphasis upon self-denial and simplicity, emanating from Ṣūfī practice and given greater urgency by the millennial climate, was also intended to safeguard the interests of the community as a whole. For according to the Mahdī, all wealth in the Sudan, from the moment of his manifestation, belonged the Anṣār collectively, and it was the responsibility of the *Bayt al-Māl* to collect, store, and distribute this wealth. (The first *Amīn Bayt al-Māl* is said to have declared that "everything in Khartoum is lawfully a possession of the Mahdī, even the souls.") This was particularly the case with booty captured during the Mahdist uprising, and included unclaimed slaves and animals. Additionally, all wealth in excess of that needed for daily living was intended—if not strictly required—to be handed over to the *Bayt al-Māl*. Since unnecessary or lavish spending squandered the resources of the community, the Mahdī lowered the bride price and recommended that wedding feasts consist only of dates and milk, prohibited prolonged and expensive funerals, and forbade extravagant dress. Further, land was to be freely distributed for the use of the Anṣār, "since it cannot be owned." The wearing of gold and silver jewelry apparently was allowed by the Mahdī, although it was considered "detaining in the Hereafter" and strongly discouraged.[6]

It is not surprising that the Mahdī expected his followers to be like the Companions of the Prophet, who "would not tolerate vanity, divert from the truth nor sleep by night," particularly since the Anṣār understood themselves to be living out a divinely guided drama. At the same time, concerned about the moral problems that might accompany a time of turmoil, the Mahdī ruled harshly on the matter of sexual misconduct. This surely is another reason for his lowering the bride price—that people might more easily marry and not be tempted to engage in adultery.[7] Significantly, however, the Mahdī imposed a variety of penalties for sexual misconduct, ranging from lashing to imprisonment and loss of property to death: As with fleeing the *jihād*, it surely was necessary to allow some flexibility in this matter, in recognition of the complicated conditions of the time. Conversely, his insistence upon women's proper dress and decorum—including even young girls—is unequivocal, as are his statements on a woman's total subordination to her husband's needs. Equally harsh are the Mahdī's rulings on the use of tobacco and alcohol, which, like sexual misconduct, were regarded as threats to society and resulted in some of the most severe punishments.

A prominent feature of the Mahdī's social order was the unity of believers, which was of crucial importance in a Sudan divided by tribal, ethnic, and regional differences. This ideal was to be achieved in a number of ways, such as mandatory attendance at the Friday communal prayers and regular recitation from the Mahdī's *Rātib*. Additionally, the Mahdī urged his followers to dress alike, in a style emblematic of personal asceticism: a patched robe of woven cotton cloth (*jibba*), loose-fitting trousers (*sirwāl*), sandals, a skull cap, and a turban with its end piece (*ᶜazaba*) hanging loose. A light sheet (*tōb*) wrapped around the waist and draped over a shoulder served a number of purposes, including use as a burial shroud: a constant reminder of the Anṣārī's commitment to *jihād* and proximity to Paradise. Men were also encouraged to shave their heads in conformity with the Prophet's practice, and both the Mahdī and Khalifa ᶜAbdallāhi criticized the Kababīsh and other Arab tribes who wore long braids in the "pagan" manner.[8]

As a further means of enforcing unity, an extremely harsh sentence of 80 lashes and seven days' imprisonment was imposed for insulting another Anṣārī, which reflects both the supreme importance the Mahdī attached to this subject as well as the fractured nature of Sudanese society. These insults include calling someone a Jew or a Christian. Apart from the measure's obvious intention to suppress discord, it reflects the idea that, at least in principle, there were no longer any "Jews" or "Christians," no longer any unbelievers in the Mahdīyya, since all had submitted and become Anṣār. In other writings, the Mahdī extended this penalty to calling a free man a slave.[9]

Likewise, the Mahdī made it the direct responsibility of all his followers to carry out his teachings, including reporting violators to the local authorities. Whether it is ceasing to pray, possessing or using alcohol or tobacco, committing a theft or any other crime, it is clear that failure to report the offense is as serious as the offense itself, resulting (again) in 80 lashes and seven days' imprisonment. And while the Mahdī did not specifically legislate the social integration of his followers, he clearly emphasized the need for the Anṣār to act as "brothers from different fathers." Among his oral teachings is a statement in which he wishes for a hundred daughters, "each one representative of a different tribe," so that he might create by means of his own family a more cohesive community.[10]

No great leveling of social distinctions was attempted by the Mahdī, although such a policy was often attributed to him and the Khalīfa. Rather, the Mahdī subordinated traditional forms of authority—such as that of Ṣūfī shaykhs, scholars, and important families—to the principle of Mahdist loyalty, even criticizing the pretensions of his relatives, the Dongola Ashrāf. In fact, the equality preached by the Mahdī was strategic and situational: Anṣār are to abandon tribalism and factionalism, cooperate in the *jihād*, turn wealth over to the *Bayt al-Māl*, etc. in return for being treated equally on earth (i.e., in the distribution of goods) and rewarded equally in heaven. While he used egalitarian rhetoric in his speeches and proclamations—addressing the Anṣār as "beloved" (*aḥbāb*) and "friends" (*aṣḥāb*) instead of "followers" (*aṭbāʿ*)—and abolished the use of certain titles favored by his opponents, such as *shaykh* and *sayyid* ("Lord"), the Mahdi did not wholly reject traditional authority but rather sought to co-opt it, as is evident in the formation of his military. Thus when the Mahdī declares that "The nobleman derives no benefit from his nobility, nor the scholar from his learning, nor the saint from his sainthood, except by following me," this does not negate the existence of nobility, scholarship, and sainthood, but rather qualifies it. Indeed, the titles of *shaykh* and *sayyid* continued to be used throughout the Mahdīyya by the Anṣār, while the titles *al-sayyid* and *al-mukarram* ("the respected") are recorded in the surviving treasury records of the Mahdist state.[11]

The penalties prescribed by the Mahdī for various offenses were harsh, and reflect both the zeal of a reformer and the tremendous disorder of the time. Although some measure of judicial discretion was allowed in the proclamations cited above, the Mahdī's judgments were usually specific and absolute. Clearly this was regarded as necessary for the creation of an ideal society from disparate and sometimes mutually hostile communities. It was the Mahdī's good fortune to die before the execution of his program became possible, and before its implications became evident.

The Khalīfa between Ideal and Reality

Expectations were extremely high among the Anṣār in 1885 after the capture of Khartoum: The "Turks" had been defeated, a British force sent to rescue General Gordon had been turned back, and belief in the mission of the Mahdī was fervent. Stories circulated among the Anṣār of the Mahdī's miracles, including the parting of the White Nile to allow soldiers to cross on dry land the morning of the attack. At least until the Mahdī's sudden death in June, the millennial dream seemed a possibility, as it must to all millennial groups. Nor did the Mahdī's death immediately change things, as the Anṣār developed explanations for this shocking turn of events: the Mahdī would return after some brief interval to lead the Believers to victory.[12]

Nonetheless, the accession of the Khalīfa ᶜAbdallāhi and the challenge of governing the Sudan necessitated certain compromises to the ideal of Mahdist society: In fact the very existence of Omdurman as a capital city was a refutation of the Mahdī's teachings, which called for continuous *jihād* by all Anṣār until the world was brought under the sway of the new Islamic order. To the Mahdī, Omdurman was merely a "place," one campsite among many; to the Khalīfa and the Anṣār, it was *Buqᶜat al-Mahdī*, a self-consciously holy city.

The conditions of the Khalīfa's 13-year reign certainly did not lend themselves to the successful implementation of the Mahdī's social order: Cycles of drought, famine, locust infestation, and cattle plague from 1888 to 1892 weakened the Khalīfa's ability to govern, as did the incessant rivalry between ᶜAbdallāhi and his western followers and the Ashrāf and their riverain followers. Meanwhile the external aggression of the Anglo-Egyptians as well as Italian and French advances in Ethiopia eventually robbed him of the time and resources needed to encourage the adoption of the Mahdī's reforms.

Moreover, from the moment the Khalīfa came to power he was forced to rely on many of the institutions, administrative practices, and especially personnel of the Turco-Egyptian regime, preventing any radical break with the "innovations" of the past. In particular, both the administrative and technical departments of the state drew heavily on Egyptians (both Muslims and Coptic Christians) and *muwalladīn* (persons of mixed Egyptian-Sudanese parentage) who had served the previous regime, and some of the technical departments attached to the dockyards, *Bayt al-māl* and *Bayt al-Amāna* were made up almost exclusively of these persons. Egyptians and *muwalladīn* were also highly represented among the clerks of the various treasuries. The names of some institutions (e.g., *Warshat al-jabkhāna* and *Hajjānat al-Bōsta*) were unchanged from the Turco-Egyptian period, and their records were usually written in the same style and kept in the same ledgers (*dafātir*). Holt remarks that "The continuity of personnel from the Egyptian to the Mahdist regimes was much greater than has generally been recognized. There was an interruption during the Mahdī's *jihād*, but the threads were picked up again during the Khalīfa's reign." Not surprisingly, even the jargon of the former regime was retained by some Sudanese during the Mahdīyya; surprisingly, the Khalifa's son and presumed heir, ᶜUthmān Shaykh al-Dīn, was among them. Bābikr Bedrī recalls that ᶜUthmān responded once in answer to a petition: "'Come tomorrow, you will find your petition *alasta*,' a Turkish word meaning 'Good! Things will be as you wish.'"[13]

The Khalīfa also was compelled to rely on the services of the *jihādīyya* whom he had inherited from the Turco-Egyptians. Many of these Sudanese soldiers of southern and Nūba mountains origin were, at best, superficially converted to Islam, eager to retain their earlier habits and cultural practices, and not easily absorbed into the ranks of the riverain and western Anṣār. (For their part, the Anṣār tended to regard the *jihādīyya* as *ᶜabīd,* slaves, although they risked punishment calling them such in public.) Practicality dictated that the Khalīfa ignore these soldiers' contravention of Mahdist teachings, while their isolation in al-Kāra, to the south of the city proper, prevented their hindering the Khalīfa's efforts to reform the rest of Sudanese society.

Acknowledging at the outset the failure of this, and indeed all attempts to create an ideal society, the issue becomes rather the degree to which the Khalīfa tried to impose the Mahdī's teachings upon the Sudanese, how his measures were implemented, and most importantly, how they were received by the Anṣār themselves. Among the areas that were of concern to the Khalīfa are adherence to Mahdist belief, including matters of worship and education; morality and propriety, including gender relations; and the social integration of the Anṣār.

At the core of Mahdist practice was, of course, the observance of the five canonical daily prayers, preferably in the main mosque in the center of Omdurman. The Khalīfa placed great emphasis on collective worship in recognition of its symbolic and spiritual values, and according to the prisoner Fr. Rosignoli, revoked the earlier practice of each neighborhood (*farīq*) praying separately under the leadership of its *amīr*. In fact not all inhabitants of Omdurman were normally required to attend the five daily prayers in the mosque: such a thing would have been impractical anyway. Rather, accounts of the period, both written and oral, make clear that two groups of people in particular were required to pray five times daily under the Khalīfa's supervision: those suspected of dubious loyalty to the Mahdīyya (e.g., many of the Masālma community and Egyptians, and certain individuals such as the Mīrghanīs), and many of the Mahdist officials and *amīrs*. Not even all of the Muslim converts prayed consistently in the central mosque: Slatin recalls that the attendance of the Masālma was not rigidly enforced and that it was only necessary for a certain number to attend as representatives of the larger community. As for the majority of the people of Omdurman, the men were expected to join the Friday communal prayer every week, but otherwise all were to perform their prayers wherever they might happen to be, usually in their own quarter if not the marketplace. Failure to pray was of course a serious offense, but most often resulted not in the death sentence prescribed by the Mahdī, but rather in a sentence of compulsory attendance at the Khalīfa's daily prayers for eighteen months.[14]

In addition to the observance of their prayers, the Anṣār were expected and required to recite twice daily from the Mahdī's *Rātib*: in the morning between the first and second prayers and in the evening between the fourth and fifth prayers, each time with a portion of the Qur'ān. This was an act, like the collective prayers, of both symbolic and spiritual value. The exact level of compliance with this requirement cannot be determined, although the European prisoners' accounts as well as oral accounts agree that most Anṣār recited from the *Rātib*, and evidence for its regular recitation outside the capital suggests the same applied in Omdurman.[15]

A cornerstone of Mahdist policy was the abolition of the various Ṣūfī orders, declared in 1301 / 1883–1884, whose practices were superseded by the appearance of the Mahdī and whose loyalties threatened the unity of his movement. The Khalīfa also forbade the use of the titles *fakī* and *fuqarā'* in 1887 in an attempt to undermine residual Ṣūfī authority. Despite these measures, the titles continued to be used, and some Sudanese continued their Ṣūfī devotions: The Khalīfa wrote in June 1888 to the people of Kassala warning them against adhering to the Khatmīyya order; while the Qādirīyya of Fitayḥāb, just south of Omdurman, claim to have continued their weekly *dhikr* from sunset on Thursday until sunrise on Friday throughout the Mahdīyya. Even the *amīr* Muḥammad al-Khayr ᶜAbdallāh Khūjalī is known to have reverted to the practices of the Tijānīyya, although this was in Dongola in 1888, when he was disaffected to the Khalīfa's regime. As for Omdurman itself, there is no evidence of Ṣūfī practices continuing there during the Mahdīyya, and such a thing seems highly unlikely. Even so, not long after the Anglo-Egyptian conquest the Ṣūfī orders (re)established themselves in the city. *The Khartoum Province Handbook* (undated, pre-1930) lists the names of six Ṣūfī orders active in Omdurman: the Khatmīyya, Sammānīyya, Aḥmadīyya, Ismāᶜīlīyya, Qādirīyya, and Rifāᶜīyya. The conventional explanation for this revival of the orders is that the Khalīfa had forcibly prevented Ṣūfī practices, and once his power was broken they returned. Another explanation, offered by the grandson of al-Fakī ᶜArabī, *amīr* of the Rikābīyya in Omdurman and *shaykh* of the

Khatmīyya, is this: During the Mahdīyya, all Ṣūfī *awrād* were replaced by the Mahdī's *Rātib*, which was read devotedly by everyone. After the conquest and the outlawing of the *Rātib*, people returned to their prior Ṣūfī practices. This represented no change in authority—the *khalīfa* of the Rikābī Khatmīyya had been their *amīr* during the Mahdīyya—nor did it represent a great change in practice, since the *Rātib* was intended as a substitute for the Ṣūfī *awrād*; nor, finally, did it represent any change in belief, since "all were means to the same end, the worship of God."[16]

The Mahdī's ideal of a Sudanese society based strictly upon Qur'ān and *Sunna* necessarily involved the eradication of certain "innovations" and "accretions" considered outside the bounds of correct Islam. Determining precisely what these are, and how to eradicate them, had been the burden of every Muslim reformer, including—not too long before the Mahdī's time—Muḥammad b. ᶜAbd al-Wahhāb (d. 1792) in Arabia and Usumān dan Fōdio (d. 1817) in Hausaland in Nigeria. The Khalīfa inherited this burden when he came to power, and he targeted in his sermons a number of practices, including the wearing of amulets, divination, and other superstitions. There is some irony in this, as the Khalīfa's father had been a respected diviner among the Taᶜāīsha years earlier. Doubtless the Khalīfa's efforts were sincere—by all accounts, he was the most devoted and loyal of the Mahdī's followers—and yet one oral account maintains that the Khalīfa regularly met with the Maḥas *shaykh* Muḥammad Ṣāliḥ wad Ūru, an authority on "the science of letters" (*ᶜilm al-ḥurūf*), a form of numerology, to seek his advice. The issue thus becomes, what constituted "correct Islamic practice" in Omdurman? The Italian prisoner Rosignoli leaves little doubt that many popular customs remained prevalent in the city, although he was most familiar with the affairs of the market quarter where the Masālma resided. An Egyptian Military Intelligence report from the time of the conquest lists "Dervish papers picked up from the streets or private homes in Omdurman." Among these were "five papers from books of astrology and superstitions, including: (a) poetry about the heavenly constellations; (b) instructions for people who would like to get rid of their enemies by putting them to death, and also for attracting the love of women; (c) instructions enabling women to bring forth children; (d) instructions for finding anything that is lost; and (e) [words of] consolation to those suffering from leprosy." Exactly how representative these papers were of general Sudanese belief is unknowable, since much of what was written down never fell into Anglo-Egyptian hands, and most of what was believed was never written down. In any case, it is apparent that the Anṣār saw no contradiction in the retention of certain popular beliefs and adherence to the Mahdīyya. Moreover, these five papers should be viewed alongside another 38 papers found in Omdurman, containing extracts from the Qur'ān and other religious works, as well as a purported work of *Ḥadīth*, "The Prophet Muḥammad's advice to his daughter Fāṭima" (discussed below). Certainly the Khalīfa attempted to impose a strict definition of *Sharīᶜa* on his followers, as indicated by the official Mahdist publications, which were entirely of a religious nature and consisted mainly of the teachings of the Mahdī. At the same time, a broader range of belief and practice apparently was tolerated than has previously been acknowledged.[17]

The state of learning in Sudan unquestionably suffered during the Mahdīyya, if learning is understood to mean active intellectual inquiry. The *General Report on the Egyptian Soudan* of 1895 stated that "with the exception of the Koran, the Mahdi's Ratib and the Mahdi's and Khalifa's proclamations, no books are allowed to be read.... There are no schools in Omdurman, but children are sent to Fikis who teach them to read the Koran and they are also taught to write." The Sudanese historian Muḥammad ᶜAbd al-Raḥīm went as far as to claim that learning stopped altogether during the Mahdīyya. These claims appear for the most part to be true. The Mahdī's abrogation of Islamic jurisprudence (*fiqh*) is well known, and he ordered that works of law and Qur'ānic exegesis (*tafsīr*) be destroyed so that nothing but the Qur'ān and *Rātib* would prevail. Intellectual inquiry in general was distrusted in Mahdist Omdurman, all scholars having been tainted by the Mahdī's derogation of certain of his enemies as "evil scholars" (*ᶜulamā' al-sū'*). Both the Mahdī and Khalīfa attempted to suppress learning on the grounds that it was a distraction from *jihād* and a possible subversion of the Mahdīyya: In 1885, the Mahdī wrote to Aḥmad Ḥājj ᶜAlī al-Majdhūb permitting him to open a *madrasa* on the condition that he not neglect the *jihād*, and that he participate in it with his local *amīr*; while the Khalīfa's correspondence reveals that he was frequently concerned about books that might "lead the people astray." Bābikr Bedrī adds that "books were among the goods the export of which to the Sudan was prohibited," and the study of Mālikī law was expressly forbidden. This did not, however, prevent Bābikr—a loyal and devout Anṣārī—and others from secretly studying a number of works of law, Qur'ānic interpretation, grammar, poetry, and mysticism under the guidance of their *shaykhs* ("in a hiding place which we found for Fakī Ḥāmid"). Quite inexplicably, a map of Omdurman drawn up by the Egyptian Military Intelligence and based upon the information supplied by Fr. Ohrwalder after his escape includes among the city's market stalls "European book shops" (*maktabāt al-Ifranj*). If this information is correct, these cannot have escaped the attention of Muḥammad Wahbī and his *muṣliḥīn al-sūq*, and hence can only have been tolerated.[18]

The Khalīfa's discouragement of learning in Omdurman must be seen alongside his encouragement of basic literacy. A survivor of the Mahdīyya recalls that "there were many *khalāwī* in Omdurman. Those who knew Qur'ān well would open a *khalwa* at their home.... They taught reading, writing, arithmetic and Qur'ān." Though the Mahdist state did not open primary schools in the manner of the Egyptian government, it did subsidize the private Qur'ān schools of Omdurman with material and monetary support. It is even claimed that "into the Anglo-Egyptian Condominium, among some western tribes only those educated under the Mahdīyya could read or write."[19] A memoir of the period describes this form of education in Omdurman:

> It is established that on Wednesday [*sic*: Saturday], the first of Muḥarram 1303 [10 October 1885], the Khalīfat al-Mahdī inaugurated the recitation of the Qur'ān, in the presence of the *khalīfas* and *amīrs* in *al-Buq*ᶜ*a al-Mubāraka*, [with the distribution of] 4,500 writing tablets. He ordered the brethren to instruct the beloved in the recitation of the *Fātiḥa*: "In the name of God, the Merciful and Compassionate, praise be to God, Ruler of the worlds," verse by verse and vowel by vowel; and the two final chapters of the Qur'ān.
>
> He ordered that the youths recite [the alphabet], *alif, bā', tā', thā'*, etc. and that 500 study circles [be established] within the mosque to recite sections of the Qur'ān, morning and evening, along with the *Rātib* of the Mahdī (Peace be upon him!).
>
> In the year five [1305 / 1887–1888] he called together all of the people in the Mahdī's mosque and ordered them to utter the *tahlīl* and *takbīr* [i.e., "There is no god but God" and "God is most great"] and to recite the Qur'ān; and [he ordered that] during the month of

> Ramaḍān they pray behind him, 70,000 prayer mats, night after night for thirty days. Ibrāhīm b. ᶜĀlim was a witness to that, [as were] Muḥammad al-Takīna, al-Qāḍī al-Hādī and Mūsa b. ᶜAqila. All of the *fuqarā'* counted and found this number correct.
>
> Every year they completed the [recitation of the] Qur'ān 6,000 times.
>
> In *al-Buqᶜa al-Mubāraka* there were 800 mosques for the recitation of the Qur'ān, and 800 riyals were paid by the *Bayt al-Māl* to the *fuqarā'* who instructed the youths in the Qur'ān from the beginning.[20]

Apart from the basic literacy taught in the city's Qur'ān schools (which were small *khalwas* rather than actual "mosques"), there was little in the way of learning available, at least legally, to the Anṣār. Ḥusayn Ibrāhīm wad al-Zahrā, who briefly served as *Qāḍī al-Islām* from 1894 to 1895, was appointed by the Khalīfa to teach inheritance law at the central mosque as a special instructor, "since nothing in this subject contradicted Mahdist teachings." At some point during the Mahdīyya, the scholar and poet Muḥammad ᶜUmar al-Bannā was allowed to read to the Khalīfa and Anṣār from the histories of the early Islamic conquests.[21] Both are exceptions, however, to the normal practice of forbidding the study of anything apart from Qur'ān, *Sunna,* and the teachings of the Mahdī. For just as the appearance and mission of the Mahdī was believed to supersede the need for conventional knowledge, so conventional instruction was replaced by the "upbringing" (*tarbīyya*) embodied in Mahdist culture.

The chief exponents of this Mahdist culture, apart from the Khalīfa himself, were the poets of Omdurman. The Mahdī gave a formal authorization (*ijāza*) in 1884 for Anṣār poets to compose poems in praise of himself and the Prophet, "since poems of praise [*madḥ*] are a source of terror for unbelievers and an exhortation and reminder for the *mujāhidīn*." Of the poets whose works survived through memorization (most written poetry was deliberately destroyed after Kararī), virtually all were from branches of the Jaᶜaliyīn and were early adherents of the Mahdī. Of these, the most celebrated were Aḥmad wad Saᶜd, known as "Shaykh al-Maddāḥ"; Muḥammad wad al-Tuwaym, named "al-Amīr" by the Mahdī at Abā Island, who has been called "the first poet of the revolution"; Aḥmad Abū Sharīᶜa, a disciple of Wad Saᶜd; Aḥmad wad Tamīm, an ascetic whose *baraka* was sought by the people of Omdurman; and Muḥammad wad Sūrkattī, whose grandfather had been a famous teacher among the Danāqla. While their most common subjects were the Prophet, the Mahdī, and the Khalīfa, they also recited poems in praise of the Mahdī's sons, the *khalīfas* ᶜAlī wad Ḥilū and Muḥammad Sharīf, the Anṣār, the mosque and *Qubba*, and Omdurman. In so doing, they reinforced the ideals of selflessness, obedience, unity, modesty, prayer, and especially devotion to *jihād*. A representative example is "The Fourth Mosque" by Aḥmad wad Saᶜd which, literally translated, begins: "The Mahdī is Imām of the Fourth Mosque, its people are ever the most God-fearing / Your humble servant is weak as he faces his end, O Khalīfat al-Mahdī, take him by the reins / O Khalīfat al-Fārūq, take hold of the bridle, O Khalīfat al-Karrār, tighten the girth / You all are his bread and you are the dip, you are his cup and you are the wine." Colloquial Arabic poetry, employing clever rhyme schemes and alliteration, was especially effective in this regard, being "a vernacular particularly suited to the conditions and ideals of the Mahdīyya." By all accounts it was extremely popular: In addition to receiving monthly payments from the *Bayt al-Māl*, poets were heavily patronized by the people of Omdurman, being hired to recite at weddings, circumcisions, and other celebrations. Bābikr Bedrī wrote that when he learned of his brother's escape from danger, he "gave thanks to God and held a party of rejoicing at which hymns of praise were sung by Shaykh Aḥmad Abū Sharīᶜa and a full chorus, and recitations of the Koran were given by the shaykhs Ibrāhīm Aḥmad Kurāᶜ al-Naᶜāma, ᶜAlī Ṭulba, al-Ṣāwī, and Egyptian reciters; and the party lasted all night."[22]

A number of Anṣār living elsewhere in Sudan sent their children to Omdurman to be educated in the city's *khalwas* and partake of the Mahdist *tarbīyya*, and the letters they wrote to the Khalīfa emphasize the value they attached to this upbringing. Most of these children lived with family members already in the city, although it was a familiar practice for students to reside at the home of their *shaykh*. Meanwhile, the children of the Muslim-convert community had a quite different experience of Mahdist education: Some apparently were compelled to attend a Qur'ān school, although it is unclear how widespread a practice this was. More commonly—and more to the liking of the Khalīfa's administration—people schooled their children themselves to be clerks or artisans and carry on the work they had begun under the Turco-Egyptian regime. The son of the

Egyptian Copt Ibrāhīm Bey Khalīl, for example, was taken to the *Bayt al-Māl* at the age of seven to observe its workings. The practical needs of the Mahdist state were thus served, while adherence to Mahdist norms, among most of the Anṣār, was enforced.[23]

The Mahdī's vision of Islamic society stressed an impeccable moral order based upon the model conduct of the Prophet's community, and both the Khalīfa and Anṣār struggled to achieve this. In particular, the Khalīfa took steps to regulate male-female relations, define a woman's role in Mahdist society, and discourage immoral practices. Ultimately, however, it is difficult to judge the state of morality in Omdurman during the Madīyya: To what should we compare it? European complaints of Sudanese "debauchery" were a staple of eighteenth- and nineteenth-century travel accounts, yet no internally generated records or accounts from Sinnār, Darfur, or Turco-Egyptian Khartoum have survived to confirm this. Recent studies however have linked the various socioeconomic changes enveloping Sudan in the eighteenth and nineteenth centuries to the rise of prostitution, lending some credence to the travel accounts. Meanwhile, the evidence from the Mahdīyya is hardly overwhelming. Very little of the scant material surviving from the papers of the *Qāḍī al-Islām* relates to moral issues, and the records of Muḥammad Wahbī Ḥusayn and his *muṣliḥīn al-sūq* were either destroyed or lost after the conquest. Nor would court records necessarily reflect on the issue, since many problems in Omdurman were quietly settled at the level of the family or the *amīr* of the local *farīq*. Among the prisoners' accounts of life in Omdurman, there is the statement of Neufeld that "very few stonings to death [for adultery] took place, and those were in the earlier days of the Mahdieh, when religious fanaticism held sway." He further remarks that a woman's confession was necessary for a sentence of death for adultery, and he knew of only three instances when the sentence was executed. The Egyptian Ibrāhīm Fawzī wrote that the Khalīfa attempted to incarcerate, and then banish to Rajjāf, all homosexuals in Omdurman, but this measure was short-lived and unsuccessful. Bābikr Bedrī makes clear that the usual vices continued (although at an unknown rate) throughout the period; while after the conquest the Darfur sultan ᶜAlī Dīnār, who had spent a brief period in Omdurman, requested that Anglo-Egyptian authorities return to him "an old flame" residing there: "She was a great favorite in the Dervish time of the

Amir Mahmud [Aḥmad] and later of [the Khalīfa's son ᶜUthmān] Shaykh al-Din. ᶜAli Dinar asserts that she is being detained by a certain Fadl al-Mawla, who, he says, is noted for his fine singing and love of women." Ultimately, the sweeping statements of Slatin and others condemning Omdurman's immorality are as suspect as sweeping statements to the contrary. More in line with the evidence is that the moral conduct of the people of Omdurman, in the aggregate, was no worse than what had previously obtained in Sudanese towns, and probably better, and definitely far more discrete. This is noteworthy, since for most Sudanese, Omdurman was their first experience of urbanization on any level, and potentially devastating to the social and moral order. Whatever efforts were made by the Anṣār to realize the Mahdī's ideal—and Bābikr and others took the issue of morality extremely seriously—it is to their credit, and it is on this basis that they must be judged.[24]

The policies of the Mahdī and Khalīfa towards male-female relations came in response to the disruptive conditions of their time. Warfare had created a situation in which women greatly preponderated in Omdurman, and it became vital to the social and moral order that all women be married and provided for. The first measure taken to encourage marriage among the Anṣār had been the Mahdī's lowering of the bride price. This artificially lowered *mahr* prevailed throughout the Mahdīyya, but not for long thereafter: E. S. Stevens noted in a 1911 visit to Sudan that "even a working man will pay a preposterous price for his wife. The cost of getting married has gone up since the days of the Mahdi." Additionally, the Mahdī had condemned the excessive presents (*shayla*) given by the groom to the bride and the sumptuous wedding feasts, recommending instead the more modest practices of the Prophet's time. Shortly after the capture of Khartoum, the Mahdī ordered that all captive women either be sent to live with relatives or else married immediately. The Khalīfa forcefully supported these measures upon coming to power, encouraging all Anṣār to marry up to the canonical limit of four wives. Neufeld writes that the Khalīfa further ordered all women without husbands to be married at once, especially the women of the Masālma community; and Ohrwalder claims that "the whole town [was] continuously occupied in marriage ceremonies," although most marriages ended in separation. One member of the Masālma community even claimed to have had five wives during the Mahdīyya: two legally recognized ones and three "common-law" wives.[25]

In addition to the women who freely (if not always willingly) settled in Omdurman as emigrants, there were numerous women classified as war booty (*ghanīma*) who were brought in during the course of the *jihād* and given by the Khalīfa and *Bayt al-Māl* to loyal Anṣār for concubines or wives. These were the widows and other survivors of "unbelievers" (e.g., Nūba, Ethiopians, etc.) killed in war, and their distribution served a political end; thus the Khalīfa jealously guarded against Anṣār marrying women of the booty without his consent. Captive women, much like *jihādiyya* and other forms of booty, were an important resource of the state and hence carefully regulated. In the event these women were deemed "useless to the Anṣār, as they are unfit for service, travel or marriage," they were released to the care of relatives either in their home region or in Omdurman. Whatever their final arrangement, the Khalīfa and Amīr Yaᶜqūb were greatly concerned with their well-being, and composed numerous letters inquiring after them, directing relatives to supervise them and ensure that they are married or otherwise provided for. Other letters express the concern that all widows and unmarried women be brought to the capital for their own safety, and that Anṣār not leave their wives and children unprotected and unsupervised. Once married, these women of the *ghanīma* were regarded as full and legal wives.[26]

Mahdist doctrine severely curtailed the range of activity for women in Omdurman. The Mahdī instructed that women remain covered at all times, not venture out of their homes unless absolutely necessary, and defer to their husbands in all matters. In a proclamation to the Anṣār shortly after the Mahdī's death, the Khalīfa reasserted these principles: women must be veiled and prevented from mingling with men unrelated to them; women are forbidden to venture into the marketplace, except for very young girls and women without family or servants to shop for them; violators of this order are to receive 100 lashes and their guardians disciplined.[27]

The idea of a woman's complete subordination to her husband was articulated by both the Mahdī and Khalīfa in their proclamations and letters, although the fullest expression of this idea was contained in a purported work of *Ḥadīth*—almost certainly a "pious forgery"—that was current in Omdurman. Entitled "The Prophet Muḥammad's advice to his daughter Fāṭima," it is an attempt to justify with prophetic practice the ideology of the Mahdīyya. Discovered after Kararī by the Egyptian Military Intelligence, it exists now only in the poor English translation prepared by the staff of the E.M.I.:

> Any woman who can gain the pleasures of her husband for one day and night will be counted to her by God as equal to one year's worship. O Fatima: Any woman who dies and her husband is pleased with her shall find her tomb a paradise. Any woman who, with her smiles, brightens up her husband's face, will rescue her soul from the fire of hell. Any woman who lies with her husband in bed with her full consent, shall have all her sins forgiven and a voice from heaven shall be heard shouting, "O woman, continue thy work, for all thy sins are forgiven thee." Any woman who spreads for her husband something to sit upon, will find the gates of mercy opened before her: Her tomb shall shine with light, and 1,000 angels will descend on it, each carrying in his hands the light and fruits of paradise, and her tomb shall also become comfortable. Any woman who receives her husband with pleasure will be counted to her as if she read the Qur'ān 1,000 times, and in heaven she will dwell in a castle built of pearls and jewels.
>
> Any woman who asks her husband to divorce her shall have all the flesh of her face decay and only the bones remain, and shall descend at last to the lowest regions of hell, except she repents for what she has done. Any woman who is called by her husband to bed and dares to refuse, shall be cursed by God and all the angels: Her prayers will fail for forty days and at last she will descend into hell. Any woman who dares to say to her husband that she never saw good in him, all her prayers will be unacceptable for forty years, although she may sit up all night and fast all day long. Any woman who deserts her husband shall be thrown ultimately into the lowest regions of hell with Pharaoh, Haman and Croesus. Any woman who leaves her house without her husband's permission, will be cursed by every[one]...[28]

Many aspects of male-female relations in Omdurman appear to have matched the Mahdist ideal—at least publicly—due to the vigilance of the Anṣār in general and the *muṣliḥīn al-sūq* in particular, although again, the account of Bābikr Bedrī reveals that no radical or absolute recalibration of women's roles took place. A survivor of the period recalls that women did not venture into the marketplace, but rather sent their young female servants to procure food for them. Specifically, however, it was the free women who kept to their homes except for special occasions, such as weddings, funerals, and circumcisions: Omdurman was teeming with slave women who shopped for food, hauled firewood and water, washed clothing along the Nile, and performed the household labor. Likewise at home, many of the *amīrs* as well as merchants and others divided their living quarters into male and female sections, employing eunuch guards (*umanā'*) to prevent the mingling of the sexes. Those of more modest means, which would include the majority of the population, also segregated themselves at home, although without the help of special servants; while the widowed or impoverished women of Omdurman, with neither male relations nor slaves, frequented a women's *sūq* created specifically for their needs. This *sūq* was a place for women to conduct business, selling among other things items specifically required by women, and men were strictly forbidden from attending this market. Initially, the women merchants were those who could lawfully venture into public, i.e., those beyond child-bearing age. Late in the period, when a dearth of funds in the *Bayt al-Māl* hindered the state's ability to support families of soldiers, the strict rules on the seclusion of women were necessarily relaxed: Other women were allowed to become merchants in the *sūq*, the most prominent of these being the women of the western Baqqāra emigrants.[29]

In the matter of *jihād*, women were of course divided into two groups: those of child-bearing years whom the Mahdī had ordered to remain at home and struggle against their "natural desires," and post-menopausal women who were instructed to take a more active role. In fact, there is some evidence of pre-menopausal women combatants throughout the period, evidence that crosses a number of social lines. The Danāqla of Qiṭayna on the White Nile recall their victory over Sāttī Bey Abū'l-Qāsim and his Turco-Egyptian force in 1884, a battle in which a number of women participated and one in particular, al-Tūma Mīyya, distinguished herself. During the revolt of the Ashrāf in Omdurman in November 1891, several of the Mahdī's widows dressed in patched *jibbas* and armed themselves with spears against an attack by the Khalīfa's forces. While after the battle of Kararī, at least one woman, a Ḥabbānīyya of the western Baqqāra, was found among the dead, with many more among the seriously wounded. Certainly women, both free and slave, had long accompanied their men on military campaigns as a support force: They swelled the ranks of al-Nujūmī's expedition to Egypt in 1889 and Maḥmūd Aḥmad's army in 1897. Their role as fighters was less common, but certainly not unknown in Sudanese tradition: The "warrior-queens" of ancient Meroë, the so-called *kandakes*, were actively involved in war, even marching at the head of their armies; the sultanates of Darfur and Sinnār provide examples of women, often the sisters of sultans, with military authority if not actual combat experience; and Mahīra bt. ᶜAbbūd, daughter of the Suwarāb *shaykh*, was celebrated as a leader of the Shāīqī resistance to the Turco-Egyptian invasion in 1820, wearing men's clothing and waving a sword to taunt and rally the men. During the Mahdīyya, when the *shaykh* of the Kabābīsh, Ṣāliḥ Bey Faḍlallāh, made his final stand against the Mahdists in Kordofan in 1887, both his mother and sister fought by his side.[30] Similar to other aspects of the social order, this less-than-literal interpretation of the Mahdī's teachings does not appear to imply a lack of devotion to the Mahdīyya. At the same time, these examples of women combatants represent exceptional behavior.

As a matter of religious principle the Mahdī had strictly prohibited the use of tobacco and alcohol, and the Khalīfa reinforced this in his letters and sermons, while the *muṣliḥīn al-sūq* were constantly seeking offenders. Even still, it is difficult to gauge the response of the Anṣār of Omdurman to these edicts. What little evidence is available in the published accounts points to the violations, as might be expected, while oral accounts uniformly insist that the Anṣār abstained from both these vices. It is clear that at least some of the Anṣār continued to drink alcohol: Yūsuf Mikhā'īl, the Coptic clerk of the Black Standard division, recalled that he used to drink wine after the evening prayers with some of the riverain Sudanese, or "at [the *farīq* of the] Funqur, where wine was always available, or at [the *farīq* of the] Baqīrma or with some of the Taᶜāīshī *amīrs*." However, it is revealing that other Anṣār wrote letters to the Khalīfa complaining of this situation: One Anṣārī in 1887 condemned the "hypocrites" using tobacco, claiming that "they don't love the *jibba*." For his part, the Khalīfa ensured that most violators caught with alcohol or tobacco were both lashed and divested of their property. As for the Taᶜāīshī *amīrs*, he is said to have accepted their backsliding out of necessity, and even laughed at their denials.[31]

Similarly, not all Anṣār strictly adhered to the Mahdī's teachings on poverty, or more accurately, their adherence diminished as the years passed and the millennial enthusiasm waned. The Mahdī had ruled against the wearing of gold and silver jewelry, and most Anṣār complied with this ruling, anxious not to attract the attention of over-zealous market and treasury officials. (Ohrwalder commented that "the richer a man is, the dirtier will his dress be.") According to a former *qāḍī* of Sinnār, the Khalīfa commissioned a merchant in 1307 / 1889–1890 to travel to Cairo to procure an embroidered cover for the Mahdī's tomb, giving him "all jewelry—rubies, diamond rings and brooches—they gathered from Hicks Pasha's army, Khartoum and other garrisons, jewelry being of no value in Omdurman." Eventually, according to Slatin, things began to change: The Khalīfa's own wives, he claimed, wore mother-of-pearl, onyx, and red coral jewelry, fulfilling the letter if not the spirit of the Mahdī's teaching, while "for the last few years, the wives of the upper classes have again taken to wearing gold and silver jewelry." Likewise, the Anṣārī patched *jibba*, which followed Ṣūfī practice and had been adopted as a symbol of asceticism and contempt for the world, eventually became a highly stylized uniform. According to one study, some *jibbas* affected a look of poverty by employing large and irregular ornamental stitches on the patches, as if the garment were crudely put together, when in fact the actual workmanship was of a highly professional nature. The color and placement of the patches often revealed an aesthetic concern for balance and symmetry. Personalized *jibbas* were even made bearing the initials of the owner (or tailor), and were sewn from imported English and Egyptian fabrics. However against these violations, both subtle and egregious, of the Mahdi's teachings, there is also abundant evidence of Anṣār who took very seriously the call to poverty: Letters were written to the Khalīfa informing him of people outside Omdurman with excessive property and "a love of this world," suggesting that they be brought to *al-Buqᶜa* to be "cured of their materialism." There is the further example of the Khalīfa ᶜAlī wad Ḥilū, leader of the White Nile Arabs and a mediating force in the political struggles between the Khalīfa ᶜAbdallāhi and his Ashrāf and riverain opponents. Known as *al-Zāhid*, "the Ascetic," Khalīfa ᶜAlī embodied the early spirit of the Mahdīyya in his manner of dress, speech, and living habits. One of the first to support the Mahdī in 1881 and one of the last to be killed alongside the Khalīfa ᶜAbdallāhi in 1899, he is said to have encouraged by his own example a stricter adherence to Mahdist norms, while retaining the respect of all factions and communities in Omdurman.[32]

Great emphasis was placed by the Mahdī on the unity of the Anṣār, and the correspondence of the Khalīfa and Amīr Yaᶜqūb indicate that they were vigilant to uncover any evidence of dissension or disharmony. In an attempt to encourage cohesiveness through collective observances, the Khalīfa limited public celebrations in Omdurman to four festivals: the Prophet's birthday, the Rajabīyya, ᶜĪd al-Fiṭr, and ᶜĪd al-Aḍḥā. As the four chief celebrations of the Muslim calendar, this represented no great transformation of practice, although with the suppression of minor feast days (e.g., saints' birthdays) and gravesite visitations (*ziyārāt*), these festivals grew in importance. The Rajabīyya in particular became an important Anṣārī celebration, due to the Mahdī's circumcision of his sons on this day in 1885: Anṣār began to celebrate circumcisions and nuptial contracts on the Rajabīyya in the hope of sharing in the Mahdī's *baraka*. A more regular Anṣārī pastime was the weekly military parade (*al-ᶜArḍa*) held on Fridays just outside the city's limits to the west. Officiated by the Khalīfa (and after 1894, increasingly by Amīr Yaᶜqūb and ᶜUthmān Shaykh al-Dīn), this event served to both drill the troops and demonstrate the might and majesty of the regime. As with prayers in the mosque, attendance at the parade was not mandatory for all Anṣār but rather required of those of suspect loyalty. Accounts from the period however suggest that a large proportion of the population attended the weekly event, enjoying what was one of the only forms of officially sanctioned popular entertainment in Omdurman.[33]

Very serious attention was paid to antisocial acts that threatened the unity of the community. The Mahdī had recommended 80 lashes for uttering words of abuse, although in fact the punishment was often less harsh: Ohrwalder wrote that the penalty for calling another "dog" was 27 lashes, while Rosignoli received 40 lashes for calling someone "filthy." However, the penalty for striking another person was severe, the cutting off of a hand, a measure that appears to have been announced only in 1891, when tensions were rising between the Khalīfa and his Ashrāf opponents. The account of Bābikr Bedrī suggests that these measures were highly effective. Equally significant, it reinforces the idea that judicial discretion and mediation, as opposed to formal court proceedings, played a significant role in resolving disputes in Omdurman. On one occasion, Bābikr was advised by a judge not to lodge an official complaint after another man had struck him:

> You are the son of your father, and your father does not injure people. If you bring this man before us, we shall confine him in the heat of the sun and the rain of the night, and when his hand is cut off his children will be orphaned while he is yet alive; and that camel—perhaps he has borrowed it from his friends on a half-share agreement, and we shall confiscate it, and his goats, if he has any, will be taken by his partner in lieu of it. Let him be, and forgive him for God's sake, as your father would do.[34]

Unquestionably, the most ambitious measure attempted by the Khalīfa to implement the Mahdī's social order was the planned intermarriage of two sections of the Omdurman population to form a more unified society. This intermarriage between the northern riverain Sudanese (*awlād al-balad*) and the western pastoralist Baqqāra (*awlād al-ᶜArab*) was an attempt to mend a major fissure in Mahdist society that dated back to the years of the Mahdī's revolt. In origin it was both a political and cultural rift: The *awlād al-balad* had been early adherents of the Mahdī from his time at Abā Island and included, most prominently, his relatives among the Ashrāf as well as other members of the Danāqla tribe and sections of the Jaᶜaliyīn. Many of these had fought under the Red Standard of the Mahdī's cousin, the Khalīfa Muḥammad Sharīf, and supported his claim to succession after the sudden death of the Mahdī. Accustomed to the village and town life of the Nile Valley as merchants, artisans, and farmers, and more affected by the modernizing developments of the eighteenth and nineteenth centuries, they often viewed the Baqqāra followers of the Khalīfa ᶜAbdallāhi with thinly veiled contempt, regarding them as vulgar in their habits, coarse in appearance and speech, and unenthusiastic in their Mahdist faith. For their part, the westerners regarded the riverain Sudanese with equal contempt, deriding them as *Jallāba* (literally "traders," but carrying a distinctly pejorative connotation) and worse: Shuqayr records an instance of the Baqqāra referring to the *awlād al-balad* as "the dogs of the world" for their supposed reluctance to wage *jihād*; while informants from Omdurman reported to the Egyptian Military Intelligence in 1894 that in a common curse, the Baqqāra associate the Danāqla with the people of the Nūba mountains, who are "the representatives of the slave class in the Sudan."

Tensions between these two groups were exacerbated by the *hijra* of the

Baqqāra and their settlement both in Omdurman and, more damagingly, in the fertile lands of the Jazīra region. The policies of the Khalīfa, who was seen to favor his western tribesmen, and the spending of the *Bayt al-Māl* to subsidize them, added enormously to these tensions, which finally erupted in the revolt of the Ashrāf in 1891. The resolution of the revolt in 1892 did nothing to ease tensions, as the Khalīfa placed Muḥammad Sharīf under arrest, banished and executed many of his followers, divested the Danāqla of a third of their goods, and confiscated many of their boats for use by the state. Thus it is not surprising that the Ja^{c}aliyīn at Matamma rose in revolt as the Anglo-Egyptian army approached in 1897, and their massacre at the hands of Maḥmūd Aḥmad and his Baqqāra troops was essentially the death-knell for the Mahdīyya.

The Khalīfa's plan to distribute some of the women of Matamma as booty to his Baqqāra followers, and the outrage this elicited among the Ja^{c}aliyīn of Omdurman, has already been discussed. Bābikr Bedrī's recollection of this event is revealing: "The western tribes made ^{c}Abdallāh Sa^{c}d's rebellion an excuse for making free of the property of 'the traders' as they called us, and there fell upon us a nightmare of fear and dismay that made us forget that it was we who had been the founders of the Mahdist state."[35]

It is in the context of this deep rift that the Khalīfa in 1893 attempted a more direct means of encouraging unity among his followers. Worried by the recent Ashrāf revolt as well as dissension in Kordofan, he proposed to intermarry a number of riverain and western Anṣār. A description of this attempt, included in an Anṣārī account of the Mahdīyya, is translated here in full. It is entitled "An account of the Khalīfa's request for 1,500 virgins from the *awlād al-^{c}Arab* and 1,000 widows and divorced women from the *awlād al-qurā*" ("town dwellers").

> The Khalīfa determined [to do this], saying, "If God wills and time permits," since in each *rāya* there were ten individuals who knew about inheritance, which is the science of obligations, such that no *rāya* was in need of another.[36]

> The Khalīfa requested the women because at times the Anṣār quarreled among themselves. The *awlād al-^{c}Arab* said, "O Khalīfat al-

Imām, the *awlād al-balad* call us 'Baqqāra,'" and the *awlād al-balad* said, "The *awlād al-ᶜArab* call us 'Jallāba.'" Al-Ḥājj Khālid al-ᶜUmarābī came forward and said, "O Khalīfat al-Imām, if only they called us 'Jallāba!' They prefer to call us 'Nūba.'" The Khalīfa became angry, and after three days he said to his *amīns*, "Announce to all of the Emigrants and Anṣār that they should heed what I say to them and what I have requested from the heads of the armies." The Khalīfa [then] called for Yaᶜqūb b. Muḥammad, who replied, "At your service," and said: "Go and collect for me the daughters of the *amīrs* and important people, and one from our daughters, their total being 1,500 virgins, free of blindness, deafness, lameness or any other defect."

The Khalīfa [also] called for al-Badawī Muḥammad Aḥmad al-ᶜIrayq, who replied, "At your service," and said to him: "Collect for me the widows and divorced women of the *awlād al-balad*, even if some of them are mothers, and your total should be 1,000. My goal is to commingle and intermarry you, that you might be brothers, sons of the Imām and hence sons of the Hereafter. I will marry the virgin daughters of the ᶜArab *amīrs* to the paupers of the *awlād al-balad*, and the widowed daughters of the *awlād al-balad* to the *amīrs* and important people of the *awlād al-ᶜArab*. The reasons for this are [first of all], the women of the *awlād al-balad* are chaste, well-tended and refined—only their paupers would be content with the daughters of the *awlād al-ᶜArab amīrs*. The *awlād al-ᶜArab* [meanwhile] lust after the townswomen. For another thing, the *awlād al-balad* are an extremely mobile people—if there are hostilities or the need to move, [their] horses are immediately saddled. [But] if one of them cannot find his slave, he is unable to saddle his charger right away. So it is my hope that the ᶜArab woman will saddle his charger for him more quickly than he or his slave are able to do, and that he will learn from her to be prompt.

My marriage of the *awlād al-ᶜArab* to the women of the *awlād al-balad* is due to the fact that [these women have been] modest and chaste by nature since before the Mahdīyya. The *awlād al-ᶜArab* [however] are without modesty or decency: The men go about half-naked in the wild, eat by the wayside, suffer privations and do not show modesty in the homes of strangers. The women of the *awlād al-balad* will teach them diffidence and when it is necessary to practice modesty,

> decency, politeness and observe the *Sunna*. Do you understand?" They said, "Yes," and he said, "Collect them for me with a list that includes their names, tribes, fathers and *rāyas*."
>
> After the Khalīfa's instructions had been issued, al-Sayyid Yaᶜqūb b. Muḥammad brought the 1,500 virgins, among them one of his own daughters whom he had selected. Every month the Khalīfa asked the *awlād al-balad*, "What about the order I gave?" and they replied, "We are working on it." After three months had passed, he asked al-Ḥājj Khālid al-ᶜUmarābī in the mosque, who replied, "O Khalīfat al-Mahdī, truly the *awlād al-balad* are untrusting, for they say that 'The Khalīfat al-Mahdī wants only to marry our daughters to the *awlād al-ᶜArab,*' and they seem not to accept that their daughters be with the *awlād al-ᶜArab* or that the daughters of the *awlād al-ᶜArab* be with their sons."
>
> So [the Khalīfa] said to al-Ḥājj Khālid, "You have spoken truthfully. May God bless you for it! The Exalted One said, 'God attains His purpose. God has appointed a measure for everything' [Qur'ān 65:3]. Our wish was that you [people] be in harmony, but God has willed your division: This because you have thought ill of us. Beware [al-Ḥājj Khālid], lest you be one of them."[37]

The Khalīfa's attempt to intermarry the Anṣār was noted at the time by Egyptian Military Intelligence, and while at least two daughters of the Amīr Yaᶜqūb did marry men of the *awlād al-balad*, no group-wide intermarriage occurred. The cultural assumptions contained in this account—e.g., the civilized *awlād al-balad* who observe the *Sunna*, versus the primitive, self-reliant *awlād al-ᶜArab* who lust after the townswomen, etc.—were common among many Sudanese both before and after the Mahdīyya. Yūsuf Mikhā'īl claimed that the Arabs of Kordofan hold the riverain people in special regard, considering them to have a sanctity like the people of Jerusalem or Mecca; while even the Mahdī is said to have referred to the western Arabs in a letter of 1884 as being "shy like wild beasts, in need of being tamed and trained." The Khalīfa for his part clearly believed the Islam of the Mahdīyya to be an essentially urban practice, with Omdurman as a model for the rest of Sudan. (For their part, and not surprisingly, the Baqqāra rejected these stereotypes unequivocally.)[38]

The failed intermarriage of the *awlād al-balad* and the *awlād al-ᶜArab* should be viewed alongside other attempts to encourage unity that met with mixed success and sometimes changed in response to conditions. For instance, the Khalīfa was determined that the Muslim-convert community of Omdurman be integrated into Mahdist society, and he specifically ordered that the Masālma men marry "black women" (*Sūdānīyyāt*), so that their offspring—necessary to the administration of the state—might be more fully accepted by the Anṣār. Many of the Masālma men subsequently married women from southern and western Sudan as well as Ethiopia. And yet, following the Mahdist defeat by the Italians at Agordat in 1893, the Khalīfa reversed this decision, apparently fearing that the same Masālma might pose a risk to the security of the state. As for the *jihādīyya*, there was never any attempt at intermarrying these soldiers of southern, western, and Nūba origin with the rest of Mahdist society since, apart from their questionable legal status, they were a vital resource of the state, to be strictly monitored. Certainly the northern Sudanese would have rejected immediately any such suggestion, since among most riverain people marriage to a "black" was considered disgraceful. Finally, the adoption of the *jibba* as the Mahdist uniform had also been an attempt to encourage unity among the Anṣār, and indeed it was worn throughout the Sudan (albeit in a sometimes stylized fashion). Even still, the Khalīfa on at least one occasion was forced to upbraid his *amīrs* for wearing colored shawls to distinguish themselves from the other Anṣār.[39]

However persistent the rifts in Mahdist society during the 13 years of the Khalīfa's reign, it is also true that many of Sudan's hostilities, tribal and ethnic, were reduced due to the power of the state and the attraction (or distraction) of *jihād*. Additionally, Holt argued that the tensions between the *awlād al-balad* and *awlād al-ᶜArab* should not be exaggerated: "It is undeniable that between the Baqqāra and the *awlād al-balad* there persisted a latent hostility which flared out in such episodes as the revolt of the Ashrāf and the resistance of al-Matamma, but these dramatic and much-publicized incidents should not conceal the more normal relationship revealed by the administrative history of the Mahdist state."[40]

Certainly the Khalīfa had limited time and ability to bring about social change of any type, much less the profound transformation envisioned by the Mahdī. However, the Mahdist social order can also be viewed in terms of the new practices adopted and the degree of social amalgamation that characterized Omdurman society. Meanwhile, if a compromise between revolutionary change and practical application marked many of the Khalīfa's efforts, there was also a discernable effort on the part of many of the Anṣār to adhere to the tenets of the Mahdī's teachings. It remains to be seen how the resources of the Mahdist state were utilized to carry out some approximation of the Mahdī's order.

The *Bayt al-Māl* and the Social Order

With the idealism of a messianic leader, the Mahdī originally had proposed to gather together all of the revenues of the Sudan in the *Bayt al-Māl* and distribute the wealth among the Anṣār according to their needs and numbers, without regard for tribal origin or status. The chief source of revenue during the revolt was of course war booty (*ghanīma*), the division of which had been determined by Qur'ān: "Know that whatever booty you take, the fifth of it is God's, and the Messenger's, and the near kinsman's, and the orphan's, and for the needy, and the traveler" (8:41). This fifth (*khums*), essentially the share of the state, was placed in the *Bayt al-Māl* for the Mahdī to use as he saw fit, while the remaining four-fifths were to be divided among the Anṣār "without distinction between rich and poor."[41]

Before very long this policy proved impractical to implement, and on occasion it was suspended. For instance after the capture of El Obeid (19 January 1883), the Mahdī blocked the collection of booty from certain merchants and allowed them to retain the money deposited with them by the people of the city before the siege. The Mahdī explained this practice by declaring that the property of El Obeid constituted tribute (*fay'*) instead of booty, since the city had ultimately surrendered. In so doing, the Mahdī was closely following the example of the Prophet Muḥammad, who also came to distinguish between plunder and tribute with a revelation that clarified that some victories are due not to the efforts of soldiers, but to divine intervention: "Whatsoever spoils of war God has given to His Messenger from the people of the cities belongs to God, and His Messenger, and the near kinsmen, the orphans, the needy and the traveler, so that it be not a thing taken in turns among the rich of you" (59:7). Although the Mahdī was exercising his prerogative as Imām in this matter, his decision caused considerable consternation among many of the Anṣār, especially since the city's capitulation followed a five-month siege and the famous Friday Battle of 8 September 1882, in which some 10,000 Anṣār had been killed. Like the Prophet before him, the Mahdī was forced to disavow any interest in personal gain and argue for the need to reconcile important individuals to the cause.[42]

As the fiscal needs of the Mahdist treasury grew with the development of the movement and an increase in followers, new sources of wealth came to be considered the exclusive property of the state. After the fall of Khartoum this wealth included the following items:

- Property of the towns captured by force.
- Property of the opponents of the Mahdīyya and of those who fled the Sudan.
- Property of employees of the former Turco-Egyptian regime.
- Property of the wealthy people and merchants in captured towns.
- Property of the Turco-Egyptian government, including buildings, dockyards, workshops, etc.
- Property of foreign merchants entering the country without official permission.
- Property of the "profiteers of war."
- Property taken away from or discarded by those fleeing besieged towns.
- Property and persons of those who do not believe in the Mahdīyya.
- Property and persons of apostates (*al-murtadd*) who go back on their belief in the Mahdīyya.
- Property of Turks and Christians, except those who surrendered prior to the battle of Shaykān (5 November 1883) and are sincere in their submission.
- Property of those who cross the borders to plunder.
- Property of those who commit mortal sins, such as using alcohol and tobacco.
- All accoutrements of war belonging to the enemy, such as weapons, *jihādīyya*, horses, and pack animals.
- All property of Khartoum that pertains to the public interest, such as

shops, caravansaries, estates, mills, gardens, houseboats, and docks.
- Property of hostile Bedouin tribes (e.g., the Kabābīsh).

Furthermore, Rosignoli indicates that building materials also came to be regarded as property of the state, particularly wood, which was extremely scarce. Moreover, "horses cannot be sold, as it is said that they belong to the government, that is they may at any time be requisitioned [for military purposes]."[43]

Noteworthy here is the redefining of "spoils of war" from battlefield trophies to economic sanctions against enemies of the state, be they "Turks," "apostates," or recalcitrant nomads. Additionally, all booty not obtained directly in battle—and even some property that was—is to be officially considered a form of tribute and essentially nationalized and administered by the *Bayt al-Māl* on behalf of the Mahdist community. Thus when the Mahdī warns the Khedive of Egypt, in a letter of 16 June 1885, that the person and possessions of a disbeliever "are a lawful spoil for the Muslims," we understand him to mean that such property belongs to the state as a trust for all Anṣār.[44]

The taking of booty was of inestimable value to the Mahdī as a threat against his opponents. In a characteristic letter, he warned an enemy that "we pray to God that you too, and all those who follow you, may be booty for the ignorant Baqqāra whom you have derided." At the same time, the collection of this booty from the Anṣār and its proper distribution by the *Bayt al-Māl* was a constant problem. After the battle of Shaykān, the Mahdī addressed a letter to his followers in which he threatened those who cheat in the matter of booty, and likewise those who fail to report the fraud of others. Invoking the threat of eternal torments, he reminded the Anṣār that "you have given me your oaths to hear and obey my orders, and to not rebel against that which is right and proper [*ma*ᶜ*rūf*]. I do not accept that anyone among you may cheat in the matter of booty, be it even [for] a needle and thread." Four days later, the Mahdī issued another letter in which he announced that those who hold back booty are not considered his companions, "for they are companions of the devil and Antichrist." Enough such letters were written by the Mahdī, and later the Khalīfa, to indicate that a comprehensive policy for the collection and distribution of booty among the Anṣār was never fully implemented. Recognition of this fact, whatever its theological implications, was for the Khalīfa an acknowledgement of reality.[45]

The situation of land use during the Mahdīyya provides another example of the need to compromise for the sake of the political and economic order. Strictly speaking, there was to be no private ownership of land, since land "cannot be owned, being the possession of the *Bayt Māl al-Muslimīn*," and "ownership of the land is with God." While Muslims were allowed the right to possess land, inherit or bequeath it and enjoy its produce, they were forbidden to tax others for occupying or working it. Legal ownership (*milkīyya*) resided with the Mahdī (and after him, the Khalīfa), as the sole representative of God's authority with the right to administer and dispose of land on behalf of the community. "Landownership" then was understood as land rights, as was the case with property that could be possessed, safeguarded, and cultivated by paying an annual tax to the government. Actual management of the lands resided with the *Bayt al-Māl*, which also leased out certain lands owned outright by the state, such as wastelands, unclaimed lands, forests, and *ghanīma* and *fay'* lands. The Mahdī clearly addressed this issue and urged his followers to give up that land which they were not in need of:

> Whoever has land, let him cultivate however much of it he is able. If he becomes incapacitated or no longer in need of it, let him not take a tax in kind [for another's use of it], because the believers are like one body: Whatever he treats equally with his brother believer will be in his balance eternally with God to a high degree....
>
> There is no competition among believers except in regard to the eternal. Every believer possesses his land. However, that he might obtain a share of the Hereafter, let him give what he does not need to his brother believer who is need. For that thing which he is incapable of using, and which brings him to the Hereafter, is better for him than the benefit of a tax, which quickly passes away.[46]

In actual practice, the Mahdist state was forced to acknowledge the differing forms of land tenure necessitated by the varied terrain of the Sudan. Particularly in the riverain north, customary usage and landownership was recognized so that cultivation might continue unhindered. According to Abū Salīm, this was also an attempt to redress the impoverishment of riverain

Sudanese brought about by the policies of the Turco-Egyptian regime. In the Jazīra region much of the land was considered either *ghanīma* or *fay'*, and the *Bayt al-Māl's* administration of these lands, which included giving plots to worthy Anṣār for cultivation and grazing, resulted in a number of legal disputes. In particular, after the *hijra* of the Taᶜāīsha and other Baqqāra tribes with their herds of cattle, some of this Jazīra land nearer to Omdurman and the White Nile was reserved for the westerners, who displaced the original occupants and farmed the land during the rainy season. Such use of the land was an obvious, even necessary response to the problem of settling and feeding the westerners, yet even by Mahdist standards it was of questionable legitimacy: Apparently not all of the appropriated land was actually *ghanīma* or *fay'*. Moreover taxes were not collected on these lands so that, implicitly at least, the Baqqāra were given ownership over their lands. At least by 1895, the Taᶜāīsha were renting out their lands in the Jazīra in exchange for an annual payment in grain, cloth, and currency. The result of this situation was the enhanced rivalry between the westerners and riverain Sudanese, as well as the elevation of the Baqqāra, against Mahdist teachings, to an economically privileged status in the hinterlands of the capital.[47]

In Omdurman meanwhile, the matter of land usage—and adherence to Mahdist ideals—was simplified by the city having been created anew from a virtually uninhabited spot: All property belonged to the *Bayt al-Māl*, which leased shops in the marketplace to individual merchants. Even here, however, enterprising Anṣār were able to lease several shops and rent them out to others: For example, the Masālma Jew Mūsa Basyūnī rented out a shop in the *sūq* to Bābikr Bedrī, while the head of the market police, Muḥammad Wahbī Ḥusayn, leased and rented out 12 shops. Homes in the residential districts meanwhile might be bought, sold, and mortgaged, but the land underneath all shops and homes belonged only to the state, and there was no ownership with regard to land. This meant that on occasion the Khalīfa was able to dictate the settlement of certain groups of people: The Baqqāra, as previously mentioned, were given land in the southern portion of the city, and the Masālma and others deemed a potential risk were required to live in their specific districts. By and large, however, settlement was a popular phenomenon in which the Khalīfa intervened as little as possible, and then only when it was dictated by security concerns. Outside the capital, apart from the appropriations of the Baqqāra, land tenure continued much as before—indeed, in some parts of the Jazīra people continued to use the title deeds (*hujjāt*) granted during the Funj sultanate. Omdurman, as the near-exemplar of Mahdist teachings, essentially constituted an anomaly in Sudanese practice.[48]

The fiscal operations of the *Bayt al-Māl* shed further light on the Mahdist social order, as might be expected from the preeminent institution in the Mahdist state. Encompassing the functions of treasury, warehouse, and general administrative office, it came to direct the entire state economy and control many aspects of society through its influence over markets and economic policies; while its chief officer, the *Amīn Bayt al-Māl*, was "the most important civil official in the Mahdist state." Unfortunately, the only surviving monthly treasury records are from the period of 18 Shawwāl 1314 until the end of Rajab 1315, i.e., 22 March–24 December 1897. Nonetheless, an examination of these records plainly reveals the Mahdist state's utter dependence upon the personnel and practices of the Turco-Egyptian regime, as well as the fiscal limitations upon its ambition to create (or "restore") an idealized social order.[49]

The growth of the *Bayt al-Māl* as an institution was a direct result of the increased administrative and economic needs of the Mahdist movement. Early in the uprising, many Anṣār were drawn to the Mahdī by both his messianic claim and his message of a more egalitarian and just society. Others, as is illustrated by the problem of booty, were attracted by the appeal of material gain. Perhaps many followers embraced all of these motivations. Confusion soon arose over the many competing claims on the movement's limited resources, prompting the first effort at organizing the Mahdīyya in a bureaucratic manner: assigning clerks to the various *rāyas* to keep lists of the Anṣār. An undated letter from this early period identifies the Black Standard of Khalīfa ᶜAbdallāhi as half the entire army, for which reason it was allotted half of the treasury's expenditure, or 15,000 *riyāls*. At least by March 1885, efforts were being made to distinguish between full- and part-time soldiers for the purpose of pay. Those who had given up everything to devote themselves to the *jihād* were to be paid over intervals at a fixed rate by the *Bayt al-Māl*, while those who left on a seasonal basis to cultivate were to receive, according to need, a share of the four-fifths of the booty held by the treasury.[50]

After the conquest of Khartoum and the accession of the Khalīfa, the *Bayt al-Māl* devoted itself to the needs of the state, particularly under Ibrāhīm Muḥammad ᶜAdlān (*Amīn* from 1886 to 1890), who expanded its operations to more effectively handle the large volume of fiscal, trade, and administrative matters and, significantly, obtained the employment of many clerks and accountants with valuable experience under the former regime. As one study has shown, with these employees came established practices of fiscal recording, accountancy, and bookkeeping (albeit "modified to suit local conditions") as well as a particular orthography that utilized Turkish and Persian technical terms. When the treasury began to mint coins, these also followed precedent, being "literally modeled on the Ottoman coins," even bearing the *tughra* (monogram) of the Ottoman sultan. From the start then, the Mahdist state—like the earliest Muslim states—acquired and adopted what was useful from its predecessors, at least to the extent that these practices "could be financed by a poor revolutionary state."[51]

Likely from the beginning, the largest share of the state's expenditures went to administrative costs and the maintenance of soldiers and their families, although compensation for soldiers at least (including currency, clothing, and grain) fluctuated according to circumstances. Additionally, several thousand people received some manner of support from the state, including former residents of Khartoum and members of the captive Masālma community, continuing a practice begun after the fall of El Obeid. Impoverished Anṣār in general, including widows, orphans, the infirm, elderly, blind, and others with no sources of income, were given relief in the form of money or slaves—almost 4,700 such individuals in 1885 alone. Payments were organized, recorded, and disbursed on a tribe-by-tribe, *rāya*-by-*rāya* basis, as befit the organizational structures of the state, and continued while funds were sufficient. (By the time Fr. Rosignoli arrived in Omdurman in May 1886, some of the subsidies had ended and the Masālma were told they would have to support themselves: "The Khalīfa ordered that all our efforts to make a living should be aided" by the treasury.) In extraordinary circumstances the state assumed other responsibilities, as in the *Bayt al-Māl's* aforementioned distribution of burial shrouds during the smallpox epidemic of 1885.[52]

With the growth of the state's resources and responsibilities, the *Bayt al-Māl* became the focus of the social and political rifts that beset the

Mahdist state. The brief terms in office of the various *amīns* reflect the incessant power struggles that consumed much of the Khalīfa's attention, as well as his inability to mediate disputes and separate political interests from administrative needs. The eventual division of the treasury into smaller units, carried out during the directorship of al-Nūr Ibrāhīm Jirayfāwī (*Amīn*, 1890–1893/1894), led to a compartmentalization of revenues and expenditures that served both bureaucratic and political ends, including greater supervision by the Amīr Yaᶜqūb. Sometime prior to 1897, these treasuries were again combined under a single *Bayt Māl al-Muslimīn*, likely to improve efficiency.

The sources of revenue and items of expenditure of the different treasuries, as they existed from 1890 onwards, are as follows.[53]

1. *Bayt Māl al-ᶜUmūm* ("The General *Bayt al-Māl*," 1890–1898)

Sources of revenue:
- *Zakāt* and *fiṭra* taxes.
- Booty and confiscated property of enemies of the state.
- Tithes (*ᶜushūr*) on imported and exported goods.
- Contributions and loans (*tabarruᶜāt*) from merchants.
- Revenue of the ferries.
- Produce of the east bank of the Blue Nile and west bank of the White Nile.
- A percentage of revenues of the regional treasuries.

Expenditures:
- Maintenance and transport of soldiers.
- Support for the households of the *khalīfas* and the widows of the Mahdī.
- Wages and salaries of government employees.
- Support for the poor and disabled.

2. *Bayt Māl al-Khums* (The Khalīfa's "Privy Treasury," 1890–1898)

Sources of revenue:
- The Khalīfa's fifth of the booty.

- A portion of the revenues of the provincial treasuries.
- Revenue of islands and all domain (*fay'*) lands.
- Tithes on goods passing between Berber and Omdurman.
- Slaves sent from the provinces.
- Revenue of most of the steamers and boats.

Expenditures:
- The Khalīfa's household.

3. *Bayt Māl al-Mulāzimīn* (1890–before 1897)

Sources of revenue:
- The Jazīra lands.

Expenditures:
- Support of the *mulāzimīn* (Khalīfa's bodyguard) and their families.

4. *Bayt Māl al-Jihādīyya* (1890–before 1897)

Sources of revenue:
- Revenues from the west bank of the Nile in the Omdurman area.

Expenditures:
- Maintenance of the *jihādīyya.*

5. *Bayt Māl al-Ḥarbīyya* (1890–before 1897)

Sources of revenue:
- Produce of the Khartoum gardens.
- Revenues of some of the waterwheels (*sāqiyyas*) in the Khartoum area.
- Equatorian ivory.

Expenditures:
- All dockyard expenses.
- Expenses of the arsenal and its related workshops.
- The refining of saltpeter and manufacture of arms and ammunition.

6. *Bayt Māl Ḍabṭīyat al-Sūq* (1890–before 1897)

Sources of revenue:
- Fines and confiscated property of gamblers and users of tobacco and alcohol.
- Tax on shops in the marketplace.

Expenditures:
- Pay of the market inspectors and judges.
- Costs associated with the state's guest house.
- Construction costs of the city wall.

This organization of state finances raises many questions, but in the absence of complete treasury records it is difficult to trace the development of fiscal policy and determine with any certainty what it all means. For example, what share of the state's revenues was controlled directly by the Khalīfa and his inner circle, and to what end? What did the Khalīfa's "Privy Treasury" actually pay for? Was there in fact a dramatic shifting of wealth from riverain Sudanese into the hands of the Taᶜāīsha and other westerners? And what percentage of the population was supported by the state, either directly or indirectly, during this period? Narrative accounts, such as the memoirs of Bābikr Bedrī and others, certainly shed light on general economic conditions, and other documentation from the Mahdist state can be employed to a degree. Otherwise, the surviving monthly treasury records from 1897 at least allow insight into the workings of the *Bayt al-Māl* prior to the state's overthrow, during a time of firm centralized control, and most particularly into its patterns of revenue and expenditure.

It is clear that some items of expenditure and sources of revenue could change dramatically with circumstances. For example, 40 percent of the total monthly expenditure of Dhū'l-Ḥijja 1314/May 1897 was devoted to new clothing for the soldiers for ᶜĪd al-Aḍḥā. One month later, in Muḥarram 1315/June 1897, most of the expenses were related to outfitting, transporting, and paying the salaries of Maḥmūd Aḥmad's expeditionary force. Revenue from booty and confiscations amounted to a mere .45 percent of total revenue in Muḥarram 1315, whereas two months later, after the massacre and pillaging of Matamma, it amounted to 60 percent of the total revenue. Additionally, a relationship seems to have existed between merchants' "contributions" and other sources of revenue: In Muḥarram 1315, with its relatively low level of income from booty and confiscations, 20 percent of the total monthly income was raised from merchants, while after the windfall of Matamma, contributions accounted for only 2.2 percent of the total income. This situation, combined with the fact that expenditures almost always equaled the revenues in any month, suggests that the Mahdist state collected whatever it needed, in whatever manner possible, to meet its obligations: or, as one study put it, the Mahdist state simply lived "hand to mouth."[54]

In general, the fines imposed on users of alcohol and tobacco, as well as the confiscation of property from "enemies of the state" (i.e., the Khalīfa's opponents), appear to have been a reliable, if relatively small, source of revenue. The collection of religious taxes (*zakāt* and *fiṭr* at the end of Ramaḍān) was by nature seasonal, while the treasury's exchange of foreign currency against Mahdist coins was a more lucrative and consistent source of revenue. Rent collected on properties seized from the former Turco-Egyptian regime or its supporters and leased out to merchants, as well as rent accruing from shops in the Omdurman *sūq*, probably constituted the most consistent source of revenue. The commodities taxes (*ᶜushūr*) imposed on all imported and exported goods, collected along the trading routes as well as in Omdurman, formed another extremely important source of revenue, particularly as such products as ivory, gum, ostrich feathers, and senna leaves were declared government monopolies and sold by the *Bayt al-Māl* to merchants at high rates. However these taxes, as well as the soliciting of "contributions" (deemed "un-Islamic" by some merchants and paid "only under duress"), were unquestionably damaging: Bābikr Bedrī estimated that the various charges levied by the government in 1894 left a merchant with only 7/60 of his original capital. Additionally, he noted that the treasury often took a half or a third of his goods, after the *ᶜushr* tax, as a "loan." This put even the most loyal Anṣār in a quandary, since "on top of these dues there were the merchant's expenses on the outward and inward journeys, and the upkeep of his family. After this, can you blame us for smuggling...?"[55]

Expenditures of the Mahdist state appear to have followed a regular pattern: Salaries and wages of government workers (including at the *Bayt al-*

Māl and related workshops, the courts, prison, *Bayt al-Amāna,* lithograph press, etc.) were the greatest expense. These were followed by various "purchases," which could include military-related needs; direct military spending, including the salaries of regular soldiers and *jihādīyya*, expenses at the dockyard, arsenal, powder factory, etc.; "miscellaneous" expenditures, such as supporting the poor and infirm, maintaining the government guest house, and providing for the needs of foreign (e.g., Ethiopian) emissaries, maintenance of the *Qubba* ("*al-Ḥaram al-Sharīf*"), and support for the households of the Khalīfa, the two junior *khalīfas,* and the Mahdī's widows; payments to irregular or seasonal soldiers from the four-fifths of the booty; and transport costs, which again could be related to military needs.[56]

The picture of Mahdist society that emerges from the treasury records and other sources is complicated. Certainly a redistribution of wealth was carried out during the Mahdīyya, involving the collection of revenues in commodities taxes, confiscations, "contributions" and rents from the riverain merchant community, and the channeling of these funds into the wartime economy to the benefit—although not exclusive benefit—of the western tribes who were devoted wholly to the *jihād.* This was never more evident than during the arrival of Maḥmūd Aḥmad's army of the west in 1897, when the population of the city as a whole was required to donate food to the emigrants, to be counted by the bowlful and recorded by clerks of the Black Standard. The result of this redistribution was enmity that approached civil war. At the outbreak of the Ashrāf revolt in 1891, Muḥammad Sharīf made the following demands: that the Khalīfa ᶜAbdallāhi abolish the taxes on trading boats and camels; restore boats taken forcibly from their owners; remove the tax on goods passing through Kōkreb, Omdurman, and Berber; abolish the tax on grain and ferries; restore Jazīra lands taken from their owners; divide arms and authority equally between the three *khalīfas*; abolish the government monopolies on export goods; and return the Mahdī's fifth-share of booty to his sons.[57]

However, at the same time that a redistribution of wealth was achieved, the essential socioeconomic structure of the Sudan did not change considerably, despite the Taᶜāīshī acquisition of land in the Jazīra: the manufacturing, agricultural, and mercantile sectors of the economy continued to be dominated by the riverain Sudanese. A familiar view of the situation, originating in the remarks of Slatin after his escape from Omdurman, held that "for [the *awlād al-balad*] there is no security of life and property, and bribery alone may temporarily stave off complete ruin." Without minimizing the hardships endured by this population, it must also be pointed out that as administrators and clerks, producers of grain, manufacturers of arms, and builders and crews of boats, they received as a regional group the largest share of the state's expenditures.[58]

The matter of boats is instructive. Following the Ashrāf revolt, a council of state in March 1892 declared the confiscation of boats in Omdurman for transporting soldiers on *jihād.* These boats were henceforth to belong to the state, with the owners paid compensation at a nominal rate per carrying capacity. Having nationalized the boats, the *Bayt al-Māl* proceeded to rent them back to the original owners to ferry goods and passengers across the Nile. The boats' crews were all given the choice to remain working on the state-owned boats, since the state required experienced boatmen. Meanwhile, on the state-owned steamers, all of the captains and pilots were either Danāqla or other Nubians. Further, in a letter to Yaᶜqūb in 1897, the *Amīn Bayt al-Māl* Ibrāhīm Ramaḍān lists the owners of boats transporting materials of war to Maḥmūd Aḥmad in Matamma: All are riverain Sudanese. Two months later, records from the state dockyard list the boat owners transporting goods from Matamma to the *Bayt al-Māl,* and again all are riverain Sudanese. Finally, a list of boats in Omdurman compiled by the Egyptian Military Intelligence after the conquest reveals that, in addition to the 136 "big boats" and ferries considered state property (*fay'*), 383 other boats were operating, of which 300 belonged to "the local people."[59]

Additionally, most of the gardens of Khartoum that had belonged to either Egyptian Copts or Sudanese loyal to the former regime ended up under the control of riverain people, leased from the Mahdist state and profitably exploited. (A smaller portion of these gardens was controlled by Taᶜāīsha, including some relatives of the Khalīfa.) Many prominent individuals—including state officeholders, associates of the Khalīfa Sharīf, and members of influential riverain families—are named in lists of the garden leasers, although none more prominent than the Mahdī's father-in-law, Aḥmad Sharfī. Given supervisory control over Khartoum's orchards and date trees by the Mahdī in early 1885, Aḥmad Sharfī eventually sublet these properties to other Anṣār. Of course he, like other businessmen, had to contend with the state's intrusions, and in letters to Amīr Yaᶜqūb in 1897 and 1898 he complains of unfair taxes on his gardens, extortionate demands for "assistance" from the *Bayt al-Māl*, and the unauthorized borrowing of his boats, asking Yaᶜqūb to intervene and restore his privileges.[60]

Unquestionably the resources of the *Bayt al-Māl* were used to the advantage of the Khalīfa and his retinue. Treasury records reveal monthly payments to the Khalīfa's household of 5,000 *riyāls*, against 300 (and sometimes 700) *riyāls* to the *khalīfas* Muḥammad Sharīf and ᶜAlī wad Ḥilū. However, the Khalīfa's "household" was understood to include a large number of families, some related to him by birth, others by marriage, and still others by loyal association. (By way of comparison, Bābikr Bedrī's household, including his family, slaves, and guests, consisted of more than 40 persons.) Slatin noted that the Khalīfa "thought it incumbent upon his position to maintain a large establishment," and naturally there were requirements to his office: When the Khalīfa's son ᶜUthmān Shaykh al-Dīn married, "almost every inhabitant of Omdurman was invited" to the wedding. Some of the expenses for the Khalīfa's household listed in the treasury records are as expected (e.g., slaves, shoes, etc.). Others, such as "silk clothes," are surprising, at least until one recalls the Khalīfa's wives' taste in jewelry. Ultimately of greater significance is the Mahdist state's creation of a highly centralized economy that supported a large segment of the Omdurman population and provided for the minimum needs of most, if not all, residents. Fr. Rosignoli observed that the *Bayt al-Māl* reflected "the socialist aspect of the Mahdist state. It centralized wealth and redistributed it." The treasury records certainly bear this out, with consistent monthly payments to disadvantaged Anṣār, including "the blind and disabled," "the elders," "the sons of the martyrs," "medical treatment for sick persons," "those separated [from their homes]," etc. Later Anṣār would recall this as a time of "social security" (*al-kafāla al-ijtimāᶜīyya*), and it is in this respect, the division of state resources to include as wide as possible a segment of the population, that the Khalīfa achieved some approximation of the Mahdī's social order.[61]

CHAPTER FIVE

Social Relations in the Mahdī's City

Then I went back to Omdurman, where I had planned to work at saddlery in the market and at home; but my wife dissuaded me, because Ḥaram bint al-Nūr had given her and her mother half an ardeb of grain, and al-Manṣūr walad Abū Kūᶜ had returned from a voyage to Bombay in India, and had given her clothes which she had sold, so that we had enough to live on.

Settlement Patterns

A hundred years after Bābikr Bedrī's experience, many descendants of the Mahdī's Anṣār were still living on the site of their family's original *hōsh*. Their recollections of the period received from parents and grandparents, combined with both Sudanese and Western written accounts as well as detailed maps drawn up by Egyptian Military Intelligence, allow us to trace the settlement patterns in Mahdist Omdurman. Thus we know with certainty where the various tribal and ethnic groups first settled, where some of them moved to after the Ashrāf revolt, and their positions relative to each other, the *sūq*, the all-important central quarter, and the riverfront. Understanding the significance of this layout for the social climate of the city is more difficult, particularly since so strong an impression of disharmony is created by many of the European memoirs of the period. What follows is a discussion of the settlement patterns of the Sudanese and other communities in Omdurman, with attention given to the conditions and alliances that created these patterns, as well as the military and administrative needs that first prompted them.[1]

As we have seen, Omdurman grew from a temporary encampment during the siege of Khartoum into a permanent capital under the Khalīfa, and hence the city's initial military character exerted the dominant influence on its layout. On the most basic level it may be viewed as a collection of tribal levies organized under the standards of the three *khalīfas*, stretched along the riverbank and positioned around the congregational mosque in the center of town. In his description of Omdurman, Abū Salīm divides the city into four quarters: (1) the southern quarter, from the village of Fitayḥāb in the south to the arsenal/storage house (*Bayt al-Amāna*) in the north, encompassing the quarters of the *jihādīyya* in al-Kāra, the port (al-Mōrida) and most of the Anṣār of western origin, Baqqāra, and others; (2) the central quarter, enclosed eventually on three sides by a stone wall, containing the mosque, the *Qubba*, the Khalīfa's bodyguard, and the homes and households of the Mahdī, Khalīfa ᶜAbdallāhi, the two junior *khalīfas*, Amīr Yaᶜqūb, the *qāḍīs,* and the chief secretaries of the administration; (3) the northwest quarter, extending north from the mosque and partially encircling the *sūq*, including the White Nile followers of Khalīfa ᶜAlī wad Ḥilū (the Kināna, Dighaym, and Laḥāwiyīn)—and after the failed Ashrāf revolt of 1891, the followers of Khalīfa Muḥammad Sharīf (Danāqla, Kunūz, and other Nubians)—plus the graves of the early martyrs and the Masālma quarter; (4) and the northern quarter, situated north of the enclosed zone along the river, including the *Bayt al-Māl* and its staff, the homes of the Egyptians and former Khartoum population, and the northern expeditionary camp. Quite differently, the author of an architectural study of Omdurman divides the city into seven areas, based upon their function and demographic distribution: (1) the urban core, including the Khalīfa's compound, the mosque, and *Qubba*; (2) al-Kāra; (3) the tribal residential quarters of the north and west, containing mainly riverain Sudanese; (4) the tribal residential quarters of the south and east, containing mainly Baqqāra; (5) the *sūq*; (6) the *Bayt al-Māl* and adjacent facilities; and (7) the village of Fitayḥāb. Both descriptions are valid, but regardless of the criteria used to analyze the city's spatial relations, an inescapable conclusion is that popular settlement originally reflected the basic differences in Anṣār composition—including regional, tribal-ethnic, cultural, and economic—that were largely, though not entirely, incorporated by the military standards of the three *khalīfas*. The general pattern of popular settlement that came to obtain in

Omdurman was hence one of a tripartite division: people of western origin (from Kordofan, Darfur, and central and western Sudanic Africa) as well as Nūba and southern Sudanese in the southern zone of the city; White Nile Arabs immediately north and west of the mosque; and all others—northern riverain Sudanese, Blue Nile and Jazīra Sudanese, Egyptians, and other foreigners—in the northern and northwest zones of the city. However, it is important to emphasize that this division was never an absolute one along tribal or regional lines, nor was it static: people sometimes switched from one *rāya* to another for a variety of reasons, and affiliation to a military standard did not last long into the period, as virtually the entire Omdurman population came to be considered a part of the Khalīfa's Black Standard. Moreover, the dynamics of social relations made for more complex and fluid settlement patterns than the E.M.I. maps, with their fixed locations for the various quarters, suggest.[2]

As already mentioned, the area occupied by each of the various tribal, ethnic or regional groups was known as a *farīq*, a term combining the sense of kinship with military organization. The *farīq* was the spatial dimension of the army unit settled there, and was known by the group (or sometimes *amīr*) living there. This division of Omdurman into tribal or ethnic quarters of course followed earlier Sudanese practice and was a function of administrative need rather than an indication of social rifts. Indeed during the revolt, when Mahdist enthusiasm was at its height, the Anṣār camps were similarly organized. Each *farīq* was located in the section of the city appropriate to the standard to which it originally belonged. Choice of a specific site within that area depended on a number of factors, including proximity to the river for access to boats, or to the outskirts of town for grazing animals, or to the *sūq*; the location of people of related tribal, ethnic, or regional origin; and eventually, the mere availability of land. In some instances, the Khalīfa was directly involved in the settlement process, as with the settlement of the recalcitrant Jazīra people in 1886–1887 and the Taᶜāīsha and other emigrants in 1888–1890. The positioning of the *farīqs* in the southern section of town was of particular interest to him, although he was mainly concerned with the location of the Taᶜāīsha relative to the strategically important *Bayt al-Amāna* and al-Kāra. In the main, however, the Khalīfa's role in the settlement of the city was minimal, limited to keeping under observation those people he deemed a security risk to the state. As with the administration of the city and the creation of a social order, the settlement of Omdurman was ultimately some combination of formal planning and spontaneous creation.[3]

After the failed Ashrāf revolt of 1891, the Khalīfa decided to resettle certain groups to enhance his personal security. Many of the relatives of Khalīfa Muḥammad Sharīf, as well as other Danāqla whose interests he championed, were made to vacate their homes east and northeast of the mosque to make room for the Khalīfa's expanded bodyguard. These people settled on the outskirts of the city, northwest and northeast of the *sūq*, although some also may have settled along the northern riverbank. According to Slatin, "The whole portion of the city lying north of the Khalifa's house had been vacated at a moment's notice by the Ashraf and their relatives; and they had not even been allowed to remove their furniture, nor had they received the smallest compensation. They had been given a patch of stony ground to the west [*sic*] of the town, where they had been ordered to build fresh houses." The purpose of this account is to provide yet another example of the Khalīfa's tyranny and cruelty, yet as ruler of the state he was obliged to remove from his midst this seditious element, while their property naturally reverted to the state as confiscated goods. Whether the Khalīfa specifically decreed where they were to resettle is unclear, although given the crowded conditions in Omdurman they did not have a great deal of choice. A large portion of the city's northern region, originally inhabited by the Kordofan tribe of the Banū Jarrār, came to be associated with the Danāqla—so much so that the neighborhood of Wad Nūbāwī, named for the *amīr* of the Banū Jarrār, has been called "the center of gravity" of the Ashrāf. Meanwhile other Sudanese of riverain origin who inhabited the area east and northeast of the Khalīfa's house, members of the merchant communities of El Obeid and Bāra, were also obliged to move in order to accommodate the *mulāzimīn* force. These settled alongside their kinsmen in the northern section of town. As a whole, this incident is mainly important for its political ramifications for the balance of power in the capital, and the Khalīfa's clearing of the area around his house to station his bodyguard only modified, but did not radically alter, the pattern of popular settlement in Omdurman.[4]

Shortly after the Anglo-Egyptian conquest, the Sudan government conducted a detailed survey of Omdurman that resulted in the division of the city by quarter (*rub*^{c}) and district (*ḥāra*). This imposed an order on the city, a precise delineation of space with straight roads, that did not exist in Mahdist times. *Farīqs* had been widely recognized according to their inhabitants, but families and households sometimes moved, while the boundaries of the *farīqs* were never fixed. A survivor of the period recalls that by the end of the Mahdīyya, the popular quarters "were not always specific to tribes. People lived everywhere." Nonetheless, it is still possible to identify the *farīqs* of Mahdist Omdurman as they were originally formed and to give an idea of their placement within the city. What follows then is a reconstruction of settlement patterns, organized according to the tripartite division that gave initial shape to the city.[5]

The Southern Zone: This area properly begins with the garrison of the *jihādīyya* at al-Kāra, a little over a mile north of the autonomous village of Fitayḥāb, containing soldiers drawn from the Nūba mountains, Baḥr al-Ghazāl, and southern regions of Sudan. The residents of al-Kāra were both spatially and socially isolated from the rest of Omdurman: They were, after all, considered "blacks" and slaves by the other Anṣār, who had no reason and no inclination to enter this area. Although individual *jihādīyya* were incorporated into the Khalīfa's bodyguard after 1891 and served until his defeat at Umm Dibaykarāt, al-Kāra stands out as a formally created quarter of the city, distinguished more by its military professionalism than its Mahdist enthusiasm.[6]

Between al-Kāra in the south and *Bayt al-Amāna* in the north existed the *farīqs* of most of the Anṣār of western origin. The largest single group within this category was of course the Baqqāra Arabs of Kordofan and Darfur, including among them the Ta^{c}āīsha. These lived in close proximity to the *farīqs* of two peoples identified as "Burqū" (i.e., from Wadai, west of Darfur) and "Takārna" (or "Takārīr," people of western Sudanic origin). Prior to the immigration of the Ta^{c}āīsha, there also existed in this mainly western area three anomalies: the *farīqs* of Shaykh Ḥamad al-Nīl of the ^{c}Arakīyīn tribe of the Jazīra, al-Ḥājj Khālid al-^{c}Umarābī of the Ja^{c}aliyīn, and Ḥasan Ḥusayn of the Egyptians and *muwalladīn* of Kordofan. Ḥamad al-Nīl al-Rayyaḥ was a *shaykh* of the Qādirīyya *ṭarīqa* and an opponent of the Khalīfa, and he was brought forcibly to Omdurman in 1887 with many of his tribesmen. Presumably he was made to settle in this section of the city in order to keep him and his followers under watch, although it is also possible that before the arrival of the Taᶜāīsha the southern zone was sparsely enough settled to permit the addition of newcomers. The Egyptians and *muwalladīn*, as a socially distinct community within the Anṣār, found this area a convenient place to settle, although after the arrival of the bulk of the westerners they resettled along the riverfront, north of the *Bayt al-Māl* where many of them were employed. As for al-Ḥājj Khālid al-ᶜUmarābī, he was a Jaᶜalī born in Kordofan, an early adherent of the Mahdī and a confidante of the Khalīfa, who relied upon him in the failed attempt to intermarry the *awlād al-balad* and the *awlād al-ᶜArab*. His association with the Egyptians and *muwalladīn* of Kordofan before the Mahdīyya, and his marriages among them, explains his settlement there. The *farīq* of al-Ḥājj Khālid remained in the southern zone after the arrival of the Baqqāra emigrants, the area eventually becoming known as "al-ᶜUmarāb."[7]

Also located in the southern quarter, on the west side of the main road extending from the mosque south towards Fitayḥāb, was a collection of western and central Sudanic peoples as well as Baqqāra and others from Kordofan and Darfur. Relations among these groups were complicated, to say the least. For instance, settled closely together in the southern half of this area were the *farīqs* of the "Fellāta" (i.e., Fulānī) of northern Nigeria, including the *farīq* of the Fulānī *amīr* Aḥmad Muḥammad "Qadaḥ al-Dām," plus a small population of Hausa people; the people of Bornu from the central Sudanic region; the "Funqur" (i.e., Fongoro) from southwestern Darfur; the Berti from western Darfur, including the *farīq* of *amīr* Ḥasan Sharaf Abū Kudōk; the Binga from western Baḥr al-Ghazāl; the people from Dār Tāma northwest of Darfur; and the Kordofan tribes of the Ḥawāra and Jawāmaᶜa. The Fulānī *amīr* Aḥmad Muḥammad, however, was descended from a family with earlier ties to Bornu, while his mother was a daughter of Sultan Muḥammad al-Ḥusayn (reg. 1838–1873) of Darfur. Additionally, the Dongolāwī *amīr* al-Nūr Muḥammad ᶜAnqara maintained a residence here, a reflection of the important social ties forged during his years of military service in Darfur and Baḥr al-Ghazāl prior to the Mahdīyya. Moreover, at least one of al-Nūr ᶜAnqara's wives was from the west: Bakhīta, another daughter of Sultan Muḥammad al-Ḥusayn of Darfur.[8]

In the northern half of this area, extending as far as the road leading west to the parade grounds, were the *farīqs* of the Kabābīsh and Ḥamar, pastoralist tribes from Kordofan with a recent history of enmity; and the

Baqqāra tribes of the Ḥumr, Habbānīyya, and Rizayqāt. The organizational structure that bound many of these groups together again issued from earlier ties: The Fulānī who settled in Sudan—originally from northern Nigeria—claimed a common ancestry with both the Kabābīsh and Ḥawāra, a claim reflected in the intermarriages among these groups. Of course claims of common ancestry are frequently a means of rationalizing political conditions, but in this case they predated the events of the Mahdīyya and were a cause, not an effect, of the settlement pattern.[9]

The Central Zone: This area was the symbolic and administrative hub of the capital, containing the mosque, *al-Qubba*, the homes of the *qāḍīs* and administrators, and homes of the Mahdist elite. Most prominently, it contained the households of the Mahdī, Khalīfa, the *khalīfas* ᶜAlī wad Ḥilū and Muḥammad Sharīf, and Amīr Yaᶜqūb. Additionally, within this zone were the households of several Taᶜāīshī *amīrs*, including Aḥmad wad ᶜAlī, Yūnis al-Dikaym and ᶜUthmān al-Dikaym, plus al-Zākī Ṭamal (of the Taᶜāīshī servile community known as the Mandala); the household of the *Qāḍī al-Islām* Aḥmad ᶜAlī, a Jaᶜalī; and (until the expulsion of the Ashrāf) the household of Sayyid Ḥāmid Muḥammad, cousin of the Mahdī and father of Khalīfa Muḥammad Sharīf. On the southern edge of this central zone, just opposite the *Bayt al-Amāna*, were the homes of the Khalīfa's secretaries Abū'l-Qāsim and al-Ṭayyib Aḥmad Hāshim, and Muddathir Ibrāhīm al-Ḥajjāz, the keeper of the Khalīfa's seal, all of them Jaᶜaliyīn. To the north and west of this zone were the White Nile tribes associated with the Green Standard of Khalīfa ᶜAlī wad Ḥilū, namely the Dighaym, Kināna, and Laḥāwiyīn, plus the homes of their various *amīrs*.

After the events of late 1891 and the resettlement of the Ashrāf and Danāqla, the central zone became the stronghold of the Khalīfa and his coterie of Taᶜāīsha supporters. Although the Mahdī's and Khalīfa ᶜAlī's families continued to reside there, they were overshadowed by the adjacent complex of the Khalīfa, which contained the quarters of the *mulāzimīn* and the very prominent homes of the Khalīfa and his son ᶜUthmān Shaykh al-Dīn. One scholar has drawn attention to the significance of the central zone's spatial relations, arguing that the enclosed core complex was designed to deliberately exclude the families of the Mahdī and Khalīfa ᶜAlī, thereby "diminish[ing] the area of the original ideological urban core" and establishing a "value-laden spatial hierarchy." This observation notwithstanding, it remains true that the central zone was at no time an exclusively Taᶜāīshī enclave.[10]

The Northern Zone: This area of the city, extending north, northwest and northeast of the mosque, was the focus of the most dense popular settlement during the Mahdīyya. Sources provide the names of a great many *farīqs*, yet here especially conditions were in flux, as seasonal soldiers moved between their farmlands and the city, merchants came and went, marriages realigned the social bonds and living arrangements, and *rāyas* became reconfigured. Three facts emerge indisputably about settlement in this area: the ethnic and tribal diversity of the inhabitants, the rapidity with which *farīqs* became integrated, and the complex social relations that affected settlement and living conditions.

Scattered throughout much of this northern zone were the *farīqs* of various Jaᶜalī *amīrs* and notables, including the *farīqs* of Ilyās Umm Birayr, the former merchant of El Obeid and an early adherent of the Mahdī, and ᶜAbd al-Raḥmān al-Nujūmī, the early Mahdist "commander-in-chief" (*amīr al-umarā'*) slain at Ṭūshkī in 1889, both of which were located northwest of the *Bayt al-Māl*; the *farīqs* of the poet Aḥmad wad Tamīm and al-Ḥājj al-Fās, Ḥusayn al-Fīl, and Ḥamad wad al-Ṭilib, all prominent traders, located north of the *Bayt al-Māl* along the river; as well as the *farīqs* of the Rubāṭāb and other Jaᶜaliyīn sub-sections located in the vicinity of the *sūq*. More so than any other tribal or ethnic group in Omdurman, there was no one residential area specific to those of Jaᶜalī identity, and they appear to have lived in virtually all parts of the northern zone, and indeed in all areas of the city.

The Sudanese from the Blue Nile region were more confined in their quarters. Situated north of the *Bayt al-Māl*, along the riverbank and extending into the interior, were the *farīqs* of the people of Kāmlīn, Masallamīyya, Wad Madanī, Abū Ḥarāz, Wad al-ᶜAbbās, and Rufāᶜa, including the pastoralist tribes of the Rufāᶜa al-Hōy, Shukrīyya, Baṭāḥīn, and Ḥalāwiyīn, as well as Jaᶜaliyīn and other sedentary people. Settled among these were also a number of western peoples (including Fūr, Zaghāwa, and Ḥumr), many of the former Khartoum population, and the Egyptians who moved here after the arrival of the Taᶜāīsha in 1888. While the Egyptians were associated with the *Bayt al-Māl* and Mahdist administration, many of the Blue Nile people were latecomers, forced to the capital in 1887, who chose to settle among relatives or former neighbors. The settlement of the westerners in this area, rather than in the southern zone, is an enigma: There are no obvious economic, political, or organizational reasons, although there may have been social contacts that are as yet unexplained. Certainly the dominant feature of this area was the sprawling compound of the *Bayt al-Māl* with its associated slave market and storehouses, but it employed mainly riverain Sudanese, Egyptians, and Sudanese Copts. The nearby port and boatyard, situated just north of the *Bayt al-Māl*, served as the economic base of the Danāqla and other riverain traders. Whether the westerners and Blue Nile Arabs were involved in the operations of the port and boatyard is unknown—oral evidence suggests that they were not—but the area came to be known for the leader of the Rufāᶜa al-Hōy, Marḍī Ab Rōf, as "Ab Rōf."[11]

While the northern interior of the city was largely populated with Jaᶜaliyīn, the area north and northwest of the *sūq* came to include the Ashrāf, their Danāqla supporters, and other Nubians after 1891, in addition to the already-present Banū Jarrār. Oral evidence also confirms the presence of several *farīqs* of Shāīqīyya (some of whom had served as irregular troops of the Turco-Egyptians) and ᶜAbābda of the Nubian desert, settled among the Jaᶜaliyīn and Danāqla in this northern zone. On the northwest perimeter of the city were the camps of local pastoralists, identified on the E.M.I. Ohrwalder map (1892) as simply "Arabs." Oral sources identify these as Jummūᶜīyya and other Arabs of the Omdurman hinterland, who made their living supplying milk, meat, cheese, and animal fat to the city's residents. Their herds and flocks were brought to Omdurman in limited numbers and for limited periods, since this area did not support the permanent grazing of a large number of animals and, being an itinerant population, they did not constitute a *farīq*. A well located just west of the parade ground likely supplied the water needs of their camps.

In the vicinity of the *sūq* there existed a number of other *farīqs*. Directly north of the market was the quarter of the Muslim converts, who were known variously as "Muslimānīyya" and, more commonly, "Masālma." (The English-language accounts tended to use the former term and Arabic-language accounts the latter.) The residents of this quarter were not exclusively members of the Masālma—for example, the Egyptian Ibrāhīm Fawzī maintained a house there—although most certainly were. Nor did all of Omdurman's Muslim converts live in the Masālma quarter: ᶜAbd al-Quddūs ᶜAbd al-Sayyid, a Copt from Kordofan, settled with other El Obeid people in the *farīq* of Muḥammad al-Makkī b. Ismāᶜīl al-Walī. The people of the Masālma community were mainly foreigners who had converted to Islam during the Mahdist uprising, some after the fall of El Obeid, most not until the fall of Khartoum. They included Egyptians, Greeks, Syrians, Armenians, Italians, Cypriots, Austrians, and Jews, and among their number were priests, nuns, and lay brothers captured at the Roman Catholic mission in Dilling in the Nūba mountains in 1882. It is clear that for security reasons they were required by the Khalīfa to live in a distinct community. (Rosignoli mentions the *farīq* of Christian "prisoners" and states that they had been ordered to live there.) The location of the Masālma quarter is significant: Most were merchants, so their proximity to the *sūq* made obvious economic sense, and also followed the earlier practice in El Obeid and other Sudanese towns.[12]

East of the *sūq* and the Masālma quarter, extending as far as the main north-south road known as *Darb al-Shuhadā'* ("Street of the Martyrs"), were the *farīqs* of the townspeople of Kordofan. The first to arrive had been Muḥammad al-Makkī, successor to his father Ismāᶜīl al-Walī, founder of the Ismāᶜīlīyya Ṣūfī order, who joined the Mahdī at El Obeid prior to the Friday Battle (8 September 1882) and accompanied him to Omdurman. Sometime in early 1885, the Mahdī wrote a letter to his cousin Maḥmūd ᶜAbd al-Qādir in El Obeid, urging him to facilitate the emigration of Anṣār there and in Bāra. Among the new emigrants were three previously mentioned families: the Danāqla of Muḥammad Ṣāliḥ Suwār al-Dhahab, the Maḥas of Muḥammad Ṣāliḥ ᶜAlī wad Ūru, and the Rikābīyya of ᶜArabī and Makkāwī Aḥmad ᶜAbd al-Raḥīm. These collectively made their way to Omdurman in 1885 or 1886 and settled adjacent to the *farīq* of Muḥammad al-Makkī. Nearby was the *farīq* of the Jaᶜalī notable Sulaymān Ḥājj Aḥmad Umm Birayr, nephew of the prominent merchant Ilyās Umm Birayr, and a *farīq* of Kunūz Nubians, also from El Obeid, who chose not to settle among the other Kunūz on the northwest outskirts or near the *Bayt al-Māl*. The final group of Kordofan townspeople to emigrate arrived sometime in early 1887, responding to an appeal sent by the Khalīfa.[13]

United by their Kordofan origin as well as a former association with the Khatmīyya order, these *farīqs* contributed to a *rāya* that served under the Black Standard. Not surprisingly, they evinced a sense of community. For example, Muḥammad al-Makkī is known to have mediated with the Khalīfa on behalf of not only his own *farīq*, but other *farīqs* as well as the Masālma, many of whom were from Kordofan and under the authority of the Coptic *muqaddam* of El Obeid, Yūsuf Mikhā'īl. A small local market served the daily needs of the area's residents. Marriage ties—it would seem inevitably—were made between the different *farīqs* and across tribal and other lines. Thus ᶜAbd al-Quddūs ᶜAbd al-Sayyid, the Copt from El Obeid, married a daughter of Dā'ūd Ṣāliḥ, a merchant from El Obeid, and settled in the *farīq* of Muḥammad al-Makkī. In essence, they appear to have formed a community within the larger community, a pattern that was duplicated in other parts of the city, such as among the "Fellāta" and other westerners in the southern zone.[14]

Enclosed within the larger Kordofan-based area was an enclave with a similar dynamic of settlement. This was Qalᶜat Fitayḥāb, a small neighborhood adjacent to the *farīq* of Wad Ūru and comprised, as its name suggests, largely of Jummūᶜīyya Arabs. The origin of this settlement lies in the Khalīfa's forced migration to Omdurman of the family of Ḥājj Nāṣir, cousin of Makk Sulaymān of Fitayḥāb, early in the Mahdīyya. The choice of the *farīq* of Wad Ūru for a Fitayḥābi settlement reflected the long-standing genealogical ties between the Jummūᶜīyya and Maḥas of the Omdurman region, ties that dated to the Funj era and were strengthened throughout the Mahdīyya with marriage alliances.

Doubtless many other examples could be found of regional, Ṣūfī-based or genealogical ties underlying the settlement patterns and social relations of Mahdist Omdurman. In any case, it is apparent that the gloomy characterization of the city's social relations so common to the European accounts cannot be accepted uncritically. (Fr. Rosignoli wrote that "each race lives in its own quarter and marriages between residents of different wards take place only with great difficulty.") To the contrary, it is clear from the accounts of Bābikr Bedrī and Yūsuf Mikhā'īl, as well as oral sources, that people moved regularly and freely between the quarters and among the different communities to socialize, and most particularly to visit relatives married and settled in other *farīqs*; while Slatin's statement about the famine of 1306 / 1888–1889 is telling, that "the actual inhabitants of the town" did not suffer most, since "the different tribes invariably assisted each other." Also, added to these earlier ties were new relations that sprang from the economic and marriage patterns of Omdurman, relations that unfolded throughout the Mahdīyya.[15]

Economic Activities

Almost from the beginning of its existence, Omdurman served as the central and chief marketplace of the Sudan. Moreover as early as 1886–1887, the Khalīfa suspended trade with Egypt in a policy that was both politically and economically motivated, seeking to ward off the contamination of the outside world but also prevent the outflow of capital. Although this policy was relaxed in 1890 in an attempt to resuscitate the economy, other policies were enacted to circumvent the provincial markets of Abū Ḥamad and Berber and compel merchants coming from Egypt to bring their goods directly to Omdurman. An informant to the E.M.I. reported in 1890 that the country between Omdurman and Berber was "quite desolate" and mentioned that trade had been prohibited south of Abū Ḥamad, "which is now the main trade depot of the north." In an undated letter to ᶜUthmān al-Dikaym, *amīr* of Berber from 1888, the Khalīfa reminds him that it is forbidden to buy and sell merchandise outside of Omdurman (i.e., except in the designated areas), and asks him to enforce this ruling. Similar rulings were pronounced with regard to the market towns of the Jazīra and also trade with British-controlled Suakin. Despite this, it is clear from the account of Bābikr Bedrī that some Sudanese merchants continued to trade not only in the Dongola region and Jazīra, but even in Suakin itself. When informed of this at a meeting with Omdurman's merchants in 1314 / 1896–1897, the Khalīfa was indignant, swearing an oath that the *Amīn Bayt al-Māl* al-Nūr Ibrāhīm Jirayfāwī had assured him that Anṣār merchants ventured only as far east as Kōkreb to exchange goods, and renewing his order forbidding merchants from entering Suakin. Whether or not the Khalīfa's indignation was genuine, and regardless of the porousness of Sudan's borders, Mahdist policy did induce merchants carrying local produce and imported goods to converge on the capital, where their merchandise was bartered for various monopolies of the state and purchased by local retailers.[16]

Ohrwalder described Omdurman as "the great wholesale and retail mart, which in turn supplies the provinces," and added that:

> Dongola and Dar Shaggieh supply Omdurman with dates; Berber sends salt, mats and baskets made of palm leaves; from Kordofan comes gum, sesame and dukhn [bulrush millet]; the Gezirah exports dhurra [sorghum millet], dammur and cotton; Karkoj supplies sesame and a small quantity of gold.... [In Omdurman] the whole population—men, women and children from eight years of age—are all dealers.

From the detailed descriptions contained in accounts of the period, it is possible to provide a comprehensive list of the economic activities that went on the city. Regarding industry, Slatin noted a "considerable manufacture and trade" in long and short spears, stirrup irons, horse and donkey bits, knives, and agricultural implements. Elsewhere he stated that "the manufacture of spears is still one of the principal industries." This is of course what one would expect in a society motivated by *jihād*, and in a state that devoted so much of its resources to the outfitting and maintenance of its troops. The concern shown by the Khalīfa towards the arms industry is revealed in an anecdote in which he is said to have told the leather- and metalworkers prior to the battle of Kararī to "go on with the work rather than fight," since he was certain of victory but aware that many arms would need to be replaced. Involved in the larger arms industry were various crafts, including blacksmiths, leatherworkers, carpenters, weavers, and tailors. Ohrwalder remarked that "blacksmiths are always busy forging spears and knives... saddlers make every description of leather ornament for horse and camel decoration; tanners prepare the leather, and dye it red or black; tailors now make much better jibbehs than before... the women spin the cotton, and the men weave the dammur from it." Leatherworkers also produced protective amulets in addition to saddles, sheaths, and reins, and in the Mahdīyya's climate of almost constant strife this constituted a brisk trade. Unrelated to warfare as such, but directly affected by the huge concentration of people in Omdurman, were the manufacture of *angarebs* [wooden frame beds], doors, windows, and boxes; the making and repairing of shoes; and the activities of tinsmiths, silversmiths, jewelers, and weavers in cotton and straw.[17]

The wholesale and retail sections of the Omdurman *sūq* were diverse. Specific areas were designated by the *Bayt al-Māl* for each good being sold, and these comprised a large number of separate markets. From the evidence of written accounts and oral sources, a list of these markets includes the following: grain, dates, honey, beans, salt, and spices; vegetables and other produce; oil and butter; butchered meat, including lamb, goat, beef, and camel; linen and other forms of woven cloth; shoes, sword and knife sheaths, purses, and amulets; knives, swords, and spears; a gold and silver market; imported goods, including rice, cloves, sugar, dried fruits, medicines, textiles, jewelry, and perfumes; woven baskets and floor mats; straw and matting for building; fodder and hay for forage; a livestock market that included goats, sheep, and poultry; animal fat; tanned skins; firewood, building wood, and *angarebs*; raw cotton for spinning; a women's market supplying the needs of elderly and indigent women, including water, sesame oil, grease (for grooming), pearls, vegetables, pharmaceuticals, grain, and dates; markets associated with the above-mentioned arms industries, including carpenters, blacksmiths, tinsmiths, and leatherworkers; and a warehouse area for the storage of grains, beans, seeds, dates, and honey. Finally, what might be termed the "services" section of the *sūq* included areas for barbers and tailors, a laundry area with washbasins for rent, cooked foods and sandwich shops, and coffeehouses.

The layout of the *sūq* conformed to a pattern familiar in Sudanic Africa, with wholesalers and craftsmen on the peripheries and retailers and services, often under covered stalls, in the interior. A large open area in the center was reserved for the selling of livestock, and around this area the individual markets were grouped. In conformity with Mahdist teaching, the women's market was placed in the extreme northwest corner of the *sūq*, allowing women to enter it with only minimal contact with the rest of the marketplace. The centrality of the Khalīfa's authority was made abundantly clear by the prominent place given to the market court and its associated prison and gallows, on the eastern perimeter of the main open area and facing into the major portion of the *sūq*.[18]

Making possible the business of the marketplace were the activities conducted (and in some cases, controlled) by various tribal and ethnic groups in Omdurman and elsewhere. Both the riverain Sudanese and Red Sea Ḥaḍāriba continued their earlier dominance of long-distance trade, plying the routes between Omdurman and outlying areas, including the Jazīra and Upper White Nile for grain, Kordofan for gum and sesame, and Egypt and Suakin for imported goods. Others were engaged in long-distance trade as well: Bābikr Bedrī refers to one ᶜAbd al-Laṭīf, "the Fūrāwī trader" in the Omdurman *sūq*, as well as the purchase of "el-Fasher slippers." ᶜUmar Kāsha of the Ḥalanqa from the Red Sea hills was particularly prominent in the ivory and munitions trade between the capital and coast. Ohrwalder reported that "all trade with the outside world is conducted by Hadarba, Jaalin, Danagla, and Barabra [Nubian] merchants, and also on the southern frontier of Egypt by Ababdeh and Kenuz people." Many items were of course brought into the city by boat, and the boat-building industry as well as the operating of boats remained the exclusive domain of such riverain tribes as the Danāqla. The Khalīfa's policy in 1892 to undermine the tribe's control of transport by nationalizing many of the boats in Omdurman depressed the boat-building industry and struck at the economic base of the Danāqla. Eventually, however, and in response to obvious need, the boat-building industry returned. Two informants to E.M.I. reported in 1894 that "all boats on the Nile were the property of the *Bayt al-Māl*, and natives were forbidden to build them, but recently the Khalīfa has given them permission to do so; but first they have to pay a tax of one dollar per meter of length, and when built, an annual tax of one dollar per *ardeb* of capacity." One year later, Slatin reported to E.M.I. that "boat building is a flourishing trade, especially at Aba Island, and the Beit el-Mal alone possesses 130 boats which are its own property." The manual labor behind the long-distance transport of goods was supplied by slaves, of southern Sudanese or Nūba origin, who hauled wood for the construction of boats, loaded the pack animals, and fed the engines of the steamers.[19]

A number of tribal and ethnic groups were represented in the *sūq*. Riverain people dominated the retail business, as one would expect, although it is clear that western and central Sudanic people as well as Fūr and even the pastoralist Baqqāra Arabs played important roles. Food was supplied to the marketplace from several sources: the government-operated steamers leased mainly by the Danāqla; the former gardens of Khartoum, seized by the government as tribute land and leased by the Danāqla as well as some Taᶜāīsha; and the population of the hinterland, such as the pastoralist Jummūᶜīyya and Jimiᶜāb supplying meat, milk, and other dairy products, and the Khawālda and other tribes of the Jazīra supplying vegetables and other produce. Manufacturing and the crafts do not appear to have been tribally specific: As with retailing, the riverain Sudanese predominated, although references to western and central Sudanic peoples in leatherworking and carpentry, and to a small gypsy ("*Ḥalaba*") population in metalwork, make clear that the Omdurman *sūq* was an economic venture in which many different peoples participated.[20]

Two population groups in Omdurman with economic roles disproportionate to their small numbers were the Egyptians and Masālma. Both were popularly known as artisans, working in jewelry and watch repair as well as tailoring and other crafts. (It is hard to imagine followers of "The Expected Mahdī" wearing watches. And yet it was the Sudanese elite, not Egyptians and Masālma, who could afford such expenses.) By at least 1895, the jewelers also became involved in minting coins and manufacturing cartridge caps for the state, the jewelry market having suffered from the isolation of the Sudan. The tailors meanwhile, in a stunning irony, were busily occupied sewing the elaborately patched *jibbas* of the wealthier Anṣār, as well as the flags of the Mahdist armies. Ohrwalder mentions that some of the captured nuns were also employed sewing *jibbas*, which were then sold by the Syrian Christian Jūrjī Istāmbūlī to the Anṣār. At least one Egyptian artisan contributed significantly to the architecture of Omdurman: ᶜUmar al-Ḥijāzī, popularly known as *al-Muhandis* ("the engineer" or "architect"), worked on the construction of the *Bayt al-Māl*, the mosque, and the *Qubba*, as well as the Mahdist fortifications at al-Qallābāt. Both the Egyptians and Masālma also operated the coffee shops and prepared food stalls in the *sūq* (e.g., Ibrāhīm Fawzī sold coffee and Fr. Rosignoli sold prepared food at one time.) This was a type of work considered shameful (*ᶜayb*) by the Sudanese (who nonetheless frequented these establishments), so much so that well into Anglo-Egyptian rule all of the coffee shops and food stalls in Omdurman were operated by Egyptians. The Masālma were also known for their weaving and dyeing of cotton cloth. A group of formerly Coptic Masālma, called "Naqāda" after the town of that name in Upper Egypt, seem to have been especially associated with both weaving and importing cloth: A Mahdist letter of 1898 mentions these Naqāda importing and exporting goods across the Sudanese-Ethiopian border. Back in Omdurman, many of their goods, including coffee and honey in addition to cloth, were bought by the state.[21]

The case of the Naqāda further highlights the important role played by the Masālma community in the Mahdist economy. Until the end of the

Mahdīyya the Naqāda were busily trading across the Ethiopian border, while other members of the Masālma also practiced long-distance trade, continuing in some cases the business associations they had developed during Turco-Egyptian rule. For example, the Masālma Jew Mūsa Basyūnī, earlier mentioned as a member of the Khalīfa's trade advisory council, spent much of the period trading across the northern border with Egypt for perfumes, which he would bring back to Omdurman for the Khalīfa's wives. Bābikr Bedrī mentions "my friend, Khalīfa Levi the Jew," with whom Bābikr frequently traded in Suakin. (It is unclear if Khalīfa Levi ventured outside of Suakin to trade in Mahdist territory.) The activities of the Naqāda merchants and Basyūnī suggest that some Masālma were permitted to cross boundaries—literally—in the interest of providing what was needed or desired. Meanwhile the wealth accumulated by the Masālma, when it was not being confiscated by the *Bayt al-Māl* as "contributions," was invested in commercial ventures in Omdurman, contributing to the growth of the local economy. In clear recognition of their commercial influence (and the limits of his own authority), the Khalīfa at one time entrusted the Jewish merchants of Omdurman to buy up all of the firearms still in private hands and sell them back to the state.[22]

In addition to the formal economy closely monitored by the state and centered in the main *sūq*, there existed an informal economy based upon household production and barter. Many of the free women of Omdurman, compelled by Mahdist teaching to remain within the *hōsh*, spent their time sewing and weaving items or raising animals for slaughter, to be exchanged within their *farīq* at informal and temporary markets for other goods. According to oral accounts, "exchange was practiced more with *dammūr* cloth than with currency," no doubt due to the shortage and constant depreciation of Mahdist coinage. (Indeed, the Khalīfa attempted at one time to replace currency with pieces of cloth as the medium of exchange, reverting to the earlier practice of both Sinnār and Darfur.) However, the economic role of Omdurman's women was clearly not limited to this informal economy: Many women sent their slaves to sell their handicrafts in the *sūq*. Ohrwalder wrote that "the latter are obliged to render full accounts when they return [from the *sūq*] in the evening; and woe to the unfortunate slave who makes a mistake in his calculations!" Additionally, both Ohrwalder and Rosignoli comment on the activities of the women's market, with Ohrwalder making particular reference to the "large share in the retail business" held by the Baqqāra women, whom he calls "naturally good dealers."[23]

Another aspect of this informal economy might be termed the "economy of *baraka*," since it involved the wide range of services provided mainly to the household of the Mahdī, but also to the households of the Khalīfa and two junior *khalīfas*, by the devoted Anṣār. Oral accounts maintain that the Mahdī's family "did not practice slavery," meaning they did not need to buy and sell slaves at the *Bayt al-Māl* as did their Anṣār: People attached themselves to the Mahdī's household out of devotion and in the hope of sharing in the Mahdī's *baraka*. Many of these servants were the young daughters of the Anṣār, known as "*Anṣārīyyāt*," brought by their fathers to Omdurman to work for the Mahdī's family. They of course neither received nor expected remuneration for their services other than the *baraka* they absorbed, but lived within the *hōsh* and received the necessities of food and shelter as well as instruction in the Qur'ān. Allegedly, these Anṣārīyyāt were virtually unique among the servants of Omdurman in their literacy.[24]

Ibrāhīm Fawzī provides an account of the practice of giving daughters as "gifts" to the Mahdī, citing the example of Muḥammad al-Ḥājj Aḥmad Umm Birayr (another nephew of the El Obeid merchant Ilyās Umm Birayr) who sought to give all three of his daughters as wives (or concubines) to the Mahdī. The Mahdī accepted only one, reminding his followers in a letter that it is forbidden to marry or take as concubines two sisters, and chastising Muḥammad al-Ḥājj for offering his daughter and then demanding a bride price! (Muḥammad al-Ḥājj certainly was not alone in doing this. At least two other wives of the Mahdī are known to have been given to him by their fathers: Maymūna bt. Muḥammad Qaylī, daughter of a Ja^calī notable, and Maḥl al-Jōd, daughter of a Dinka leader. Others of his wives likely were given to him as well.) Fawzī understood the motive for this "reprehensible practice" to be simple profit. In fact, the giving of daughters to the Mahdī's household followed an established practice of honoring holy men and endowing their *khalwas* with land, slaves, livestock, shares of produce, and voluntary labor. Moreover, people often would ask a holy man to marry from the local women, in order to honor their households. For instance, it was said of Aḥmad ibn Idrīs, the nineteenth-century Ṣūfī teacher in Arabia, that "He made many marriages since the people sought blessing and honour from him through a relationship by marriage with him, so that he sired many children, although none reached maturity." Additionally, one scholar notes that it had been customary "for parents to donate children, particularly little girls, to the holy man as gifts of alms. Each community leader had a pool of these 'Daughters of the House' with which to reward himself or other deserving men." Quite clearly the Anṣār of the Mahdī sought not material gain but rather spiritual and social advancement, the height of which was achieved through a marriage union, particularly if it produced children who passed the *baraka* on to their family. (At the same time, this social advancement could, and did, lead to material gain.) Thus, when the Mahdī married Āmina bt. Abū Bakr al-Jarkūk, daughter of a prominent Egyptian merchant killed at Khartoum, Āmina's brothers were considered relatives of the Mahdī, given formal pardons (i.e., their captive family members were released to them), and joined to a *rāya* led by a member of the Ashrāf. The Mahdī's household, of course, benefited from these gifts of daughters in labor and other services, as did the households of the three *khalīfas*, while the daughters' offspring had a social value that is discussed more fully below.[25]

Unlike the Mahdī's family, the families of the Khalīfa ᶜAbdallāhi and other Mahdist elites cannot claim to have eschewed "slavery," since they obviously owed much of their considerable affluence to slave labor. In Omdurman as in other parts of the Sudan, the labor of "blacks" formed the productive base of society, and to these were added the women of the *ghanīma* captured during war. In a document dated 1309 / 1892, the senior member of the Ashrāf, Aḥmad Muḥammad Sharfī (who was indeed the Mahdī's relative and father-in-law), listed among his possessions 98 slaves employed in cultivation at Ḥalfāya, Khartoum, Omdurman, Abā Island, and elsewhere. Among the Taᶜāīsha, the *amīr* Maḥmūd Aḥmad, cousin to the Khalīfa, made claim to 33 female slaves in Omdurman and 59 female slaves in Kordofan. These were needed "to assist Maḥmūd in giving hospitality to the Anṣār" and to be given to "the Companions who deserve them." Maḥmūd notes in a letter to the Khalīfa that the wealth of his household consists only of slaves and cattle, since he "has paid no heed to money since he joined the Mahdīyya." Countless other Anṣār are said to have had large numbers of slaves laboring on their behalf, among them the *Qāḍī al-Islām* Aḥmad ᶜAlī (Slatin claimed "upwards of a thousand slaves," an obvious exaggeration) and the *Amīn Bayt al-Māl* al-Nūr Ibrāhīm Jirayfāwī ("a village of slaves" near Masīd, according to his family). Meanwhile, even among the common people of Omdurman, slave labor seems to have been the normal means of feeding and maintaining the household. Ohrwalder's statement has already been cited, that "Omdurman is full of slaves; even in the poorest houses one female slave at least will be found." Rosignoli also observed that "farming is exclusively the work of slaves," and slaves who did not farm hired themselves out for the day "in order to earn money for [their] master," or else collected grass and firewood to be sold in the *sūq*. Oral evidence fully corroborates these testimonies.[26]

A great deal of labor in the Mahdist state was also supplied by the *jihādīyya*. Moved about the capital area as needed, they were utilized by the state as guards and laborers at the soap factory, market court, central prison, the ports and boatyards of Omdurman and Khartoum, the storehouses, *Bayt al-Māl*, *Bayt al-Amāna,* and the Khalīfa's house; as herders of livestock, cutters and haulers of wood, collectors of straw, and farmers; as military tailors and guards for messengers and tax collectors; as haulers of bricks and other materials from Khartoum; and as builders of the fortifications, walls, homes of the Mahdist elite, *Bayt al-Māl,* and *mulāzimīn* complex, etc. around Omdurman. Taken as a distinct social group—and certainly the other Anṣār viewed them this way—the *jihādīyya* constituted the largest single category within the state's work force. For example, of the approximately 794 state employees at the time of the Anglo-Egyptian conquest, inclusive of menial laborers and encompassing all of the facilities and departments, 389 of these (48%) were *jihādīyya.* At the dockyard alone, the *jihādīyya* comprised 59 of 131 laborers (45%), while among the steamer crews they totaled 81 of 105 laborers (77%). These figures do not include laborers identified in the Mahdist and E.M.I. documents as "*Sūdānī,*" so that the percentage of non-Arab Sudanese of southern or Nūba origin was certainly much higher than that given here. Regardless of their actual legal status, which was vague, or their social status, which was crystal clear, the functions of the *jihādīyya* make plain that they were essentially the slaves of the state.[27]

At the other end of the socioeconomic spectrum were the riverain and Taᶜāīsha elites, who respectively dominated administrative and political authority through their prestige, power, and influence. While they were (at least publicly) jointly committed to the Mahdī's vision of reform and mission of *jihād*, they were also competing against each other for dominance. Significantly, they were also joining their households in alliances of marriage, as part of a process of elite formation encouraged by the conditions of Omdurman. The particular elite that they created is the next aspect of social relations examined here.

The Integration of the Elite

Given the Mahdī's determination to create a more egalitarian society, the existence of elite groups in Omdurman may seem contradictory until one recalls the practical needs of *jihād* and governance. Joined to the social order that the Mahdī and Khalīfa inherited and adopted was a specifically Mahdist hierarchy: the ranking of Anṣār according to when they first joined the Mahdīyya. Thus the students (*talāmidha*) of the Mahdī who had known him prior to the Mahdīyya occupied the highest rank, known as *Abkār al-Mahdī* (literally, "the eldest"). Next came those who had been present at the battle of Abā Island (12 August 1881), known as *Anṣār Abā*. Following them were the emigrants to Jabal Qadīr (1881–1882), the *Anṣār Qadīr*; those who left El Obeid during the siege (September 1882–January 1883) to join the Mahdī at Kābā (*Anṣār Kābā*); and the rest of the Anṣār, also ranked according to when they joined, e.g., *Anṣār El Obeid*, *Anṣār Khartoum*, etc. It is not clear how tangible a benefit this status was in Omdurman society: Did it confer high office, sway business decisions, or elevate marriage prospects? Oral sources confirm that the rank signified a degree of honor, something not easily quantified but also not easily ignored. Illustrative of this was the experience of Ibrāhīm Fawzī at the home of al-Ḥājj Khālid al-ᶜUmarābī: The Egyptian Yūsuf Manṣūr was told by al-Ḥājj Khālid that he should drink his coffee before Ibrāhīm Fawzī, his former superior in military rank, since Yūsuf now surpassed Ibrāhīm with his longer allegiance to the Mahdīyya. On the other hand, the terms were sometimes loosely applied: Yūsuf Mikhā'īl mentions that he and his brothers got on well with the other Anṣār, "who respected us because we were among the *Abkār*." Yūsuf was of course a Copt and not a student of the Mahdī, so perhaps *Abkār* came to mean all Anṣār who joined the Mahdī at "an early date," e.g., prior to the fall of El Obeid. Certainly many of the most prominent members of Omdurman society (including al-Ḥājj Khālid, Ilyās Umm Birayr, the *Amīn Bayt al-Māl* Ibrāhīm Muḥammad ᶜAdlān, Muḥammad al-Makkī Ismāᶜīl, etc.) were former residents of El Obeid, and they owed their prestige in part to having been early adherents of the Mahdī.[28]

Additionally, there were many other people in Omdurman with claims to authority and prestige, people whom we might term "notables," who may or may not have been among the *Abkār al-Mahdī*. The *amīr* of every *rāya*; the *shaykh* of every *farīq*, tribe, or extended family; the government officials at the *Bayt al-Māl,* Sharīᶜa court and *sūq*; the religious teachers and holy men who operated the *khalwas* for Qur'ān instruction; the leading merchants: All had a claim to the loyalty, respect, and services of those under their authority. A collection of these important people formed the Khalīfa's two councils in 1892, confiscating the boats in Omdurman and condemning Khalīfa Muḥammad Sharīf for his part in the Ashrāf revolt. Their numbers included several important scholars and merchants, many of whom served as *qāḍīs* in Omdurman and the provinces, and a small number of *amīrs*. Some of these same people signed a letter addressed to the Sirdār of the Egyptian army, General H. H. Kitchener, shortly after Kararī, requesting him to restrain the army's "Sudanese" soldiers (including former *jihādīyya*) who were engaged in acts of vengeance and looting. The early Anglo-Egyptian government, in its concern to rule a people over whom it had limited control, selected many of these same individuals to serve as *qāḍīs*, *ᶜumdas,* and other officials in its administration. From the earliest days of the Mahdīyya—and in some cases, since Funj times—the families of these individuals have represented the select population of the capital and the northern Sudan at large.[29]

At the top of Omdurman society were those who had been closest to the Mahdī, who best knew his intentions and had benefited most from his *baraka*, including those who closely served his chosen successor. This elite, combining religious prestige, political influence, and economic power, formed the households of the Mahdī's extended family, including the Ashrāf, the households of the Khalīfa ᶜAbdallāhi and his relatives among the Taᶜāīsha, the household of Khalīfa ᶜAlī, and the households of several of the leading *amīrs*. Despite their well-known strife and antagonism, there were important bonds that joined these families together, and by the end of the period, numerous common interests as well.

The people of these households shared a similar experience of the Mahdīyya in Omdurman. For instance, a survivor of the period, the youngest son of the *amīr* ᶜAbd al-Raḥmān al-Nujūmī, recalled attending a *khalwa* in the Khalīfa's compound for instruction in Qur'ān and other subjects, alongside the sons of the Mahdī, the Khalīfa, Amīr Yaᶜqūb, and the *amīrs* al-Zākī ᶜUthmān, Ḥamdān Abū ᶜAnja, ᶜUthmān Ādam, Muḥammad Khālid al-Zuqal, and Yūnus al-Dikaym. Rather than being exclusively Taᶜāīshī, this group included, besides the sons of the Mahdī, the Jaᶜalī sons of al-Nujūmī and the Dongolāwī sons of Muḥammad Khālid, a member of the Ashrāf. Furthermore, the Khalīfa is said to have had the sons of al-Nujūmī circumcised alongside his own sons, to dispel any notion that he bore the family ill will. The *khalīfas* ᶜAlī wad Ḥilū and Muḥammad Sharīf meanwhile established their own *khalwas* to accommodate the large number of children in their extended families. Contrary to practice in most of the city, the girls in the Mahdī's household and the households of at least the *khalīfas* ᶜAlī and Muḥammad Sharīf were also instructed in reading and writing, with Khalīfa ᶜAlī and the Mahdī's wife Fāṭima bt. ᶜAbd al-Raḥmān Ḥusayn personally supervising the girls' education. (The Mahdī's daughter Maryam, in fact, is alleged to have known most of the Qur'ān by heart.)[30]

Naturally the people of these households took a sterner approach to the Mahdī's teachings than many of the other Anṣār, despite the well-known shortcomings of such individuals as ᶜUthmān Shaykh al-Dīn. As previously mentioned, al-Nujūmī's son recalled that "all important households had *umanā'* [eunuch guards]. This was because it was forbidden for males and females to mix unobserved, even fathers and daughters and brothers and sisters." These *umanā'* lived within the *hōsh*, preventing strangers from entering and keeping mature youths out of the women's quarters. A document compiled by E.M.I. immediately after Kararī lists the households containing eunuchs in Omdurman and the number of eunuchs remaining with them after the battle. This is virtually a list of the Mahdist elite, and includes the homes of the Mahdī (17 eunuchs), al-Bushrā, son of the Mahdī (one), Khalīfa ᶜAbdallāhi (18), Amīr Yaᶜqūb (five), ᶜUthmān Shaykh al-Dīn (three), Hārūn Muḥammad, brother of the Khalīfa (one), al-Sanūsī Aḥmad, brother of the Khalīfa (one), *amīr* Maḥmūd Aḥmad, cousin of the Khalīfa (five), *amīr* Ibrāhīm al-Khalīl Aḥmad, cousin of the Khalīfa (one), *amīr* Yūnus al-Dikaym (four), *amīr* ʿUthmān al-Dikaym (two), *amīr* ʿAbd al-Raḥmān al-Nujūmī (one), *amīr* al-Zākī Muḥammad ʿUthmān (five), *amīr* Musāʿid Qaydūm (two), *amīr* Ḥāmid ʿAlī (one), *amīr* al-Ṣāliḥ Ḥammād (one), *amīr* Hārūn Mūsa (one), *amīr* Ab Sām (one), *amīr* Ḥamdān Abū ʿAnja (one), *amīr* ʿAbd al-Bāqī ʿAbd al-Wakīl (two), Khalīfa ʿAlī wad Ḥilū (three), and Khalīfa Muḥammad Sharīf (three). Missing from the list are Aḥmad Sharfī, the Ashrāf patriarch, and Ḥāmid Muḥammad, the Mahdī's cousin and father of Khalīfa Sharīf, as well as several other important *amīrs*, but the document is still revealing.[31]

Moreover, the members of these households were aware of belonging to a distinct and select group. The Mahdī is said to have proclaimed that the members of his household (*ahl baytī*) include his own family, the families of his brothers Muḥammad and Ḥāmid, the families of his three *khalīfas,* and the family of Amīr Yaʿqūb. While such a sentiment is certainly possible—Yaʿqūb was, like ʿAbdallāhi, an early adherent of the Mahdī and one of his most important and trusted commanders—it is also possible that this statement was a later invention to validate the Khalīfa's near-monopoly of political power and the integration of their families.[32] Similarly, we might view the claims of both ʿAbdallāhi and ʿAlī wad Ḥilū to Sharīfī status, claims that were much publicized during the Mahdīyya, as obvious fictions to enhance the prestige of their families while they were creating marriage alliances with the Dongola Ashrāf. (For example, the Khalīfa often signed his letters "al-Khalīfa ʿAbdallāhi ibn al-Sayyid Muḥammad.") Perhaps it matters less what the Mahdī actually said—which in any case is unknowable—and from whom ʿAbdallāhi and ʿAli wad Ḥilū were descended, and more what the Anṣār in general, and families of the elite in particular, chose to believe. If their marriage alliances are any indication, they eventually chose to believe that they had much in common.[33]

The exact composition of some of these families is uncertain, since many people who are identified in accounts of the period as relatives of the Mahdī and Khalīfa were in fact their associates or "retainers." For example, Shuqayr (following Slatin) mentions among the relatives of the Khalīfa the following: Yūnus al-Dikaym, ʿUthmān al-Dikaym, al-Zākī ʿUthmān, Ḥāmid ʿAlī, Musāʿid Qaydūm, Muḥammad Bishāra, Ab Sām, and Ibrāhīm Mālik. All of these important *amīrs*, as well Ḥamdān Abū ʿAnja and al-

Zākī Ṭamal, are recalled by the grandchildren of the Khalīfa as "members of the household," although not related by marriage or descent. Complicating matters is the complexity of relations, the ways in which people came to be considered related. For example, in an undated letter written to the Khalīfa, one Ibrāhīm al-Daqīqa asks the Khalīfa's permission to marry the daughter of the Dongolāwī *amīr* al-Nūr ᶜAnqara. The Khalīfa replies that he can neither accept nor refuse, but that Ibrāhīm must first demonstrate his worthiness for the girl, since "al-Nūr ᶜAnqara is related to us." The suitor is advised to seek the intercession of al-Zākī Ṭamal in the matter. In fact the marriage relation between the Khalīfa and al-Nūr ᶜAnqara was not very close: al-Nūr's daughter Āmina was married to the Khalīfa's cousin, Maḥmūd Aḥmad. A relationship of trust and history, however—further reflected in al-Nūr's settlement in the southern zone of the city—may be the more compelling one in this instance.[34]

Examined here are the marriage alliances created during the Mahdīyya of the most prominent Mahdist elite. They include the wives of the Mahdī, Khalīfa ᶜAbdallāhi, *khalīfas* ᶜAlī wad Ḥilū and Muḥammad Sharīf, Aḥmad Sharfī, Ḥāmid Muḥammad, Amīr Yaᶜqūb, and Maḥmūd Aḥmad. Included also are the marriages of the sons and daughters of many of these, as well as the nieces and nephews of the Mahdī. In the case of the second generation, some of the marriages were contracted in the early years of Anglo-Egyptian rule, but it has been thought useful to include them here to show a continuation of the process begun during the Mahdīyya. Although a small sample, it is indicative of the general tendency of social integration among the elite, a tendency further displayed in the marriages of the siblings and cousins of most of these individuals. No broader statement about the social integration of Omdurman as a whole is intended, although there is some evidence for that as well.

(1) *The Mahdī's Wives*: Apparently at the time of his death the Mahdī had some 100 women in his *ḥarīm*. (Shuqayr estimated the number to be "about one hundred," while the Mahdī's brother-in-law, Maḥmūd al-Qabbānī, told E.M.I. in 1893 that it was 105.) Based upon written and especially oral accounts, this study identifies 72 of these. While the Mahdī claimed the authority to fashion his own *Sunna*, he was still bound by Qur'ānic dictate, hence four wives only were considered *sharᶜīyyāt* or "legal wives," the rest being *sarārī* (concubines). The legal wives consisted of Fāṭima bt.

Aḥmad Sharfī, daughter of the Ashrāf patriarch married at Khartoum before the Mahdīyya, who died at Jabal Qadīr; ᶜĀ'isha bt. Aḥmad Sharfī, married after the death of her sister; Fāṭima bt. al-Ḥājj Sharīf, a relative married at Kararī before the Mahdīyya; Fāṭima bt. ᶜAbd al-Raḥmān Ḥusayn, an Egyptian married at Shāṭṭ or Abā Island before the Mahdīyya; and ᶜĀ'isha bt. Idrīs, daughter of a Fulānī *shaykh* of Sinja, married at Jabal Qadīr. Whether legal wife or concubine, all of the Mahdī's women were regarded by the people of Omdurman as his wives, and of course their offspring were fully his children. At various times, many were referred to by the honorific *Umm al-Mu'minīn* ("Mother of the Believers"). Ohrwalder comments that after the Mahdī's death the widows were forbidden to remarry and held in virtual captivity. It is more likely that the Mahdī's wives chose to remain his widows, since only four of the approximately 100 are known to have remarried.[35]

The Mahdī married these women—for indeed, all were considered "married"—under varied circumstances. As already mentioned, many devoted Anṣār gave, or sought to give, their daughters to the Mahdī in the hope of benefiting from his *baraka*. The Mahdī had also expressed a desire to more fully integrate Sudanese society through the example of his own family. The effect of his marriages to the widows of former Turco-Egyptian officials and merchants was to destroy the authority of the old regime, while also setting an example for his Anṣār to solve the problems of warfare. Holt mentions the Mahdī's attempt "to restore stability to a society in dissolution," and this is the context in which many of these marriages should be viewed. At the same time, the advantages gained by marriages to families of religious, economic, and tribal authority were not inconsequential.[36]

Of the 72 women identified as wives of the Mahdī by this study, only three (Fāṭima and ᶜĀ'isha bt. Aḥmad Sharfī and Fāṭima bt. al-Ḥājj Sharīf) were close relations, while three others (Bakhīta bt. ᶜAlī al-Fakī Muḥammad, Umm Salama bt. ᶜAbdallāh Shūsh, and Ḥaram bt. al-Nūr Ḥusayn Baṣīr) were distant relatives from the Ashrāf settled in Qiṭayna on the White Nile. At least 12 women were survivors of Turco-Egyptian officers or administrators (including a daughter, a niece, and a concubine of the Mahdī's former enemy, Yūsuf Pasha Ḥasan al-Shallālī), while at least another ten were the daughters or survivors of important traders from Darfur, Kordofan and Khartoum. Among these were the daughters of

Muḥammad Abū'l-Su^cūd al-^cAqqād, al-Nūr Bey al-Khabīr, Muḥammad al-Ḥājj Aḥmad Umm Birayr, Ḥasan Mismār, Abū Bakr al-Jarkūk, and Muḥammad Ṣāliḥ al-Qabbānī. Several were the daughters of men of considerable political or religious authority, including al-Ni^cma bt. Shaykh al-Qurashī wad al-Zayn, daughter of the Mahdī's teacher; al-Surra bt. Shaykh Muḥammad al-Ṭayyib al-Baṣīr of the Ḥalāwiyīn; and Maqbūla bt. Nūrayn, granddaughter of Sultan Muḥammad al-Faḍl of Darfur (d.1839). Several others were of southern Sudanese or Nūba origin, the daughters of important political leaders. The Sudanese tribes represented in the Mahdī's *ḥarīm* reflect the regions in which he waged his campaigns—almost a third each came from the Jazīra region, Kordofan, and the Khartoum area—but also include others. Among the wives were the following tribal, ethnic, or regional affiliations: Danāqla, Ja^caliyīn, Shāīqīyya, Maḥas, Kunūz, Ḥalāwiyīn, Jawāma^ca, Masallamīyya, Fūr, Nūba, Dinka, Fulānī, Ethiopian, Egyptian, and Syrian. Doubtless more were represented than this study was able to uncover.

(2) *The Khalīfa's Wives:* Like the Mahdī, the Khalīfa had many women in his *ḥarīm*. Slatin, who served as one of his attendants, wrote that the Khalīfa had over 400 wives, but this surely is an exaggeration: This study identifies 29 of the wives based upon oral and written sources, among whom 25 bore him children, while the *Sudan Intelligence Report* drawn up after Kararī—which presumably approached accuracy—listed only 25 women at that time. The same brother-in-law of the Mahdī, Maḥmūd al-Qabbānī, told E.M.I. in 1893 that the Khalīfa's *ḥarīm* included 200 wives, but Maḥmūd would have been more familiar with the Mahdī's household than the Khalīfa's. Four of the wives were *shar^cīyyāt*: Zahrā', a Ta^cāīshīyya married before the Mahdīyya; Umm Kulthūm bt. al-Mahdī; Āmina bt. Ḥāmid ^cAbdallāh, the Mahdī's niece; and Nafīsa bt. Bābikr, a Ja^calīyya from Masīd wad ^cĪsā. As with the Mahdī, some of the Khalīfa's wives are identifiable as daughters of former Turco-Egyptian officers and administrators, including Fāṭima bt. Aḥmad Aghā Yāsīn and Asma' bt. Muḥammad Khashm al-Mūs Pasha. Others were the daughters of tribal *shaykhs*. The Khalīfa does not appear to have married many daughters or survivors of prominent Khartoum merchants—the only known example being Fāṭima bt. Badran Ḥasan—although this list is admittedly incomplete. Unquestionably the marriage of the Khalīfa to a daughter of the Mahdī was of the

greatest symbolic importance: For a short period of time while he was divorced from Umm Kulthūm, the Khalīfa married her sister Maryam ("in order to remain close to the Mahdī's *baraka*"), but this union was dissolved when he and Umm Kulthūm reconciled and remarried. In addition to the Mahdī's daughters and niece, the Khalīfa married two women who were sisters of the Mahdī's wives: Fāṭima bt. Badran Ḥasan, an Egyptian from Khartoum, and Āmina bt. Karamallāh Kirkusāwī, daughter of the Dongolāwī *amīr*. Again, Slatin claimed that the Khalīfa's *ḥarīm* "comprises almost every tribe in the Sudan." At least the known tribal, ethnic, or regional affiliations include the following: Ja^{c}aliyīn, Danāqla, Shāīqīyya, Rikābīyya, Maḥas, Kunūz, Shukrīyya, Ḥabbānīyya, Ta^{c}āīsha, Jimi^{c}āb, Fūr, Nūba, Dinka, Egyptian, and Ethiopian. Despite his close personal and political ties to the Ta^{c}āīsha, the Khalifa appears to have married only one woman, his first wife, from that tribe, while the preponderance of his *ḥarīm* (three of his four *shar^{c}īyyāt* and 13 of the known 29) represents the riverain tribes.[37]

(3) *Khalīfa ^{c}Alī wad Ḥilū's Wives:* One of the earliest and most devout followers of the Mahdī, Khalīfa ^{c}Alī was known as "The Ascetic" for the simplicity of his manners and household. His following was the smallest of the three initial standards of the army, and his role in Mahdist politics was that of mediator between the Khalīfa and Muḥammad Sharīf. Not surprisingly his *ḥarīm* was the smallest of the leaders of the Mahdīyya. The same Maḥmūd al-Qabbānī told E.M.I. in 1893 that Khalīfa ^{c}Alī had 20 wives, but only nine are remembered by his family, of whom eight bore him children. Among them, only three were tribal relations, two of the Dighaym and one of the Kināna. Two of his wives were of obvious symbolic importance: Nūr al-Shām bt. al-Mahdī and Ḥalīma bt. Muḥammad, the sister of the Khalīfa ^{c}Abdallāhi, both of whom were *shar^{c}īyyāt*. One wife, Ḥafsa bt. Jubāra Aḥmad Jifūn, was the daughter of a *shaykh* of the Jimi^{c}āb of the White Nile. At least two *sarārī* were of southern or Nūba origin.[38]

(4) *Khalīfa Muḥammad Sharīf's Wives*: Perhaps 15 women formed the *ḥarīm* of Khalīfa Muḥammad Sharīf, a relatively small number attributable to the instability of his short life, although he may have had other *sarārī* whose names have been lost. His first wife was Zaynab, the eldest child of the Mahdī. Two other *shar^{c}īyyāt* also came from his Ashrāf relations, Fāṭima bt. Ḥāmid ^{c}Abdallāh, a niece of the Mahdī, and Umm Kulthūm bt. Ṣāliḥ, of the Ashrāf of Labab Island in Dongola. Two wives were daughters

of *amīrs* of the Shanābla and Funj. (Āmina bt. Saᶜīd Muḥammad Faraḥ was the daughter of the *nāẓir* of the Funj under Turco-Egyptian rule, who later became *amīr* of the Funj during the Mahdīyya.) Two of his wives had sisters married to the Mahdī: Naṣra bt. al-Burra and a daughter of Muḥammad Ṣāliḥ al-Qabbānī, the Khartoum merchant. Two wives, Zaynab bt. al-Mahdī and his relative Fāṭima bt. Ḥāmid ᶜAbdallāh, had sisters married to the Khalīfa ᶜAbdallāhi. These were presumably his only marriage links to the Khalīfa.

(5) *The Ashrāf*: Aḥmad Muḥammad Sharfī, the patriarch of the Dongola Ashrāf and father-in-law of the Mahdī, married 12 women. Of the *sharᶜīyyāt*, three were relatives from the Ashrāf, including Ruqayya bt. ᶜAbd al-Karīm, sister of the *amīr* Muḥammad ᶜAbd al-Karīm. The fourth was Āmina bt. Muṣṭafā Nimayrī, from a Khartoum family that claimed Sharīfī status. At least one wife, Burra bt. al-Nūr al-Khabīr (sister to a wife of the Mahdī), was from an important Khartoum trading family. The remaining wives were *sarārī* of riverain, southern Sudanese, Nūba, and Ethiopian origin.

The Mahdī's first cousin Ḥāmid Muḥammad, father of Khalīfa Muḥammad Sharīf, is known to have married seven women. Three of the *sharᶜīyyāt* were relatives from the Ashrāf, including a daughter of Aḥmad Sharfī. Three others were from the Maḥas, Jaᶜaliyīn and Kabābīsh emigrants to Omdurman. The final wife was a daughter of Ḥasan Mismār, a prominent trader killed at Khartoum, whose sister was married to the Mahdī.

(6) *The Taᶜāīsha*: Amīr Yaᶜqūb, the elder half-brother of Khalīfa ᶜAbdallāhi, is unique in that of the 13 women he is known to have married, not one was a relation, nor even of the Taᶜāīsha. The reason for this is unclear, although one possibility is that such an alliance was simply unnecessary. Among his wives were daughters of Shaykh Nuwāy of the Ḥawāzma of Kordofan; of Ḥasabū Muḥammad, the *amīr* of the Zaghāwa of Darfur; and of ᶜUmar Tarḥū, a Shāīqī Turco-Egyptian official in Darfur who became a Mahdist *amīr*. The remaining wives were from the western tribes of the Ḥumr and Ḥabbāniyya, the White Nile Jaᶜafra, the Nūba and Dinka, a woman of Khartoum (identified as a "Turkīyya"), and two Ethiopians.

The Khalīfa's first cousin, Maḥmūd wad Aḥmad, is known to have married seven women, all of whom are remembered as coming from affluent or influential families established prior to the Mahdīyya. Only one wife, his first, was a relative: ᶜĀ'isha bt. Muhammad, sister of the Khalīfa. Of the remainder, one was from the family of Malik Kanbal, a Shāīqī leader of irregular cavalry during the Turco-Egyptian regime. One was the daughter of a wealthy Dongolāwī merchant in Bāra, and another the daughter of a wealthy man of the Shukrīyya ("the owner of many camels"). The remaining wives were a daughter of the Dongolāwī *amīr* al-Nūr ᶜAnqara and two riverain women of the Dongola region. Differently put, five of Maḥmūd's seven wives were riverain Sudanese.

(7) *The Mahdī's Children*: The nine daughters of the Mahdī who survived and married represent a three-way split in their marriages between the three *khalīfas*, the sons of the three *khalīfas* and their relatives from the Ashrāf. Zaynab, the Mahdī's eldest, married Muḥammad Sharīf, Umm Kulthūm married Khalīfa ᶜAbdallāhi, and Nūr al-Shām married ᶜAlī wad Ḥilū. ᶜĀ'isha married Muḥammad Aḥmad b. al-Khalifa ᶜAlī, Umm Salama married ᶜUthmān Shaykh al-Dīn b. al-Khalīfa ᶜAbdallāhi, and Maryam married Muḥammad b. al-Khalīfa Sharīf. Finally, Nafīsa ("Kinayn") married her cousin Ḥāmid b. Ḥāmid ᶜAbdallāh, the nephew of the Mahdī; Zahrā' married her relative Muḥammad Ṣāliḥ b. Muḥammad ᶜAbd al-Karīm; and Qamr al-Dīn married her relative Maḥmūd ᶜAbd al-Karīm.

Of the six sons of the Mahdī who married, four did so during the Mahdīyya: Al-Faḍl married two wives, Zaynab bt. Muḥammad Ibrāhīm, the granddaughter of the *amīr* of the Funj, plus his cousin Miyāsa bt. Ḥāmid ᶜAbdallāh. The other three sons, Muḥammad, al-Bushrā and al-Ṭāhir, all married daughters of the Khalīfa ᶜAbdallāhi. The two other sons, ᶜAlī and ᶜAbd al-Raḥmān, married nine women during Anglo-Egyptian rule, of whom only one was a relative (ᶜAbd al-Raḥmān's wife Khadīja bt. Khalīfa Muḥammad Sharīf). Seven of their wives were daughters of Jazīra and White Nile tribal leaders and holy men, including Dār al-Naᶜīm bt. ᶜAbd al-Bāqī, from a Kawāhla holy family descended from ᶜAbd al-Bāqī al-Nayl al-Walī (fl.1750).

(8) *Khalīfa ᶜAbdallāhi's Children*: Of the nine daughters of the Khalīfa who survived and married, five married within the family, marrying sons of either Amīr Yaᶜqūb (Ḥawā, Nūr al-Shām, and Maryam), Maḥmūd wad Aḥmad (Nafīsa), or Ismāᶜīl wad Aḥmad (Saᶜdīyya). Two other daughters married sons of ᶜAlī wad Ḥilū (Ṣāfīyya and al-Ṭāhira), one daughter

(Zahrā') married a Jaᶜalī of Shendi (her mother was a Jaᶜalīyya, so this husband may have been a relative), and the ninth daughter Khadīja "al-Raḍīyya" married Muḥammad b. al-Mahdī, and after their divorce, his brother al-Bushrā. Khadīja's marriage to al-Bushrā after her divorce from Muḥammad resembles the Khalīfa's marriage to Maryam bt. al-Mahdī after his divorce from Umm Kulthūm, and underlines the importance of remaining close to the source of *baraka* and font of Mahdist inspiration. Additionally, one daughter was briefly married to al-Ṭāhir b. al-Mahdī, who died a month after their marriage.

Eighteen sons of the Khalīfa married a total of forty wives, either in the Mahdīyya or Anglo-Egyptian periods, and their choice of wives illustrates the interconnectedness of the Mahdist elite. Of these wives, at least nine were relatives from the family of Amīr Yaᶜqūb. Others were relatives from the sons' maternal side, and encompass a variety of western, eastern, and riverain tribes, including the Taᶜāīsha, Rizayqāt, Zaghāwa, Jimiᶜāb, Jaᶜaliyīn, Maḥas, Danāqla, Kināna, and Banī ᶜĀmir. Nine were daughters of Taᶜāīshī *amīrs*, others were the daughters of other western *amīrs*, and one was the daughter of the Dongolāwī *amīr* al-Nūr ᶜAnqara. At least three wives were Egyptians, and at least two wives came from important trading families: Fāṭima bt. Wad Tātāy (daughter of Faḍl al-Sīd, the market and port official) and Khadīja bt. al-Ḥājj Aḥmad al-ᶜAqqād. Four wives were members of the Mahdī's extended family, of whom the most important was Umm Salama bt. al-Mahdī, wife of ᶜUthmān Shaykh al-Dīn. Otherwise, Dā'ūd married Badūr bt. ᶜAbdallāhi al-Faḍl al-Mahdī, ᶜAbd al-Salām married Qūt al-Qulūb bt. ᶜAbd al-Raḥmān al-Mahdī, and al-Ṭayyib married a daughter of Ḥāmid b. Ḥāmid ᶜAbdallāh, the Mahdī's nephew.

(9) *Khalīfa ᶜAlī wad Ḥilū's Children*: Of the seven daughters of Khalīfa ᶜAlī, three married relatives from either the maternal or paternal side: Ṣāfīyya married her mother's cousin Muḥammad al-Mahdī b. Aḥmad (the brother of Maḥmūd Aḥmad), ᶜĀ'isha married her mother's cousin Ḥusayn b. al-Khalīfa Sharīf, and Ḥawā married her paternal cousin Shaykh Bilāl Maḥl of the Dighaym. Of the other four daughters, Zaynab married ᶜĪsā Aḥmad Jifūn, a former *amīr* of the Shankhāb section of the White Nile Jimiᶜāb (Khalīfa ᶜAlī had married a woman of this group, but she was not the mother of Zaynab); and Nūr al-Shām married ᶜAbd al-Bāqī b. Aḥmad al-Mikāshfī, son of a Mahdist *amīr* from the Kawāhla holy family of ᶜAbd

al-Bāqī al-Nayl and a relative of the wife of ᶜAbd al-Raḥmān al-Mahdī; the Mikāshfīs also claimed Sharīfī descent. Finally, Umm Maḥl and Batūl both married sons of Amīr Yaᶜqūb.

The 11 sons of Khalīfa ᶜAlī married a total of 32 women. The eldest son, Muḥammad Aḥmad, married all nine of his wives during the Mahdīyya. His four *sharᶜīyyāt* were ᶜĀ'isha bt. al-Mahdī, Āmina ᶜĪsā Aḥmad Jifūn of the Shankhāb Jimiᶜāb (a daughter of his sister Zaynab's husband from a previous marriage), and two relatives from the Dighaym. His five *sarārī* included at least one southern Sudanese and one of Nūba origin. The other sons of Khalīfa ᶜAlī married between them two granddaughters of the Mahdī, four women from the families of Khalīfa ᶜAbdallāhi and Amīr Yaᶜqūb (including two daughters of the Khalīfa and one daughter of Amīr Yaᶜqūb), four relatives of the Dighaym, and women of the Shankhāb Jimiᶜāb, Rufāᶜa al-Hōy, Maḥas, Ḥawāzma and Taᶜāīsha.

(10) *Khalīfa Muḥammad Sharīf's Children*: Four daughters of Khalīfa Muḥammad Sharīf married, all from the extended family, and their husbands include a son and grandson of the Mahdī, a nephew of the Mahdī, and the *amīr* Muḥammad ᶜUthmān Abū Qarja of the Ashrāf of Qitayna. Of the five sons of Muḥammad Sharīf known to have married, their wives include Maryam bt. al-Mahdī, ᶜĀ'isha bt. al-Khalīfa ᶜAlī, a daughter of Muḥammad ᶜUthmān Abū Qarja, a daughter of an *amīr* of the Dighaym (from the *Anṣār Abā*), a woman of the Kināna, and ᶜĀ'isha bt. ᶜAbd al-Bāqī, sister of ᶜAbd al-Raḥmān al-Mahdī's wife from the Kawāhla holy family.

(11) *The Mahdī's Nephews and Nieces*: The Mahdī's brothers died early in the Mahdīyya, of whom two, Muḥammad and Ḥāmid, had married. Their children, the nieces and nephews of the Mahdī, made a number of significant marriages. Of the five nieces, their husbands include Khalifa Muḥammad Sharīf (Fāṭima bt. Ḥāmid), Khalīfa ᶜAbdallāhi (Āmina bt. Ḥāmid), al-Faḍl b. al-Mahdī (Miyāsa bt. Ḥāmid), an Ashrāf relative (Zahrā' bt. Muḥammad), and a man of the Baqqāra married after the Mahdīyya (Batūl bt. Muḥammad). After the death of al-Faḍl al-Mahdī at Shukkāba in 1899, Miyāsa bt. Ḥāmid married a man of the Kināna. The five nephews of the Mahdī married a total of 22 women, of whom only two were from the Ashrāf relations, including Nafīsa bt. al-Mahdī. At least 13 wives were from important families of the White Nile and Jazīra region (including the

Kināna, Dighaym, ^{c}Arakīyīn, Masallamīyya, Laḥāwīyīn, and Ḥusaynāt), in part a reflection of the circumstances of the Mahdī's family in the early years of Anglo-Egyptian rule. Three other wives were from the Rizayqāt Baqqāra, one from the Baṭāḥīn, and only three from the riverain tribes of the Danāqla and Ja^{c}aliyīn.

(12) *Amīr Ya^{c}qūb's Children*: Thirteen daughters of Amīr Ya^{c}qūb are known to have married. Of their spouses, six were relatives, including four sons of Khalīfa ^{c}Abdallāhi, a brother of Maḥmūd Aḥmad, and a nephew of the Khalīfa. Two daughters married the sons of Ja^{c}alī and Shāīqī *amīrs*, fulfilling the Khalīfa's wish to intermarry the *awlād al-balad* and the *awlād al-^{c}Arab*. One daughter married a son of Khalīfa ^{c}Alī, another a son of Ibrāhīm Mukhayyir (the *amīr* of the Zayyādīyya of Darfur), and others married Ta^{c}āīsha who do not appear to have been relatives. Ten sons of Amīr Ya^{c}qūb are known to have married a total of 21 women. Of these, at least five wives were relatives, including three daughters of Khalīfa ^{c}Abdallāhi, a sister of Maḥmūd Aḥmad and a daughter of ^{c}Uthmān Shaykh al-Dīn. Nine other wives were the daughters of Ta^{c}āīshī and other Baqqāra *amīrs*. Three married women from the Dighaym, including two daughters of Khalīfa ^{c}Alī. Only one son of Amīr Ya^{c}qūb appears to have married a riverain Sudanese, a woman of the Maḥas. As with the daughters of Amīr Ya^{c}qūb, the sons' marriages seem intended to strengthen alliances with the western tribes and the family of Khalīfa ^{c}Alī.

A Society in Transition

Taken as a whole, the social relations of Mahdist Omdurman suggest the continuation of several trends that had emerged over the previous two centuries, but also the creation of something different and larger, responding to the ethos and conditions of the Mahdīyya. The settlement of the city, for example, follows an earlier pattern of spatially distinct tribal and ethnic quarters with a centrally located, enclosed "royal quarter." And yet across the southern, central and northern zones appear examples of a dynamic mixture that in a short 13-year period, and in close quarters, created new affiliations. The economic activities of Omdurman meanwhile confirm the dominance, especially in long-distance trade, of Sudan's northern riverain and Red Sea populations, and yet we notice as well the involvement of western and central Sudanic people, Fūr, and most surprisingly, Baqqāra in trade and the crafts. In a larger sense, the Mahdist state's intrusion into the economy resembles the centralized policies of the earlier Sudanic states; and yet these policies were only partially successful, especially after the removal from office of Ibrāhīm Muḥammad ᶜAdlān, the *Amīn Bayt al-Māl,* such that the practices of the Mahdīyya ultimately came to resemble a mixture of things, including public welfare and private smuggling.

In the marriages of the Mahdist elite the formation of a multi-ethnic, multi-tribal ruling group is apparent. If the Mahdī's and Khalīfa's intentions were to create a more unified Anṣār through common cause and intermarriage, some success was achieved, as the families of the upper echelon came to include tribal and ethnic groups that were formerly beyond their social or geographic limits. Of course the distribution of daughters in marriage to form an elite group, create alliances, and improve fortunes was already a familiar practice in Sinnār and Darfur; and certainly among most Sudanese the most common form of marriage remained within the extended family. However, as a consequence of the Mahdīyya, the extended families of many northern elites now bridged tribes of the riverain, Jazīra, and western regions. This is most obvious in the marriage alliances made with the extended family of the Mahdī, as the Khalīfa and his Taᶜāīshī relations, and ᶜAlī wad Ḥilū and his Dighaym and Kināna relations, sought to benefit from the various advantages of the Mahdī's *baraka.* Added to the direct marriage ties between families were the larger number of indirect associations: previously unrelated individuals marrying sisters, be they women of the Mahdist elite, prominent trading families, or local holy families. For example, although the family of Muḥammad Sharīf had few associations with the family of Khalīfa ᶜAbdallāhi during the Mahdīyya—a consequence of their sustained political tension—they were nonetheless encompassed within the same extended family by the period's end. The marriages of the elite appear also to have encouraged a centralization of *baraka*, as various claimants to Sharīfī descent were joined to the Dongola Ashrāf, including the Qiṭayna Ashrāf, Khartoum and White Nile Jaᶜafra, Jazīra Mikhāshfīs, and (with the children of Aḥmad Sharfī) the Shinqīṭṭīs. This process was to the immediate benefit of the extended families of Khalīfa ᶜAbdallāhi and ᶜAlī wad Ḥilū, who "uncovered" their own Sharīfī origins even as they were marrying into the Dongola and other Ashrāf families.

The Mahdist elite used their influence in familiar ways. Bābikr Bedrī recalls seeking patronage in a difficult time, when he and a relative "went to the Khalīfa Sharīf to ask him to give us a slave-girl to sell, because we were very hard up. He asked us which official he should write to for us." Later, Bābikr mentions the aftermath of the failed Ashrāf revolt of 1891, when many Danāqla of the Jazīra, including relatives of the Mahdī, were arrested for their complicity: "I wept to see such humiliation after such great prosperity in the days of their power, while the Mahdī was yet alive, and after his death too. Then they lived in great houses with servants and retainers, and the finest horses; they were the influential patrons of their friends, who placed their hopes in them." Meanwhile, the Taᶜāīsha elites had begun to extend their own influence through patronage. Bābikr recalls that a fellow merchant "had a special concession from ᶜUthmān Shaykh al-Dīn, allowing him to pay only a half of the customs due on his goods." (Bābikr quite willingly labeled his own goods with the other merchant's name.) This merchant, al-Ṣādiq ᶜUthmān, had previously served in the irregular cavalry of the Turco-Egyptian regime, yet "because of his friendship with Shaykh al-Dīn, [he] achieved a fortune of 60,000 *riyāls*." Understandably Bābikr bristled at the Khalīfa's favoring of the Baqqāra and their subsequent rise in status. Yet unnoticed by him, something profound was taking place: the integration of many of these western Arabs into the social order of the riverain Sudan.[39]

One measure of this integration was linguistic. ᶜIsmat Ḥasan Zulfō writes that many of the Baqqāra began to adopt the riverain dialect of Arabic, which was prevalent in Omdurman, as a result of their settlement. ᶜUthmān Shaykh al-Dīn spoke this form of Arabic—he could not speak Baqqārī dialect, in fact—and was dubbed "Ibn al-Madīna" ("son of the city"). To further Shaykh al-Dīn's education, the Khalīfa assigned his secretary, al-Ṭayyib Hāshim, to teach him classical Arabic. Needless to say, the poetry of the Mahdīyya, an important component of the Mahdist *tarbīyya*, was largely recited in the riverain vernacular. Even communities removed from Omdurman were affected by its conditions: The Kunūz of al-Kawwa on the White Nile, earlier migrants from the Nubian north, effectively replaced their native Kenzī with Arabic during this period, as they did their traditional monogamous marriages with the polygamy encouraged by the

Mahdīyya. Fr. Ohrwalder, the most observant (if not unbiased) of the European prisoners, comments on this process of integration:

> It is only right that the Baqqara, who have been brought up in the forests and plains, and who are far more simple-minded, honest individuals, should rule the corrupt Aulad-belad; their emigration to Omdurman and their submission to the Khalifa's rule has had the advantages of taming them, and their advances in civilization are quite astounding. Being now possessed of power and money, they have begun to build better houses, to wear cleaner clothing, and to occasionally wash their jibbehs, which were reeking and besmeared with oil and fat; the Khalifa has done much to improve their manners and customs in this respect. Their west-country Arabic dialect has greatly improved; now the two opposition parties can thoroughly understand each other, and the Aulad-belad no longer make a laughingstock of their western brethren.

Ohrwalder also wrote that the Baqqāra have become proficient merchants, and have taken a large share of the retail business in Omdurman. "Although they have scarcely ever owned a piastre in their lives, the shining dollar has excited the most inordinate cupidity amongst them. They are very quick to learn, and already surpass the Aulad-belad in many branches of trade."[40]

The changes that were occurring in Omdurman emerged out of, and intensified, the social ferment of the late Funj and Turco-Egyptian periods. Most obviously, this involved the growth of a Sudanese Arab-Muslim society by means of acculturation and urbanization: what one scholar has described as a "progressive homogenization of culture and social organization." Likewise if it is true, as this scholar writes, that during Turco-Egyptian rule "adherence to Islam and an Arab social idiom was no longer simply a matter of prestige; it was the prerequisite for membership and survival," the statement is particularly true for the Mahdīyya: To survive and be a member was to be an Anṣārī, to adopt the Islamic practice and Arabic culture of the Mahdīyya, epitomized by the society of Omdurman. This greater "homogenization" was arguably the most significant outcome of the Mahdī's teachings and the Khalīfa's rule, whether intended or not, and it outlasted the violent destruction of the Mahdist state in 1898.[41]

CHAPTER SIX

The Omdurman Experience

I who had risked my life against the steamers, I who had never feared to meet the enemy, I who had started out to take Ḥalfā with only eight companions—today I rubbed my face into the sand trying to bury my head in it, thoughtless of suffocation, so distracted was I by the fear of death, which in dangers no less acute than this I had sought so eagerly. Then Bābikr Muṣṭafā, the man on my right, received a wound in the left hand, and I came to my senses at last and remembered what I had promised my comrades. I slipped off my turban, smeared it in my neighbor's blood, and bound it on my left arm; then I called to my companions, 'Now two of us are wounded!'

British correspondents who accompanied Kitchener's victorious army found nothing to like about Omdurman, which to them resembled a labyrinth of crudely made huts. Perhaps the most hostile description was given by G. W. Steevens, a writer for the *Daily Mail*, who likened the city to a menagerie, referring to its dwellings as "a rabbit-warren," a "teeming beehive," "piggish dwelling-holes," "mud kennels," "birds' nests," and "a gibbering monkey-house." (Lest his point be unclear, he pronounced "the whole city" to be "a monstrosity of African lust.") Others were slightly less vehement: F. Maurice granted the Sudanese "the heroism of the beast of prey," although "they had been the most atrocious set of tyrants that ever darkened the face of the earth." R. W. Felkin meanwhile wondered if it was possible to make the site of old Khartoum a "salubrious and a fitting residence for Europeans," since "it is of vital importance for the whole Nile Valley to be permanently under the control of either Egypt or Great

Britain." Quite differently, the correspondent for the *Westminster Gazette*, Ernest Bennett, ignited a firestorm of controversy with his denunciation of the Anglo-Egyptian army's treatment of the Sudanese wounded on the battlefield, using such phrases as "wholesale slaughter" and "gratuitous bit of butchery." Worse, Bennett accused the British as well as Egyptian and "Soudanese" troops of looting and acts of violence against civilians, a clear contravention of international law, and condemned Kitchener's decisions to bombard the *Qubba* and exhume the Mahdī's body from its grave. Bennett's scathing comments ("The act is nothing more or less than a return to the barbarism of the Middle Ages") were rebutted by the British military, apparently to the satisfaction of government and the public. The Mahdī's head, which had been severed from its body, was quietly buried in Wādī Ḥalfā; and the British authorities were free to consider how to govern their newly won territory. Among their many concerns was Omdurman, with its large population of western Arabs "without any regular means of subsistence." Seeking to return as many people to the land as possible, the authorities moved quickly to settle land claims and, in the words of Lord Cromer, to empty Omdurman and the Jazīra of "the useless mouths." In a further sign of the return of civilization, the Sudan was opened to foreign trade: The first issue of *The Sudan Gazette* (7 March 1899), the official government organ, advertised the establishment of four wine, spirits, and general merchandise purveyors in Omdurman (two at the former parade grounds and two at the market). Five months later, *The Gazette* announced the granting of liquor licenses to six merchants in the Khartoum administrative district, joining 16 others granted in Kassala, Berber, Dongola, and Ḥalfā. If any Sudanese objected to this policy, they did so quietly, at least for the time being.[1]

For their part, the people of Omdurman were trying to survive the pillaging and settling of scores in the three days following Kararī, most of it carried out by former *jihādīyya* in the service of the Egyptian army. After order was restored, there was great concern to recover their runaway slaves, some of whom had joined the army and others fled to parts unknown. While Naᶜūm Shuqayr and other staff of the Intelligence Department were searching house-to-house for Mahdist documents, many Anṣār were burning their papers (as well as their patched *jibbas*), hoping to avoid being associated with a regime that had been so thoroughly vanquished. Eventually, most left the city and returned to their original towns and villages, or else settled in the Jazīra; but thousands, perhaps 50,000, remained. That they chose not to move to the new Khartoum, with its neat and shady streets, seemed puzzling to some. The American missionary J. Kelly Giffen, who arrived in 1899, reasoned that in Omdurman "property was cheap, living expenses less than in Khartoum, and above all else, the restrictions imposed by the municipality of Khartoum were dreaded. The people loved their savage liberty." Doubtless the expense of Khartoum was a major consideration: Why else would the majority of Egyptians and Masālma (now mostly returned to Christianity and Judaism) remain in Omdurman? But Giffen also fervently hoped that Omdurman would disappear: "It was built of the most perishable materials, and it is well. A few more seasons of rain and wind and much of it will not be traceable. Like the Mahdi and his cause, let it perish forever from the face of the earth." Missing from Giffen's thinking was the fact that, simply put, to many Sudanese "the Mahdī's city" was more than a place to live: it was a vital part of their history and it was an idea.[2]

As a town, Omdurman owed much to its precolonial predecessors, just as the Mahdīyya owed much to the states of Sinnār and Darfur. The distinct settlement pattern and market organization, the enclosed "royal" quarter with adjoining administrative district and elite slave guard, the office of *Sirr al-tujjār* and the titles of *amīn* and *muqaddam*: All follow a Sudanic precedent. We can see in Sinnār's honorific title, *Sinnār al-Maḥrūsa al-Maḥmīyya* ("Sinnār the divinely protected and guarded"), a foreshadowing of such names as *al-Buqᶜa al-Ṭāhira*. Like the kings of old, the Mahdī and Khalīfa were believed to have the power to heal and bestow life on their subjects; they intervened in the economy in a variety of ways, including sumptuary laws and trade monopolies, and struggled to control their merchants; and they restricted travel when necessary or advantageous. Quite directly, Omdurman was built on (or better, *with*) the former towns, since most of its brick and wood came from Khartoum, which in turn had taken many of its materials from both Sōba and Sinnār. (Of the famous carved doors of Sinnār, however, there was no reported trace.) Omdurman also drew upon the population that had served the earlier states. This included the descendants of some of the *makks* of Nubia, but most notably the *Amīn Bayt al-Māl* Ibrāhīm Muḥammad ᶜAdlān, who undertook the vast reorganization of the Mahdist treasury and was the son of the last Hamaj regent of Sinnār. Even one of the symbols of office from the Funj period, the double-horned headdress (*taqīyya umm qarnayn*) worn by *makks,* survived into the Mahdist period, although it is not known how often it was worn.[3]

Omdurman's debt to Turco-Egyptian Khartoum is also clear, especially its combination of administrative and market functions in one town, although ideologically Omdurman defined itself in opposition to "The city of the Turks" where, in the words of one visitor, "everything is to be had." The Mahdist state's reliance upon the personnel and administrative techniques of the former regime, of course, is an established fact. In a more general way, the success of the Mahdīyya owed much to the developments of the Turco-Egyptian period, especially the growth of the Ṣūfī orders and their contribution to a common Islamic discourse in the Sudan. In addition, the spread of such groups as the Khatmīyya (and its offshoot, the Ismāᶜīlīyya in Kordofan) created a social network, especially among merchants, as well as a fluidity of identity that made possible the Mahdī's widespread appeal.[4]

At the same time that Omdurman's debt to its predecessors is acknowledged, it is important to recall that many features of its governance, organization, and daily life bore little in common with earlier practices. The social distance between noblemen and subjects so common to the Sudanic states, for example, had no place in a city where the *Amīr al-umarā'* might walk arm-in-arm with an anonymous foot-soldier, as happened to Bābikr Bedrī. At least in its early years, Omdurman seemed to the Anṣār a place where their millennial idea was possible.

Reputations often outlast a city. Well into the twentieth century, more than 400 years after its destruction, there were still people swearing oaths by "Sōba, the city of my ancestors." Omdurman under Anglo-Egyptian rule, by comparison, was a vibrant town, the commercial center of the country, the acknowledged "popular capital" where literary groups and popular media (e.g., Radio Omdurman) gave rise to a nationalist movement, transforming the holy city into a national symbol. No such national awareness had existed in the nineteenth century. Fr. Giovanni Beltrame, visiting Khartoum in 1853, had observed that "There are many amusements, dances and songs in Khartoum by day and night. It must be said that such amusements give spontaneous joy to all classes, but despite this the common feeling of citizenship is missing; it may be true that each loves his own house and his district, but nevertheless they recognize no country." Certainly a sense of larger identity was developing. Yūsuf Mikhā'īl, part of the Coptic community in Turco-Egyptian Kordofan, recalled an incident in El Obeid when he and other students set upon an unpopular teacher. Yūsuf wrote that "We were not afraid of him, because he was an Egyptian and a coward." (The teacher, for his part, proclaimed that he did not understand "these Sudanese boys.") A more directly nationalist sentiment was expressed in a work of Mahdist propaganda published in Omdurman in 1305 / 1887–1888, entitled *Naṣīḥat al-ᶜAwwām* ("ᶜAwwām's Advice"). Written by Aḥmad al-ᶜAwwām, a former participant in Egypt's ᶜUrābī revolt, it defended the Mahdīyya as a religiously warranted uprising of "the Sudanese nation" (*umma Sūdānīyya*). It would take a few more years for such discourse to become commonplace in the northern Sudan, but a significant start had been achieved, at least among the Arab Muslim population, in the experience of the Mahdist period.

In his memoir, ᶜAlī al-Mahdī recorded the speech of an Anṣārī who had accompanied a Sudanese delegation to Egypt in 1888:

> They asked me my nationality [*jinsī*], and I told them 'I am one of the Companions of the Mahdī.' They said, 'We would like to know your tribe before the Mahdī. Are you a Jaᶜalī or Shāīqī or what?' I said to them, 'I do not know my tribe before the Mahdī.' So they asked me about my hometown [*baladī*], and I told them 'Umm Durmān, Buqᶜat al-Mahdī.'[5]

APPENDIX

Informants to the Study

^{c}Abbās Aḥmad Muḥammad: Son of Aḥmad Muḥammad "Qadaḥ al-Dām," Mahdist *amīr* and *shaykh* of the Omdurman Fellāta (Fulānī) community during the Condominium; an authority on the Fellāta community; in Omdurman, 1987.

^{c}Abbās Aḥmad ^{c}Umar: Son of a Turco-Egyptian *sanjak* and Mahdist *amīr*; a life-long resident of Abā Island and former aide to Sayyid ^{c}Abd al-Raḥmān al-Mahdī and Imām al-Hādī; on Abā Island, 1987.

^{c}Abd al-Qādir Sharīf ^{c}Abdallāhi ^{c}Abd al-Qādir Maḥmūd: Relative of Khalīfa Muḥammad Sharīf, born ca. 1895 in Omdurman; in Omdurman, 1987.

^{c}Abd al-Raḥmān Isḥāq Khidr: Grandson of Khidr Da^{c}ūd, an Iraqi Jewish trader during the Turco-Egyptian period and a member of the Masālma community during the Mahdīyya; in Omdurman, 1987.

Abūnā Daniel: Archbishop of the Coptic church in Sudan and son of Ibrāhīm Bey Khalīl, a prominent merchant in Turco-Egyptian Khartoum and a member of the Omdurman Masālma community during the Mahdīyya; in Khartoum, 1986.

Aḥmad Makkī ^{c}Arabī: *Khalīfa* of the Rikābīyya Khatmīyya of Omdurman and grandson of al-Fakī ^{c}Arabī Aḥmad ^{c}Abd al-Raḥīm who, together with his brother al-Fakī Makkāwī, brought the Rikābīyya of El Obeid and Bāra to Omdurman during the Mahdīyya; in Omdurman, 1987.

Aḥmad Muḥammad wad Badr Shaykh Aḥmad Sulaymān: *Khalīfa* of the

Qādirīyya in Fitayḥāb and grandson of Shaykh Aḥmad Sulaymān, a Zanarkhī who took the Qādirī *ṭarīqa* from Shaykh Wad Badr of Umm Dubbān; in Fitayḥāb, 1987.

ᶜAlī Ḥasan Jamīl: Dongolāwī born in Omdurman in 1919 to a family of merchants and boat builders who, like the Mahdī's family, had settled during Turco-Egyptian rule near Kararī and collected and shipped wood from Abā Island; in Omdurman, 1987.

ᶜAlī Ṣiddīq and Ḥasan ᶜUmar wad Ūru: Grandsons of Muḥammad Ṣāliḥ wad Ūru, a leader of the Maḥas community of El Obeid during Turco-Egyptian rule, *shaykh* of a Qur'ān school in Mahdist Omdurman and a confidant of the Khalīfa; in Omdurman, 1987.

ᶜAlī Yaᶜqūb al-Khalīfa Ḥilū: Grandson of both Khalīfa ᶜAli and Khalīfa ᶜAbdallāhi (through Ṣāfīyya bint al-Khalīfa) and an authority on the family of Khalīfa ᶜAlī; in Khartoum, 1986–1987.

Allegra Harūsh Basyūnī: Wife of the late Daᶜūd Basyūnī, who was the son of Mūsa Basyūnī (born Moshe Ben Zion), a Jewish merchant during Turco-Egyptian rule and a prominent member of the Masālma community as well as a confidant of the Khalīfa; in Khartoum, 1986–1987.

Āmina bint Farajallāh Yūsuf: Widow of Sayyid ᶜAbd al-Raḥmān al-Mahdī; in Omdurman, 1986–1987.

Farīda bint Isḥāq Isrā'īl: Granddaughter of Isrā'īl Daᶜūd Binyamī, an Egyptian Jewish trader during Turco-Egyptian rule and a member of the Masālma community during the Mahdīyya; in Omdurman, 1987.

Hillāla Ādam Sulaymān: Daughter of Ādam Sulaymān, of "Kunjarī" origin from Kutum in Darfur, who was enslaved during the Mahdīyya and eventually taken into the household of Mūsa Basyūnī; in Khartoum, 1987.

Ibrāhīm Bushrā Abū Kudōk: Grandson of the Mahdist *amīr* Ḥasan Sharaf Abū Kudōk of the Berti; in Omdurman, 1987.

Ibrāhīm Sulaymān and Da^{c}ūd Ādam Mandīl: Grandsons of Da^{c}ūd Mandīl, a Jewish merchant of Algerian origin who was a trader during Turco-Egyptian rule and a member of the Omdurman Masālma community; in Omdurman, 1987.

Isḥāq Muḥammad al-Khalīfa Sharīf: Grandson of both Khalīfa Muḥammad Sharīf and the Mahdī (through Maryam bint al-Mahdī) and an authority on the Mahdī's family; in Omdurman, 1986–1987.

Ismā^{c}īl Ṣāliḥ Da^{c}ūd: Grandson of Da^{c}ūd Ṣāliḥ, an Egyptian from Isnā who traded in El Obeid during Turco-Egyptian rule and settled in Omdurman during the Mahdīyya; in Omdurman, 1987.

^{c}Izz al-Dīn Abū'l-Qāsim Aḥmad Hāshim: Son of the Khalīfa's secretary Abū'l-Qāsim Hāshim and elder member of the Hāshimāb clan; in Omdurman, 1987.

^{c}Izz al-Dīn al-Ḥāfiẓ al-Fakī Muḥammad: Grandson of al-Fakī Muḥammad, the eldest son of Aḥmad Hāshim, founder of the Hāshimāb clan of Berber; in Omdurman, 1987.

al-Jīlānī Khidr ^{c}Abdallāhi: Resident of al-Qōz, from a Khawālda family that has long practiced cultivation and animal husbandry along the White Nile south of Khartoum; in al-Qōz, 1987.

Khālid Aḥmad Sharfī: Son of Aḥmad Sharfī, patriarch of the Mahdī's family and father-in-law of the Mahdī; in Omdurman, 1987.

Muḥammad Aḥmad Ismā^{c}īl: Great-grandson of Muḥammad Wahbī Ḥusayn, the official in charge of the market court and police in Mahdist Omdurman; in Omdurman, 1987.

Muḥammad Da^{c}ūd al-Khalīfa: Grandson of Khalīfa ^{c}Abdallāhi and an authority on the Khalīfa's family; in Khartoum and Omdurman, 1987.

Muḥammad Ibrāhīm al-Nūr: Retired High Court judge born in Jirayf 1901;

son of Ibrāhīm al-Nūr Ḥāmid, an *ᶜāmil* of the Buṭāna region during the Mahdīyya and a confidant of Amīr Yaᶜqūb, descended from the Maḥasī *shaykhs* of Tūtī Island; maternal grandson of the Mahdist *Amīn Bayt al-Māl* al-Nūr Ibrāhīm Jirayfāwī; in Omdurman, 1987.

Muḥammad Yūsuf Ḥamad al-Nīl: Grandson of Shaykh Ḥamad al-Nīl, the Qādirī *shaykh* of the ᶜArakīyīn tribe; in Omdurman, 1987.

Al-Qurashī Muḥammad Ḥasan: Nephew of the Khalīfa Muḥammad Sharīf and an authority on the poetry (*madḥ*) of the Mahdīyya; in Omdurman, 1987.

Ṣādiq Ḥāmid Ḥāmid: Grandson of the Mahdī's brother and Director of the Office of the Anṣār, Abā Island; on Abā Island, 1987.

Ṣādiq al-Mahdī: Former Prime Minister of the Sudan and great-grandson of the Mahdī; in Khartoum, 1987.

Sharīf ᶜAbd al-Raḥmān al-Nujūmī: Son of Amīr ᶜAbd al-Raḥman al-Nujūmī; born pre-1885 in Dongola and raised in Omdurman; in Omdurman, 1987.

Sharīf Maḥmūd Ḥasan: Elder of the Nubian village of Qarīyat al-Kunūz on the White Nile; in al-Kawwa, 1987.

Ṣiddīq Ibrāhīm Mukhayyir: Son of the Mahdist *amīr* Ibrāhīm wad Mukhayyir, *shaykh* of the Zayyādīyya of northern Darfur; in Omdurman, 1987.

Al-Ṭāhir ᶜAbdallāhi al-Nūr: Member of the Danāqla Ashrāf of Qiṭayna along the White Nile and nephew of the Mahdī's wife Ḥaram bint al-Nūr; in Qiṭayna, 1987.

Al-Ṭāhir Muḥammad al-Nayl: A relative of the Mahdī's wife ᶜĀ'isha bint Idrīs and an authority on the history of the Ashrāf; in Omdurman, 1987.

Al-Ṭayyib Muḥammad al-Ṭayyib: An authority on Sudanese folklore and history; in Khartoum, 1986.

Al-Tijānī ᶜAmr: Born in Omdurman in 1911, related to the *amīr* Muḥammad al-Khayr ᶜAbdallāh Khūjalī of the Jaᶜaliyīn; veteran columnist for the newspaper *al-Siyāsa* and author of many articles on Omdurman; an authority on the Mahdīyya in Omdurman; in Khartoum, 1986–1987.

Al-ᶜUmda Yaḥyā Bābikr Sulaymān al-Makk: Grandson of *Makk* Sulaymān, leader of the people of Fitayḥāb during the Mahdīyya; in Fitayḥāb, 1987.

Al-Waṣila al-Sammānī, Ḥasan al-Nūr and Ibrāhīm al-Nūr Shaykh Birayr: Grandsons of Shaykh Birayr, the Jaᶜalī *shaykh* of the Sammānīyya who founded the settlement of Shabasha on the White Nile during the Turco-Egyptian period; in Shabasha, 1987.

Yūsuf Bedrī: Son of Bābikr Bedrī; born in Rufāᶜa in 1912, raised in Rufāᶜa and Omdurman; a 1931 graduate of Gordon Memorial College and long-time headmaster of Aḥfād School; in Omdurman, 1986–1987.

Zakārīyya Ḥannā al-Ṣarrāf: Son of Ḥannā Mikhā'īl, a Coptic Egyptian trader in Sudan during Turco-Egyptian rule and a member of the Masālma community during the Mahdīyya; in Omdurman, 1986.

Zaynab ᶜAbd al-Qādir Bān Naqā: Granddaughter of a Jaᶜalī *shaykh* and an Austrian Catholic woman of the Masālma community, regarded as an authority on Omdurman's history; in Omdurman, 1987.

NOTES

Chapter One

1. John Lewis Burckhardt, *Travels in Nubia* (London: 1822), second edition, 236. Al-Maqrīzī quoted in P. M. Holt, *The Sudan of the Three Niles: The Funj Chronicle* (Leiden: 1999), 153. Jay Spaulding and Stephanie Beswick, "Sex, bondage and the market: the emergence of prostitution in northern Sudan," *Journal of the History of Sexuality*, 5:4 (1995), 516–517. O.G.S. Crawford, *The Fung Kingdom of Sennar* (Gloucester: 1951), 134–142. S. Hillelson, "David Reubeni, an early visitor to Sennar," *S.N.R.*, 16 (1933), 60.

2. For Sinnār and Darfur, see R. S. O'Fahey and J. L. Spaulding, *Kingdoms of the Sudan* (London: 1974); R. S. O'Fahey, *State and Society in Dār Fūr* (London: 1980); and Jay Spaulding, *The Heroic Age in Sinnār* (East Lansing: 1985). The following studies by Spaulding are particularly revealing: "The evolution of the Islamic judiciary in Sinnar," *The International Journal of African Historical Studies,* 10:3 (1977), 408–426; "Slavery, land tenure and social class in the northern Turkish Sudan," *I.J.A.H.S.,* 15:1 (1982), 1–20; and "The misfortunes of some—the advantages of others: land sales by women in Sinnar," in Margaret Jean Hay and Marcia Wright, eds., *African Women and the Law* (Boston: 1982), 3–18. For the socioeconomic developments of the Turco-Egyptian period, see Anders Bjørkelo, *Prelude to the Mahdiyya: Peasants and Traders in the Shendi Region* (Cambridge: 1989).

3. Holt, *Sudan of the Three Niles,* 4. O'Fahey and Spaulding, *Kingdoms*, 32–33, 79–80. Lidwien Kapteijns and Jay Spaulding, "Precolonial trade between states in the eastern Sudan, ca.1700–ca.1900," *African Economic History*, 11 (1982), 36. Jay Spaulding, "The management of exchange in Sinnār, c.1700," in Leif Manger, ed., *Trade and Traders in the Sudan* (Bergen: 1984), 36, 46. Arbajī may in fact have been founded a century later, on the site of an earlier town: Crawford, *The Fung Kingdom*, 68.

4. Crawford, *The Fung Kingdom*, 296, 319–321, 324. Theodoro Krump, *Hoher und fruchtbarer palm-baum des heiligen evangelij* (Augsburg: 1710), 273, 284–

290, trans. Jay Spaulding and available at www.kean.edu/~jspauldi/krump2one.html. James Bruce, *Travels and Adventures in Abyssinia*, ed. J. M. Clingan (Edinburgh: 1860), 307, 313. O'Fahey and Spaulding, *Kingdoms*, 99. Holt, *Sudan of the Three Niles,* 25.

5. O'Fahey and Spaulding, *Kingdoms, passim*. Crawford, *The Fung Kingdom*, 65–69, 296. Krump, *Hoher und fruchtbarer*, 266–267. Bruce, *Travels*, 314–315.

6. Crawford, *The Fung Kingdom*, 61–62. Bruce, *Travels*, 315–316. Burckhardt, *Travels*, 247–289. Bayard Taylor, *A Journey to Central Africa*, tenth edition (New York: 1856), 259–260. For Shendī's history and economy before Turco-Egyptian rule, see Bjørkelo, *Prelude*, 7–33.

7. O'Fahey and Spaulding, *Kingdoms*, 84. Burckhardt, *Travels*, 236–239. Regarding the Majādhīb of al-Dāmir, see Albrecht Hofheinz, "Internalising Islam: Shaykh Muḥammad Majdhūb, scriptural Islam and local context," unpublished doctoral dissertation (University of Bergen: 1996), and especially 2:576–579 for the destruction of al-Dāmir in 1823.

8. Burckhardt, *Travels*, 194–220.

9. O'Fahey and Spaulding, *Kingdoms*, 63–65, 93, 136. The history of Taqalī and its relation to the larger Nile Valley is the subject of Janet Ewald, *Soldiers, Traders and Slaves* (Madison: 1990). For the derivation of the word "Nūba," see *Soldiers*, 48.

10. Ignatius Pallme, *Travels in Kordofan* (London: 1844), 50, 56, 258–277. For the Maghribīn (or Maghārba), see H. A. MacMichael, *A History of the Arabs in the Sudan* (Cambridge: 1922), 1:316–318.

11. Pallme, *Travels*, 186, 267–277, 292–293.

12. O'Fahey and Spaulding, *Kingdoms*, 141, 146, 160–161. For the symbolic significance of the sultan's *fāshir*, see O'Fahey, *State and Society*, 23ff.

13. W. G. Browne, *Travels in Africa, Egypt and Syria* (London: 1799), 234–245, 297.

14. Browne, *Travels*, 236–240, 284–288. O'Fahey, *State and Society*, 139–144.

15. Gustav Nachtigal, *Sahara and Sudan*, trans. A.G.B. Fisher and H. J. Fisher (Berkeley: 1971), volume 4, 251–258. O'Fahey, *State and Society*, 23–28.

16. Crawford, *The Fung Kingdom*, 118–126. Burckhardt, *Travels*, 389–403.

17. Neil McHugh, *Holymen of the Blue Nile* (Evanston: 1994), 85–95, 116–128. El Sayed El-Bushra, "Towns in the Sudan in the 18th and early 19th centuries," *S.N.R.*, 52 (1971), 63–70. O'Fahey, *State and Society*, 26.

18. R. C. Stevenson, "Old Khartoum, 1821–1885," *S.N.R.*, 47 (1966), 1–38.

19. Elias Toniolo and Richard Hill, eds., *The Opening of the Nile Basin* (New York: 1975), 31–33. Taylor, *A Journey*, 269–278.

20. Stevenson, "Old Khartoum." Joseph Churi, *Sea Nile, the Desert and Nigritia* (London: 1853), 130. Toniolo and Hill, *The Opening*, 35–38. J. A. Grant, *Khartoom as I Saw It in 1863* (Edinburgh: 1885), second edition, 10, 24.

Chapter Two

1. Bābikr Bedrī, *Memoirs*, trans. Y. Bedri and G. Scott (London: 1969), 20–21. F. Rehfisch, "A sketch of the early history of Omdurman," *S.N.R.*, 45 (1964), 35–47. Stephanie Beswick, *Sudan's Blood Memory:The Legacy of War, Ethnicity and Slavery* (Rochester, NY: 2004), 18–26. The name "Washal" appears in an elegy written for the Mahdī: Qurashī Muḥammad Ḥasan, *Qaṣā'id min shuᶜarā' al-mahdīyya* (Khartoum: 1974), 290. Additionally, it is mentioned in the memoir of a Coptic eyewitness to the Mahdīyya, Yūsuf Mikhā'īl: Ṣāliḥ Muḥammad Nūr, "A critical edition of the memoirs of Yūsuf Mikhā'īl," unpublished D.Phil thesis (University of London: 1962), 164. On the identity of the ᶜAnaj, see O'Fahey and Spaulding, *Kingdoms*, 29. Rehfisch mentions the idea that Washal was an ᶜAnaj king and Umm Durmān his wife.

2. Muḥammad al-Nūr b. Ḍayfallāh, *Kitāb al-ṭabaqāt fī khuṣūṣ al-awliyā' wa'l-ṣāliḥīn wa'l-ᶜulamā' wa'l-shuᶜarā' fī'l-Sūdān,* third edition, ed. Yūsuf Faḍl Ḥasan (Khartoum: 1985), 288. The Maḥas produced a number of teachers around whom schools and eventually villages were formed. Two of these were in the Khartoum area: Shaykh Idrīs wad al-Arbāb at ᶜAylafūn and Shaykh Khūjalī ᶜAbd al-Raḥmān Ibrāhīm at Tūtī. See Richard A. Lobban, "A genealogical and historical study of the Maḥas of the Three Towns," *S.N.R.*, 61 (1980), 89–109. Well into the nineteenth century villages were being formed in this manner, such as Shabasha on the White Nile settled by the Jaᶜalī *shaykh* al-Birayr wad al-Ḥasīn.

3. W. G. Browne, *Travels*, 180, 459–460. Bayard Taylor, *A Journey,* 371, also mentions Kordofan merchants at Omdurman. Holt, *The Sudan of the Three Niles*, *passim*. Rehfisch, "A sketch." Churi, *Sea Nile*, 138–140.

4. A. E. Hake, ed., *The Journals of Major General C .G. Gordon at Khartoum* (London: 1885), 173. See Ismā^{c}īl b. ^{c}Abd al-Qādir's *Kitāb sa^{c}ādat al-mustahdī bi-sīrat al-Imām al-Mahdī*, ed. M. I. Abū Salīm (Beirut: 1982), 343–345. *Al-Āthār al-Kāmila,* 4:473. P. M. Holt, *The Mahdist State in the Sudan*, second edition (Oxford: 1970), 101.

5. Holt, *Mahdist State*, 104. The Mahdī's family claimed descent from the Hāshimite clan of the Prophet Muḥammad, hence their adoption of the honorific title "Ashrāf."

6. *Al-Āthār al-Kāmila*, 1:124, 4:594, 4:636. Qur'ān 14:44–46, translated by N. J. Dawood, *The Koran*, fifth revised edition (London: 1995), 183. See also M. I. Abū Salīm, *Ta'rīkh al-Kharṭūm* (Beirut: 1979), 84.

7. Gordon, *Journal*, *op.cit*., 160. The Sudanese soldier ^{c}Alī Jifūn recalls in his memoirs that Sayyid Ḥasan al-Mīrghanī (d.1869) had prophesied "the final struggle for supremacy in the Soudan" at Kararī, in which the English would prevail and regenerate the Sudan. See Percy Machell, "Memoirs of a Soudanese Soldier," *Cornhill Magazine* 74/n.s.1 (1896), 338. Charles Neufeld, a German prisoner in Omdurman, writes of Mahdist expectations of a final confrontation at Kararī: *A Prisoner of the Khaleefa* (London: 1899), 260–261. This point is echoed by ^{c}Ismat Ḥasan Zulfō, *Kararī* (Khartoum: 1973), 339–340, 349.

8. Bayard Taylor, *A Journey*, 278–280, noted Khartoum's unhealthiness and said "the opposite bank of the river is considered more healthy." The idea of moving the capital during the Turco-Egyptian era is mentioned by R. W. Felkin in "The Soudan Question," *Contemporary Review,* 74 (1898), 488. See also Richard Hill, *Egypt in the Sudan* (London: 1959), 114.

9. *Daftar al-ṣādir* 2/42.

10. *Daftar al-ṣādir* 2/326, 513, 514, 575.

11. Ibrāhīm al-Būrdayn, "Report on the fall of Khartoum," CAIRINT 1/10/52. Fr. Joseph Ohrwalder claimed that only three days were given to abandon Khartoum, but he refers to the initial order of evacuation, which was enforced upon all Europeans and others of suspect loyalty: F. R. Wingate (from Fr. Ohrwalder), *Ten*

Years' Captivity in the Mahdi's Camp, third edition (London: 1892), 151.

12. F. Rehfisch, "Omdurman during the Mahdiya," *S.N.R.*, 48 (1967), 34.

13. Descriptions of Omdurman are to be found in most of the European memoirs from the Mahdīyya, especially in Rosignoli (ed. Rehfisch, "Omdurman during the Mahdiya") 34 and *passim*. Bennet Burleigh, *Khartoum Campaign 1898* (London: 1899), 130.

14. Interview with al-Tijānī ᶜAmr, 23 December 1986, Khartoum. See Abū Salīm, *Ta'rīkh*, 94, 108. Expeditions going east mobilized at the tomb of Shaykh Khūjalī in Ḥalfayāt al-Mulūk, on the east bank of the main Nile.

15. Similarly, the Mahdist *jihādīyya* at Sinnār lived apart from other troops drawn from the villagers and tribal levies, and their garrison was known as al-Kāra: see *Daftar al-ṣādir* 2/342. Several explanations have been offered for the origin of the name, including French, Turkish, and Sudanese derivations. More simple (and convincing), *Kāra* is the name of an ethnic group in southwestern Darfur and Bahr al-Ghazal that contributed many professional soldiers, and as far back as the Funj sultanate it was common to name a settlement or fortress after its dominant people: Abū Salīm, *Ta'rīkh*, 39. For the practice of military slavery in the Sudan, see Douglas Johnson, "Sudanese military slavery from the eighteenth to the twentieth century," *Slavery and Other Forms of Unfree Labour*, ed. Léonie Archer (London: 1988), 142–156.

16. Rosignoli, *op.cit.*, 38. The Khalīfa wrote to his *amīr* Ḥamdān Abū ᶜAnja of plans to build a wall for the mosque on 14 September 1885 (*Daftar al-ṣādir* 2/426). Egyptian Military Intelligence estimated the mosque to be 1,000 yards by 800 yards: *General Military Report 1890* (London: 1891). Extensive accounts of the prison and its keeper, Idrīs al-Sāyir, are given in the memoirs of the European prisoners. See also Burleigh, *Khartoum Campaign*, 216–226.

17. CAIRINT 1/10/52. *General Military Report 1890* mentions that postal service camels were also kept there. Ibrāhīm Muḥammad ᶜAdlān served as *Amīn Bayt al-Māl* from 1886 to 1890.

18. Market court: *Daftar al-ṣādir* 9/160 and Rosignoli, *op.cit.*, 37. Treasury court: *Daftar al-ṣādir* 13/3/355. See also Holt, *Mahdist State*, 131–132, 261ff. Abū Salīm, *Ta'rīkh*, 104.

19. *Daftar* of ᶜAlī al-Mahdī (MAHDIA 8/10/70), 166ff. See also Naᶜūm Shuqayr,

Ta'rīkh al-Sūdān al-qadīm wa'l-ḥadīth wa jughrāfīyatuhu (Cairo: 1903) 3:534.

20. Holt, *Mahdist State*, 193.

21. Rosignoli, *op.cit.*, 44. Letter of Muḥammad ᶜUthmān Khālid to the Khalīfa (MAHDIA 2/20/1/15). Ibrāhīm Fawzī, *al-Sūdān bayna yadāy Ghurdūn wa Kitshanir* (Cairo: 1901), 2:200–204.

22. Rosignoli, *op.cit.*, 42.

23. Abū Salīm, *Ta'rīkh*, 86ff., Shuqayr, *Ta'rīkh*, 3:528.

24. Bābikr Bedrī, *Memoirs*, 222. The role of F. R. Grenfell, Sirdar of the Egyptian army, in planting the idea of the Khalīfa's treachery in the minds of Sudanese is discussed by ᶜAbd al-Wahhāb Aḥmad ᶜAbd al-Raḥmān in *Ṭūshkī* (Khartoum: 1979), 154–162.

25. Rosignoli, *op.cit.*, 40. Bābikr Bedrī, *Memoirs*, 144–145. The Khalīfa's involvement in the economy follows the precedent of earlier Sudanic kingdoms: See O'-Fahey and Spaulding, *Kingdoms*, 54ff, 160ff. Abū Salīm, *Ta'rīkh*, 86.

26. *General Report on the Egyptian Soudan 1895* (London: 1895), 9, states that the *mulāzimīn* enclosure measured 900 yards by 1,500 yards.

27. Two chief judges were arrested and executed at this time, Aḥmad ᶜAlī in 1894 and Ḥusayn Ibrāhīm wad al-Zahrā in 1895. Between 1892 and 1897, three men headed the *Bayt al-Māl*: al-Nūr Ibrāhīm Jirayfāwī (1889–1892), al-ᶜAwaḍ al-Marḍī (1893–1896 and three months in 1897), and Ibrāhīm Ramaḍān (1896–1897).

28. Rosignoli, *op.cit.*, 58–59. *General Report 1895*, 4, 9–10.

29. Bābikr Bedrī, *Memoirs*, 222. The other two events were the fall of Dongola in 1896 and the massacre of the Jaᶜaliyīn at Matamma in 1897.

30. P. M. Holt, ed. and trans., *Calendar of Correspondence of the Khalifa Abdullahi and Mahmud Ahmad* (Khartoum: 1950 [sic: 1956]), 25 n.39, 80 n.280, 120 n.411.

31. Bābikr Bedrī, *Memoirs*, 226. *Sudan Intelligence Report No.60* (Cairo: 1898), 47–48.

32. See for example the Mahdī's letter to Muḥammad al-Ṭayyib al-Baṣīr: *al-Āthār al-Kāmila*, 1:15. Holt, *Mahdist State*, 54. For the concept of *hijra* in the West

African *jihād* movements, see the treatise by ᶜUthmān ibn Fūdī (Usumān dan Fōdio), *Bayān wujūb al-hijra ᶜala'l-ᶜibād,* ed. and trans. F. H. El Masri (Khartoum: 1978).

33. See for example *al-Āthār al-Kāmila*, 1:139. John O. Voll, "The Mahdi's Concept and Use of *Hijra*," *Islamic Studies*, 26:1 (1987), 31–32.

34. Interview with al-Ṭāhir ᶜAbdallāhi al-Nūr, 16 July 1987, Qiṭayna. *Intelligence Report Egypt* (I.R.E.), no.1,2,4 (1892).

35. Interviews with ᶜIzz al-Dīn al-Ḥāfiẓ Muḥammad Aḥmad Hāshim, October 1987, Omdurman and ᶜAlī al-Ṣiddīq Muḥammad Ṣāliḥ wad Ūru, April–October 1987, Omdurman. Yūsuf Mikhā'īl, *Memoirs*, 178–180.

36. Invitations to *hijra* are contained in the *Dafātir al-ṣādir*, 1–6. For the settlement of disputes and hearing of complaints, see for example 2/219, 2/232, 2/288.

37. *Daftar al-ṣādir* 3/4.

38. *Daftar al-ṣādir* 10/133, 134. The letters of 1304 are addressed mainly, though not exclusively, to the Arab tribes of the west. See the *Dafātir al-ṣādir* 10–11.

39. From Aḥmad ᶜAlī to al-Nujūmi, 1 Rajab 1304, in the papers of the *Qāḍī al-Islām* (MAHDIA 1/42/5). Ewald, *Soldiers*, 118–129.

40. *Al-Āthār al-Kāmila*, 4:594, 5:783. *Daftar al-ṣādir* 2/247, 2/428, 11/61, 11/178.

41. Ibrāhīm al-Būrdayn, "Report on the fall of Khartoum," CAIRINT 1/10/52.

42. Letters of safe conduct are found throughout the *Dafātir al-ṣādir.* See for example *Daftar al-ṣādir* 2/545.

43. H. A. MacMichael, *The Tribes of Northern and Central Kordofan* (Cambridge: 1912), 43–44. Gordon, *Journal, op.cit.*, 221. MAHDIA 2/26/2/27, 2/26/2/33 and 8/10/70.

44. MAHDIA 2/3/2/31, 2/3/3/12, 2/77/22.

45. MAHDIA 2/2/1/2, 2/3/3/2. Bābikr Bedrī, *Memoirs*, 213–215.

46. MAHDIA 2/1/1/6. *Daftar al-ṣādir* 2/229, 301. Bābikr Bedrī, *Memoirs*, 196.

47. *General Report 1895,* 24. Ibrāhīm Fawzī, *al-Sūdān*, 2:82. CAIRINT 1/17/97/1. Interview with ᶜAlī Ṣiddīq wad Ūru, 24 April 1987, Omdurman.

48. Holt, *Mahdist State*, 104. Muḥammad ᶜUthmān Khālid to the Khalīfa, April 1897 (MAHDIA 2/27/80). Interviews with al-Jīlāni Khidr ᶜAbdallāhi, November 1987, al-Qōz.

49. Ibrāhīm al-Būrdayn, "Report," *op.cit.* Sir William Garstin, *Report on the Soudan*, Command Paper, Egypt n.5 (London: 1899). Bābikr Bedrī, *Memoirs*, 141–142. Bjørkelo, *Prelude*, 82 ff. and 137–147.

50. Muḥammad Saᶜīd al-Qaddāl, *al-Sīyāsa al-iqtiṣādīyya li'l-dawla al-Mahdīyya* (Khartoum: 1986), 80ff. *Daftar al-ṣādir* 2/304, 404, 490; 3/31; 6/18. Holt, *Mahdist State*, 176. MAHDIA 1/42/5.

51. MAHDIA 2/8/1/108, 2/20/3/67. Apparently Sudanese also made the *ziyāra* to Abā Island, birthplace of the Mahdīyya, at this time: Interview with al-Ṭayyib Muḥammad al-Ṭayyib, 17 November 1986, Khartoum.

52. MAHDIA 2/6/2/68, 2/8/2/79. Qurashī Muḥammad Ḥasan, *Qaṣā'id*, 297. Wad Sūrkattī's removal of his shoes is reminiscent of the ritual before entering the Keira sultan's *fāshir*: See Nachtigal, *Sahara and Sudan*, 4:258.

53. Qurashī Muḥammad Ḥasan, *Qaṣā'id*, 167 and MAHDIA 2, *passim*. See also Ibrāhīm Fawzī, *al-Sūdān*, 2:25, 292.

54. MAHDIA 2/21/2/71, CAIRINT 1/20/113, 3/10/190.

55. *General Military Report on the Egyptian Sudan, 1891* (London: 1892), 16. Bābikr Bedrī, *Memoirs*, 61. Bennett Burleigh, *Khartoum Campaign 1898* (London: 1899), 237.

56. Qurashī Muḥammad Ḥasan, *Qaṣā'id*, 116–117. Interview with ᶜAbd al-Qādir Sharīf ᶜAbdallāh, April 1987, Omdurman. MAHDIA 2/16/2/30, 2/17/2/18, 2/18/2/58, 2/19/1/8, 2/27/80. For the tradition of the Ṣūfī *khalwa* as a place of healing, see ᶜAlī Ṣāliḥ Karrār, *The Sufi Brotherhoods in the Sudan* (Evanston: 1992), 140ff. O'Fahey and Spaulding, *Kingdoms*, 42–43.

57. INTEL 2/41/341/21. Bābikr Bedrī, *Memoirs*, 224, 236ff.

58. Holt, *Mahdist State*, 254. Lord Cromer, *Report on the Finances, Administration and Conditions of Egypt and Sudan, 1904* (London: 1905), 115.

59. Gordon estimated the Khartoum population at 34,000 in Sept. 1884: *Journal*, 8, 171. The figure of 30,000 was given at the trial of Ḥasan Bey Bahnasāwī in

1887: CAIRINT 1/14/86.

60. CAIRINT 1/4/20, 1/8/38. Ibrāhīm Fawzī, *al-Sūdān*, 2:2. Rosignoli, *op.cit.*, 34, 42. Wingate (Ohrwalder), *Ten Years' Captivity,* 283. *General Report 1890*, 17. *General Report 1895*, 3.

61. F. R. Wingate (Rudolf C. Slatin), *Fire and Sword in the Sudan*, second edition (London: 1896), 421, 455. Shuqayr, *Ta'rīkh* 3:454, 534. Wingate (Ohrwalder), *Ten Years' Captivity*, 225, 283. Yūsuf Mikhā'īl, *Memoirs*, 173. *General Report 1895*, 6. MAHDIA 8/10/70. Ibrāhīm Fawzī, *al-Sūdān*, 2:200. CAIRINT 1/13/87.

62. Neufeld, *A Prisoner*, 139. MAHDIA 2/1/3/1, 2/3/2/43, 2/3/3/12, 2/17/1/20. F. Rehfisch, "An Unrecorded Population Count of Omdurman," *S.N.R.*, 46 (1965), 33–39.

63. Taj Hargey, "The suppression of slavery in the Sudan, 1898–1939," unpublished D.Phil. thesis (Oxford: 1981), 5–16, 52–70. Hargey estimates that there were 75,000 slaves in the city in 1898. Wingate (Ohrwalder), *Ten Years' Captivity*, 386. Bayard Taylor, *A Journey*, 278. Richard Hill, *Egypt in the Sudan,* 161–162.

64. CAIRINT 3/10/190, 1/10/52, 1/16/96. *General Report 1890*, 17. *General Report 1891*, 7. Rosignoli, *op.cit.*, 38. Aḥmad wad Saᶜd statement in Yaḥya Muḥammad Ibrāhīm, *Ta'rīkh al-taᶜlīm al-dīnī fī'l-Sūdān* (Beirut:1987), 433–434.

65. *Sudan Intelligence Report* n.60 (May–December 1898), 52. Muḥammad ᶜAbd al-Raḥīm, *Al-Nidā' fī dafᶜ al-iftirā'* (Cairo: 1953), 255–256. Giffen, *Egyptian Sudan*, 67. W. H. McLean, *The Planning of Khartoum and Omdurman* (London: 1911). Ḥasan Zakī account: SAD 407/6/1–14.

66. MAHDIA 2/3/3.

67. *S.I.R.* 60, 54–58, 70–74 and CAIRINT 1/63/328.

Chapter Three

1. Bābikr Bedrī, *Memoirs*, 31, 213, 228. Wingate (Slatin), *Fire and Sword*, 522. *Daftar al-ṣādir* 11/231.

2. Burleigh, *Khartoum Campaign*, 239–40.

3. MAHDIA 1/42/11/1 and 7. A defective version of this list is given in *S.I.R.* 60,

54. Holt, *Mahdist State*, 244ff.

4. Zulfō, *Kararī*, 10. Ḥusayn Sīd Aḥmad al-Muftī, *Taṭawwur niẓām al-qaḍā' fī'l-mahdīyya* (Khartoum: 1959), 134, 144. Interview with [c]Abbās Aḥmad Muḥammad, 13 October 1987, Omdurman.

5. Yūsuf Mikhā'īl, *Memoirs*, 219. Bābikr Bedrī, *Memoirs*, 214, 238.

6. *S.I.R.* 60, 44–48, and Zulfō, *Kararī*, 130–150.

7. Yūsuf Mikhā'īl, *Memoirs*, 147, 168. *Daftar al-ṣādir* 11/135. *Al-Āthār al-Kāmila*, 4:476.

8. Wingate (Ohrwalder), *Ten Year's Captivity*, 46, 360, and Wingate (Slatin), *Fire and Sword*, 293, 577. Yūsuf Mikhā'īl, *Memoirs*, 189–191. Rosignoli, *op.cit.*, 56.

9. Ḥusayn Sīd Aḥmad, *Taṭawwur,* 152–153. CAIRINT 1/40/242. Rosignoli, *op.cit.*, 38, 61.

10. Zulfō, *Kararī*, 543. Ya[c]qūb Abū Zaynab survived Kararī, was wounded at Umm Dibaykarāt and died in Omdurman some years later. Bābikr Bedrī, *Memoirs*, 235.

11. Holt, *Mahdist State*, 160ff. PMH 1/4/84, 109. *Daftar al-ṣādir* 2/379–380; 5/52–53. MacMichael, *Tribes*, 125–128. *Al-Āthār al-Kāmila*, 5:910. Interviews with Khalīfa Aḥmad Makkī [c]Arabī, 11 October 1987, Omdurman; Muḥammad Yūsuf Ḥamad al-Nīl, 14 October 1987, Omdurman; Ṣiddīq Ibrāhīm Mukhayyir, 9 October 1987, Omdurman. Yūsuf Mikhā'īl, *Memoirs*, 100ff. R. Dekmejian and M. Wyszomirski, "Charismatic leadership in Islam: The Mahdi of the Sudan," *Comparative Studies in Society and History,* 14 (1972), 193–214. The authors rely exclusively on R. L. Hill's *Biographical Dictionary of the Sudan* (London: 1967), second edition, a work that did not claim to be comprehensive—indeed, many significant figures from the Mahdīyya are missing from it. Additionally, the categories "merchants," "slave traders," and religious leaders" are not mutually exclusive in Sudan's history.

12. [c]Alī Ṣāliḥ Karrār, *The Sufi Brotherhoods*. Lidwien Kapteijns, "The religious background of the Mahdi," *African Perspectives*, 2 (1976).

13. *General Report 1890,* 15. *I.R.E.* 32 (1894). SAD 430/6/4. MAHDIA 2/8/2/11. Interview with Khalīfa Aḥmad Makkī [c]Arabī, 11 October 1987, Omdurman. Bābikr Bedrī, *Memoirs*, 170–171. Wingate (Ohrwalder), *Ten Years' Captivity,* 359.

14. Muḥammad al-Makkī was *khalīfa* of his father, the founder of the Ismāʿīlīyya *ṭarīqa*, which was an offshoot of the Khatmīyya. Among the Hāshimāb with Tijānī connections were Abū'l-Qāsim Aḥmad Hāshim, his brother al-Ṭayyib, their cousin the *amīr* ʿAbd al-Ḥalīm Musāʿid, and Muddathir Ibrāhīm al-Ḥajjāz. Interview with al-Ṭayyib Muḥammad al-Ṭayyib, 17 November 1986, Khartoum. Bābikr Bedrī, *Memoirs, passim.*

15. R. Hill, *Egypt in the Sudan*, 49. Cf. SAD 404/10/1–22.

16. *Daftar al-ṣādir* 6/6. Bābikr Bedrī, *Memoirs*, 184, 202. Cambridge Ms. Or. 234. MAHDIA 2/19/1/28.

17. CAIRINT 3/10/197 and MAHDIA 1/43. Interview with Zaynab ʿAbd al-Qādir Bān Naqā, 10 May 1987, Omdurman.

18. Holt, *Mahdist State*, 251. Wingate (Slatin), *Fire and Sword*, 408 and *General Report 1895*, 29. *Daftar al-ṣādir* 2/142, 226, 500, 11/108. MAHDIA 1/35, 2/6/4/12, 2/8/3/28, 2/17/2/27, 2/20/2/43, 2/78/22.

19. Wingate (Ohrwalder), *Ten Years' Captivity*, 224, 297, 304.

20. Shuqayr, *Ta'rīkh*, 3:608. Wingate (Ohrwalder), *Ten Years' Captivity*, 61. Interview with Sharīf al-Nujūmī, 25 September 1987, Omdurman. Yūsuf Mikhā'īl, *Memoirs*, 187–188.

21. Shuqayr, *Ta'rīkh* 3:553, 627. Hearing complaints (*naẓr al-maẓālim*) is a traditional prerogative of the ruler in an Islamic state. See R. Levy, *The Social Structure of Islam* (Cambridge: 1957), 347–350. Perhaps more relevant, it was also the practice in Sinnār: see Krump, *op.cit.*, 300. Interview with Allegra Basyūnī, 8 December 1986, Khartoum. Holt, *Mahdist State*, 251 and Wingate (Ohrwalder), *Ten Years' Captivity*, 301. Yūsuf Mikhā'īl, *Memoirs*, 221–222.

22. Rosignoli, *op.cit.*, 38–39.

23. Wingate (Ohrwalder), *Ten Years' Captivity*, 275–77.

24. Wingate (Slatin), *Fire and Sword*, 430. Collective responsibility, an important feature of Mahdist teaching, was significantly also the practice in Sinnār: see Spaulding, "Taxation," 130, and Spaulding and Beswick, "Sex, bondage," 517.

25. Qaddāl, *al-Siyāsa*, 161–193. Holt, *Mahdist State*, 252. Al-Nūr Ibrāhīm Jirayfāwī was three-quarters Maḥasī (both maternal grandparents were Maḥas of

Tūtī Island and his paternal grandmother was a Maḥasīyya), but his paternal grandfather was from the region of Dār Ṣilayḥ (Wadai) in the central Sudan. He was born and raised in Jirayf Nūrī above Dongola, from where he got his name. He is often misidentified as "Takrūrī" or Shāīqī. Interview with Muḥammad Ibrāhīm al-Nūr, 28 September 1987, Omdurman.

26. MAHDIA 1/43 and *S.I.R.* 60, 54–58, 64. Holt, *Mahdist State*, 252–254.

27. Wingate (Slatin), *Fire and Sword*, 544–546, and Ḥusayn Sīd Aḥmad, *Taṭawwur*, 133, 139–147.

28. *Daftar al-ṣādir* 13/3/355 and MAHDIA 1/43.

29. Mahdist *jihādīyya* were not the first slave soldiers to misuse their authority for extortion: Cf. Holt, *Sudan of the Three Niles*, 126. MAHDIA 2/7/4/44. Bābikr Bedrī, *Memoirs*, 217–218.

30. Rosignoli, *op.cit.*, 37–38. Interview with Muḥammad Aḥmad Ismāᶜīl, 7 June 1987, Omdurman. Ḥusayn Sīd Aḥmad, *Taṭawwur*, 177–181. M. I. Abū Salīm, "*Al-Būlīs fi'l-mahdīyya,*" *Majallat al-Būlīs* (July: 1966), 33–34. Wingate (Ohrwalder), *Ten Years' Captivity*, 339–40. Ḥusayn Sīd Aḥmad writes of the "*maḥkamat al-muḥtasib,*" which strictly speaking is incorrect since there was no official by that name in Omdurman, although such a title is true to the spirit of Muḥammad Wahbī's office. *I.R.E.*, 41 (1895) names one Ḥasan Khalīl as "head of the market," presumably replacing Muḥammad Wahbī.

31. Wingate (Slatin), *Fire and Sword*, 570. PMH 1/1/16.

32. MAHDIA 1/42/12, 1/43 and *S.I.R.* 60, 58.

33. *Daftar al-ṣādir* 2/268–269, 507. Interview with Allegra Basyūnī, 14 March 1987, Khartoum.

34. *Daftar al-ṣādir* 2/14, 516–517 and Ḥusayn Sīd Aḥmad, *Taṭawwur*, 177–181. *Al-Āthār al-Kāmila*, 5:864. Interview with Muḥammad Yūsuf Ḥamad al-Nīl, 14 October 1987, Omdurman. Aḥmad al-Rayyiḥ was likely a descendant of Muḥammad Madanī Dushayn (*fl.* 1680), the founder of Wad Madani.

35. *General Report 1895*, 9. Wingate (Ohrwalder), *Ten Years' Captivity*, 304. Report of Major Penton, Principal Medical Officer, *Report on the Finances, Administration, and Condition of Egypt and the Soudan, 1899* (London: 1900), 53–54. SAD 646/4/1–83, 679/2/1–88. Samuel Baker, *The Albert N'yanza: Great Basin of*

the Nile (London: 1888), reprint of the 1866 edition, 7.

36. *Al-Āthār al-Kāmila*, 5:822. *Daftar al-ṣādir* 10/183 and CAIRINT 1/13/87.

37. J. B. Christopherson, "Description of Sudanese native remedies in the Mahdi's and Khalifa's time in Omdurman," typescript, 1907, SAD 407/6/1–28. PMH 1/4/10.

38. Christopherson, *op.cit.* Yūsuf Mikhā'īl, *Memoirs*, 168.

39. Wingate (Ohrwalder), *Ten Years' Captivity*, 289, 304, and Wingate (Slatin), *Fire and Sword*, 455. Interview with Ibrāhīm Sulaymān Mandīl, 15 September 1987, Omdurman. Fr. Rolleri comments upon the water-filled "holes and ditches" in Khartoum in 1881, also caused by home building: *op.cit.*, 42.

40. *General Report 1895*, 10. Interviews with al-Tijānī ᶜAmr, 23 December 1986, Khartoum and ᶜAbbās Aḥmad Muḥammad, 13 October 1987, Omdurman.

41. Abū Salīm, "*al-Būlīs*." Interview with al-Tijānī ᶜAmr, 23 December 1986, Khartoum. ᶜAlī al-Mahdī, *Daftar*, 171. Shuqayr, *Tā'rīkh*, 3:649. Interview with Sharīf al-Nujūmī, 19 June 1987, Omdurman.

Chapter Four

1. Bābikr Bedrī, *Memoirs*, 194. Shuqayr, *Ta'rīkh* 3:139. Other versions of the Mahdī's oath (*bayᶜa*), slightly different in wording although similar in meaning, are given in the accounts of Wingate (Slatin), *Fire and Sword*, 288–289, and Bābikr Bedrī, *Memoirs,* 29.

2. Shuqayr, *Ta'rīkh* 3:366–371, and *al-Āthār al-Kāmila*, 1:91, 5:806.

3. Arabic: *al-Rīf*, literally "countryside." In Sudan it referred specifically to Egypt, and Egyptians were known as *Awlād al-Rīf.* Since the Mahdī is warning against the allure of material comforts, "civilization" seems an appropriate translation.

4. *Al-Āthār al-Kāmila*, 1:108.

5. See Soad el-Fatih, "The teachings of Muhammad Ahmad, the Sudanese Mahdi," unpublished M.A. thesis (University of London: 1961), and Aharon Layish, "The

legal methodology of the Mahdī in the Sudan, 1881–1885," *Sudanic Africa,* 8 (1997), 37–66. Needless to say, the Mahdī's status *as Mahdī* implies that his practice, his *Sunna*, transcends ordinary jurisprudence.

6. Ibrāhīm Fawzī, *al-Sūdān*, 1:225–229, 2:8. *Al-Āthār al-Kāmila*, 1:76, 1:158, 2:244, 3:350. Bābikr Bedrī, *Memoirs*, 33–34. Shuqayr claims the Mahdī forbid the wearing of gold and silver, *Ta'rīkh*, 364–366.

7. The Mahdī was certainly not the first Sudanese leader to regulate bride prices: for the sumptuary laws of Sinnār, see Spaulding, *The Heroic Age,* 104ff., and Spaulding and Beswick, "Sex, bondage," 517.

8. Griselda al-Tayyib, "An illustrated record of Sudanese national costumes," unpublished M.A. thesis (Khartoum University: 1976). This style of shaven head, known as a *jabana* after the coffee pot it resembled, is visible in a sketch made of the slain *Amīr* ᶜAbd al-Raḥmān al-Nujūmī at Tūshkī: Wingate (Ohrwalder), *Ten Years' Captivity*, 264. *Al-Āthār al-Kāmila*, 5:995.

9. Soad el-Fatih, *op.cit.*, 178.

10. Interview with Āmina bint Farajallāh Yūsuf, 1987, Omdurman. *Al-Āthār al-Kāmila*, 5:947, 7:4d.

11. *Al-Āthār al-Kāmila,* 3:325, 3:359, 5:905. Aḥmad Ibrāhīm Abū Shouk and Anders Bjørkelo, eds. and trans., *The Public Treasury of the Muslims: Monthly Budgets of the Mahdist State in the Sudan, 1897* (Leiden: 1996), xiv and *passim.*

12. Interviews with Isḥāq Muḥammad al-Khalīfa Sharīf, 1987, Omdurman. The Anṣār's development of a new explanation in response to a situation of "cognitive dissonance" is typical of millennial communities across time and space: See for example Eugen Weber, *Apocalypses* (Cambridge, MA: 1999).

13. Bābikr Bedrī, *Memoirs*, 213). Holt, *Mahdist State*, 253–254. See also P. M. Holt, "Modernization and reaction in the 19th century Sudan," in W. Polk and R. Chambers, eds., *The Beginnings of Modernization in the Middle East* (Chicago: 1968).

14. Rosignoli, *op.cit.*, 45. Wingate (Slatin), *Fire and Sword*, 526, 577. Wingate (Ohrwalder), *Ten Years' Captivity*, 297. Interview with Sharīf ᶜAbd al-Raḥmān al-Nujūmī, 19 June 1987, Omdurman. Interview with ᶜAlī Ṣiddīq wad Ūru, 24 April 1987, Omdurman. The *amīr* ᶜAbd al-Ḥalīm Musāᶜid had a similar policy in

Dongola, requiring the suspect Qarārīsh men to attend mosque prayers five times a day "or else be considered spies and executed": Bābikr Bedrī, *Memoirs*, 45.

15. MAHDIA 2/15/1/9. *Al-Āthār al-Kāmila*, 4:538. Interview with Isḥāq Muḥammad al-Khalīfa Sharīf, 18 September 1987, Omdurman. See also Wingate (Slatin), *Fire and Sword*, 548, and Ibrāhīm Fawzī, *al-Sudan*, 2:78. Bābikr Bedrī, *Memoirs*, 160.

16. *Al-Āthār al-Kāmila*, 2:287, 3:326, 3:437. *Daftar al-ṣādir* 3/99, 11/243. Interview with Khalīfa Aḥmad wad Badr, 21 October 1987, Fitayḥāb. Interview with Khalīfa Aḥmad Makkī ᶜArabī, 11 October 1987, Omdurman. Al-Tijānī ᶜAmr, *Darāwīsh wa firsān* (Khartoum: n.d.), 40.

17. Rosignoli, *op.cit.*, 51ff. Interview with ᶜAlī Ṣiddīq wad Ūru, 24 April 1987, Omdurman. Holt, *Mahdist State*, 51. CAIRINT 11/1/23. *S.I.R.* 60, 63.

18. *General Military Report 1895*, 24–25. Muḥammad ᶜAbd al-Raḥīm, *Nafathāt al-yarāᶜ fī'l-ādab wā'l-ta'rīkh wā'l-ijtimāᶜ* (Khartoum: 1931), 1. MAHDIA 1/42. *Al-Āthār al-Kāmila*, 1:58, 1:160, 4:552, 5:863, 5:940, 5:944. Bābikr Bedrī, *Memoirs*, 158, 195, 225–226. *Daftar al-ṣādir* 2/225. The map of Omdurman at the end of Ohrwalder's *Ten Years' Captivity* includes "European Book Shops" (#102). The map, prepared by E.M.I., was drawn "from descriptions given by natives and revised by Fr. Ohrwalder."

19. Interview with Sharīf ᶜAbd al-Raḥmān al-Nujūmī, 19 June 1987, Omdurman. Interview with Isḥāq Muḥammad al-Khalīfa Sharīf, 17 October 1986, Omdurman.

20. Testimony of the Mahdist poet Aḥmad wad Saᶜd, in Yaḥyā Muḥammad Ibrāhīm, *Ta'rīkh al-taᶜlīm al-dīnī*, 433–434. Interview with al-Khalīfa Aḥmad Makkī ᶜArabī, 11 October 1987, Omdurman.

21. Ḥusayn Sīd Aḥmad, *Taṭawwur*, 146. *Al-Āthār al-Kāmila*, 3:331. Wingate (Ohrwalder), *Ten Years' Captivity*, 299, 401.

22. Qurashī Muḥammad Ḥasan, *Qaṣā'id*, 16, 116–117 and *passim*. *Al-Āthār al-Kāmila*, 3:308, 4:495, 5:949. Qurashī Muḥammad Ḥasan, "*Al-Madkhal ilā shiᶜr al-thawra al-Mahdīyya*," unpublished article. Bābikr Bedrī, *Memoirs*, 202, 228. "Khalīfat al-Fārūq" refers to ᶜAlī wad Ḥilū and "Khalīfat al-Karrār" refers to Muḥammad Sharīf.

23. MAHDIA 2/10/1/51, 56 and 2/78/55. Yūsuf Mikhā'īl, *Memoirs*, 22, 28. Wingate (Slatin), *Fire and Sword*, 577. Interview with Abūnā Daniel, 30 October 1986, Khartoum.

24. Burckhardt, *Travels*, 201. Spaulding and Beswick, "Sex, bondage," 525–527. Spaulding, "Misfortunes," 7ff. Neufeld, *A Prisoner*, 136. Ibrāhīm Fawzī, *al-Sūdān*, 2:173–175. Bābikr Bedrī, *Memoirs*, 178, 180, 219 and *passim*. *S.I.R.*, 85 (1901). For a discussion of European views of the Mahdīyya and its morality, see Norman Daniel, *Islam, Europe and Empire* (Edinburgh: 1966), 416–458.

25. E. S. Stevens, *My Sudan Year* (London: 1912), 97. *Al-Āthār al-Kāmila*, 1:76. Neufeld, *A Prisoner*, 189. Wingate (Ohrwalder), *Ten Years' Captivity*, 342. Bābikr Bedrī, *Memoirs*, 33. Interview with Allegra Basyūnī, 8 December, Khartoum.

26. *Daftar al-ṣādir* 3/100, 11/33, 11/229, 246. Holt, *Calendar*, 63 n.222. MAHDIA 2/2/1/2, 2/6/1/45. PMH 1/4/73. Bābikr Bedrī, *Memoirs*, 40.

27. *Daftar al-ṣādir* 6/4.

28. CAIRINT 11/1/23. This work is deemed a forgery since no part of it is included in A. J. Wensinck's *Concordance et indices de la tradition Musulmane*, 7 vol. (Leiden: 1936–1939). A version of it was current in Hausaland during the reign of Muḥammad Bello (1817–1837), son and successor of Usumān dan Fōdio, and can be found in the ᶜUmar Falke Collection at Northwestern University's Africana Library. Interestingly, *another* version of this Ḥadīth was cited by Bello in his *Kitāb al-naṣīḥa* (1836) as a justification for women's leadership roles in the Sokoto state: See Jean Boyd, *The Caliph's Sister: Nana Asma'u* (London: 1989), 42. For the socioeconomic developments in Sudan that such a work justifies, see Lidwien Kapteijns, "Islamic rationales for the changing social roles of women in the western Sudan," in M. W. Daly (ed), *Modernization in the Sudan* (New York: 1985), and Spaulding, "The misfortunes of some."

29. Interviews with ᶜAbd al-Qādir Sharīf ᶜAbdallāhi, 21 April 1987, Omdurman; al-Tijānī ᶜAmr, 23 December 1986, Khartoum; Muḥammad Aḥmad Ismāᶜīl, 7 June 1987, Omdurman; and Sharīf ᶜAbd al-Raḥmān al-Nujūmī, 11 July 1987, Omdurman. Qaddāl, *al-Siyāsa al-Iqtiṣādīyya*, 79, 176. Wingate (Ohrwalder), *Ten Years' Captivity*, 282–283, 380, 399.

30. Interview with al-Ṭāhir ᶜAbdallāhi al-Nūr, 16 July 1987, Qiṭayna. CAIRINT 1/13/81, 1/40/246. Shuqayr, *Ta'rīkh*, 3:580. Bābikr Bedrī, *Memoirs*, 61ff. Holt, *Calendar*, 36 n.99. See also William Adams, *Nubia: Corridor to Africa* (Princeton: 1977), and P. L. Shinnie, *Meroe, a Civilization of the Sudan* (New York: 1967). O'Fahey and Spaulding, *Kingdoms*, 150. On campaign with al-Nujūmī in 1889, Bābikr Bedrī was accompanied by his mother, his married sister and her small daughters, his 12-year-old sister, his two half-sisters, and his stepmother.

31. Yūsuf Mikhā'īl, *Memoirs*, 227. Rosignoli, *op.cit.*, 48–49. MAHDIA 2/15/1/87, 2/26/2/39. Interview with Allegra Basyūnī, 14 March 1987, Khartoum. The Funqur (Fongoro) and Bagirma are ethnic groups from the central Sudanic region. W. G. Browne (*Travels*, 291) noted a similar situation in Darfur: "But though the Sultan hath just published an ordinance (March 1795) forbidding the use of that liquor under pain of death, the plurality, though less publicly than before, still indulge themselves in it."

32. Wingate (Slatin), *Fire and Sword*, 521. Wingate (Ohrwalder), *Ten Years' Captivity*, 381. S.A.D. 232/1/406. Griselda al-Tayyib, "An illustrated record." MAHDIA 2/15/1/42. Interviews with ᶜAlī Yaᶜqūb al-Khalīfa Ḥilū, 1986–1987, Khartoum, and Isḥāq Muḥammad al-Khalīfa Sharīf, 1986–1987, Omdurman.

33. CAIRINT 1/40/240. *I.R.E.* 43:4, 5:3. Interview with ᶜAbd al-Qādir Sharīf ᶜAbdallāhi, 21 April 1987, Omdurman. Shuqayr, *Ta'rīkh*, 3:354. Ibrāhīm Fawzī, *al-Sūdān*, 2:59.

34. Wingate (Ohrwalder), *Ten Years' Captivity*, 17, 333. Rosignoli, *op.cit.*, 54. Bābikr Bedrī, *Memoirs*, 138–140.

35. Shuqayr, *Ta'rīkh*, 3:373. *I.R.E.* 24:5. Bābikr Bedrī, *Memoirs*, 146, 215. The rift between the riverain and western Sudanese is the subject of Muḥammad Sayyid Dā'ūd, "*Al-Ṣirāᶜ baynā awlād al-balad wa awlād al-ᶜArab fī ᶜahd al-Khalīfa ᶜAbdallāhi, 1885–1898*," unpublished M.A. thesis (Khartoum University: 1971). See also Muḥammad Maḥjūb Mālik, *al-Muqāwama al-dākhilīyya li-ḥarakat al-Mahdīyya* (Beirut: 1987).

36. I.e., the legal complications arising from this forced intermarriage could be settled within each affected *rāya* by its own authorities.

37. ᶜAbd al-Wahhāb Aḥmad b. al-Ḥājj al-Amīn, *Sayf al-mujāhidīn al-ḥāsim fī aᶜnāq al-mulḥidīn*, 2:144–146, MAHDIA 8/11/71. E.M.I. noted this attempt by the Khalīfa in a monthly intelligence report, *I.R.E.*, 14 (May 1893), 3. (In that account, the Khalīfa intends to marry 3,000 women of the *awlād al-balad* to the Taᶜāīsha.) The Khalīfa's choice of his brother Yaᶜqūb to collect the Baqqāra women was likely due to his position as commander of the Black Standard. Al-Badawī Muḥammad Aḥmad al-ᶜIrayq was a Jaᶜalī notable and former *Sirr al-tujjār* at El Obeid who had informed the Khalīfa of the intended Ashrāf revolt in 1891: *I.R.E.*, 1 (April 1892) called him "*amīr* of the Jaᶜaliyīn." Al-Ḥājj Khālid al-ᶜUmarābī was a Jaᶜalī follower of the Mahdī who became a confidante of the Khalīfa

in Omdurman. For [c]Abd al-Wahhāb Aḥmad, see R. S. O'Fahey, ed. *Arabic Literature of Africa: The Arabic Writings of Eastern Sudanic Africa* (Leiden: 1997), vol. 1, 332.

38. Yūsuf Mikhā'īl, *Memoirs*, 65. Mūsa al-Mubārak al-Ḥasan, *Ta'rīkh Dār Fūr al-siyāsī* (Khartoum: n.d.), 71, 77.

39. Rosignoli, *op.cit.*, 58. *Daftar al-ṣādir* 2/358 and MAHDIA 2/11/1/7. Holt, *Calendar*, 120 n.412. Interview with Abūnā Daniel, 30 October 1986, Khartoum. Bābikr Bedrī, *Memoirs*, 117–118, 131.

40. Muḥammad Maḥjūb Mālik, *al-Muqāwama, passim*. Holt, *Mahdist State*, 254.

41. Shuqayr, *Ta'rīkh*, 3:356–357. *Al-Āthār al-Kāmila*, 2:253.

42. Ibrāhīm Fawzī, *al-Sūdān*, 1:130, 2:225–229. *Al-Āthār al-Kāmila*, 2:176, 2:274, 5:845. Despite the efforts of Muslim jurists to precisely distinguish booty from tribute, it has traditionally been up to the Imām to decide how to exploit these and other revenues: Ibn Juzayy, *Qawānīn al-aḥkām al-shar[c]īyya* (Beirut: 1974), 166ff. The Prophet's defense of his use of alms offerings (*zakāt*) for political purposes as well as the needs of the poor is in Qur'ān 9:60.

43. *Al-Āthār al-Kāmila*, 3:345, 4:684, 4:687, 5:809. See M. I. Abū Salīm, *al-[c]Arḍ fī'l-mahdīyya* (Khartoum: 1970), 35ff. Rosignoli, *op.cit.*, 61.

44. Shuqayr, *Ta'rīkh*, 3:347–51.

45. *Al-Āthār al-Kāmila*, 1:31, 1:121, 2:176, 2:181, 2:197.

46. Abū Salīm, *al-[c]Arḍ*, 61ff. *Al-Āthār al-Kāmila*, 1:95, 3:345.

47. Qaddāl, *al-Siyāsa al-Iqtiṣādīyya*, 61ff. Abū Salīm, *al-[c]Arḍ*, 62-63. *General Report, 1895.*

48. Bābikr Bedrī, *Memoirs*, 158, 219. Abū Salīm, *al-[c]Arḍ*, 46. *Report on the Sudan*, Command Paper, Egypt no.5 (1899), PRO 2HC1 6251. Interviews with [c]Alī Ya[c]qūb al-Khalīfa Ḥilū, 11 November 1986, Khartoum; Abūnā Daniel, 30 October 1986, Khartoum; [c]Alī Ṣiddīq w. Ūru, 9 July 1987, Omdurman; Muḥammad Aḥmad Ismā[c]īl, 7 June 1987, Omdurman. Funj charters authenticated during the Mahdīyya are discussed by Neil McHugh in "Land, lords and holymen in eighteenth century Sinnār," *Bulletin Fontes Hist. Afr.*, 7/8 (1982–1983), 12–32.

49. Abū Shouk and Bjørkelo, *The Public Treasury*, xv–xvi .

50. *Al-Āthār al-Kāmila*, 1:139, 2:197, 4:664, 4:687.

51. Abū Shouk and Bjørkelo, *The Public Treasury*, vii–xi, xvii–xxi.

52. *Dafātir al-ṣādir* 4/11–14, 19. Qaddāl, *al-Siyāsa al-Iqtiṣādīyya*, 168–169, 175ff. Yūsuf Mikhā'īl, *Memoirs*, 169. CAIRINT 1/10/52, 1/14/86. Wingate (Slatin), *Fire and Sword*, 293–294. Rosignoli, *op.cit.*, 35–36. *Al-Āthār al-Kāmila*, 3:441, 4:638, 5:885, 5:977.

53. Wingate (Slatin), *Fire and Sword*, 538–540. Qaddāl, *al-Siyāsa al-Iqtiṣādīyya*, 220–226. There are some disagreements concerning the names of the treasuries and their sources of revenue: Cf. Abū Shouk and Bjørkelo, *The Public Treasury*, xiii–xiv.

54. Qaddāl, *al-Siyāsa al-Iqtiṣādīyya*, 185 ff. Abū Shouk and Bjørkelo, *The Public Treasury*, xix.

55. Bābikr Bedrī, *Memoirs*, 190–191 and *passim*. Rosignoli, *op.cit.*, 36. Abū Shouk and Bjørkelo, *The Public Treasury*, xxvii–xxxiv. Abū Shouk and Bjørkelo add that such government monopolies followed the practice of the early Turco-Egyptian administration, xxix.

56. Abū Shouk and Bjørkelo, *The Public Treasury*, xxxiii–xxxvi.

57. Yūsuf Mikhā'īl, *Memoirs*, 174, 232–236. *Intelligence Report Egypt*, 1 (1892).

58. Qaddāl, *al-Siyāsa al-Iqtiṣādīyya*, 64. *General Report 1895*, 31.

59. Cambridge Ms Or. 234. MAHDIA 1/43/7–8, 2/8/2/115, 2/10/1/97, 4.

60. MAHDIA 2/7/4/42,44, 5/1,2. *Al-Āthār al-Kāmila*, 4:583.

61. Wingate (Slatin), *Fire and Sword*, 400, 519. Rosignoli, *op.cit.*, 60. Bābikr Bedrī, *Memoirs*, 204. Abū Shouk and Bjørkelo, *The Public Treasury*, *passim*. Interview with ᶜAbbās Aḥmad ᶜUmar, 22 July 1987, Abā Island.

Chapter Five

1. Bābikr Bedrī, *Memoirs*, 142. In addition to the written and oral sources already employed, this chapter makes use of an architectural study of Omdurman that draws upon both published works and observation: James Deemer, "Umm Durman during the Mahdiyya," unpublished doctoral dissertation (Harvard University: 1987).

2. Abū Salīm, *Ta'rīkh*, 88ff. Deemer, "Umm Durman," 371–372.

3. The spatial dimension of *farīq* in Sudanese usage is noted by ^{c}Awn al-Sharīf Qāsim, *Qamūs al-lahja al-^{c}ammīyya fī'l-Sūdān* (Cairo: 1985), second edition, 854. ^{c}Alī al-Mahdī stresses the Khalīfa's role in the settlement of these peoples but implies its rarity: *Daftar*, 106, 166 in MAHDIA 8/10/70. Interviews with Zaynab ^{c}Abd al-Qādir Bān Naqā, 28 September 1987, and ^{c}Alī Ṣiddīq wad Ūru, 9 July 1987, Omdurman.

4. Wingate (Slatin), *Fire and Sword*, 494. Interview with ^{c}Alī Ḥasan Jamīl, 6 October 1987, Omdurman, and al-Ṭāhir Muḥammad al-Nayl, 5 June 1987, Omdurman. Abū Salīm, *Ta'rīkh*, 96. Deemer's description (744) of the forced resettlement of the Danāqla as a "general program of ethno-political reorganization" seems a bit exaggerated.

5. W. H. McLean, *The Planning of Khartoum*, 594ff. Interview with Sharīf ^{c}Abd al-Raḥmān al-Nujūmī, 19 June 1987, Omdurman. Reconstruction of the settlement of Omdurman is based on the two E.M.I. maps (1892 and 1896, according to the information supplied by Ohrwalder and Slatin) and interviews with Zaynab ^{c}Abd al-Qādir Bān Naqā, September–October 1987; al-Tijānī ^{c}Amr, 23 December 1986; ^{c}Abbās Aḥmad Muḥammad, September 1987; ^{c}Alī Ṣiddīq wad Ūru, 24 April and 9 July 1987; Sharīf ^{c}Abd al-Raḥmān al-Nujūmī, 18 September 1987; and ^{c}Alī Ḥasan Jamīl, 6 October 1987.

6. See Johnson, "Sudanese military slavery."

7. ^{c}Umar al-Naqar, *The Pilgrimage Tradition in West Africa* (Khartoum: 1972). For the relations of the Mahdīyya with the central Sudanic region, see Lidwien Kapteijns and Jay Spaulding, eds., *After the Millenium: Diplomatic Correspondance from Wadai and Dar Fur on the Eve of the Colonial Conquest*, (East Lansing: 1988). Interview with Muḥammad Yūsuf Ḥamad al-Nīl, 14 October 1987, Omdurman. Ibrāhīm Fawzī, *al-Sūdān*, 1:127–128 and 2:188, 259, 293.

8. Personal communication, Prof. R. S. O'Fahey, 23 June 1992.

9. Interview with ^{c}Abbās Aḥmad Muḥammad, 22 September 1987, Omdurman. For relations between these groups and their identification with ^{c}Uqba the common ancestor, see MacMichael, *Tribes*, 172 ff. On the uses of genealogy, see Ian Cunnison, "Classification by genealogy: a problem of the Baqqāra belt," in Yūsuf Faḍl Ḥasan, ed., *Sudan in Africa* (Khartoum: 1985), second edition, 186–196.

10. Deemer, "Umm Durman," 400, 423.

11. Bābikr Bedrī, *Memoirs*, 52 and *passim*. Interview with ^{c}Alī Ḥasan Jamīl, 6 October 1987, Omdurman.

12. Both names *Masālma* and *Muslimānī* derive from the third form of the Arabic verb *salama*, meaning "to surrender peacefully." *Masālma* seems to have been used more as a group reference, with *Muslimānī* as an individual identifier. Thus the Mahdī wrote of sending a Muslim convert, ^{c}Abdallāhi al-Muslimānī, to Egypt to propagandize the Mahdīyya: *al-Āthār al-Kāmila*, 5:932. Ibrāhīm Fawzī, *al-Sūdān*, 2:193–194. Rosignoli, *op.cit.*, 35. Yūsuf Mikhā'īl, *Memoirs*, 29, 216–218, 247. Interview with Zaynab ^{c}Abd al-Qādir Bān Naqā, 28 September 1987, Omdurman. Interview with Ismā^{c}īl Ṣāliḥ Dā'ūd, 19 October 1987, Omdurman.

13. *Al-Āthār al-Kāmila*, 4:594. Interview with ^{c}Alī Ṣiddīq wad Ūru, 24 April 1987, Omdurman. MAHDIA 2/1/1/6. Ismā^{c}īl b. ^{c}Abd al-Qādir, *Kitāb ṣa^{c}ādat,* 17–18.

14. Yūsuf Mikhā'īl, *Memoirs*, 248. Interview with Ismā^{c}īl Ṣāliḥ Dā'ūd, 19 October 1987, Omdurman.

15. Interviews with al-^{c}Umda Yaḥyā Bābikr Sulaymān al-Makk and Khalīfa Aḥmad Muḥammad wad Badr, 21 October 1987, Fitayḥāb. Rosignoli, *op.cit.*, 42. Richard Lobban, "A genealogical and historical study," 89–109. Wingate (Slatin), *Fire and Sword*, 421, 455.

16. MAHDIA 2/31/4/112, 2/77/259. CAIRINT 3/10/197. Qaddāl, *al-Siyāsa al-Iqtiṣādīyya*, 80–81, 107–132. Bābikr Bedrī, *Memoirs*, 202–203.

17. Wingate (Ohrwalder), *Ten Years' Captivity*, 379–381. Wingate (Slatin), *Fire and Sword*, 558–559. *General Report 1895*, 19. Rehfisch, "A sketch," 43.

18. Cf. The E.M.I. maps in the *General Military Reports* and the Rosignoli map.

19. *I.R.E.* 27, 4. *General Report 1895*, 20. For earlier Ḥaḍāriba traders, see Burckhardt, *Travels*, 285–287 and O'Fahey and Spaulding, *Kingdoms*, 79. Wingate (Ohrwalder), *Ten Years' Captivity*, 398–399. Interviews with ^{c}Alī Ḥasan Jamīl, 6 September 1987, Omdurman; Shaykh Ḥasan al-Nūr Shaykh Birayr, 18 July 1987, Shabasha; and Zaynab ^{c}Abd al-Qādir Bān Naqā, 14 October 1987, Omdurman. Bābikr Bedrī, *Memoirs*, 171, 216 and *passim.*

20. Wingate (Ohrwalder), *Ten Years' Captivity*, 276, 381, 399. MAHDIA 5/1/1. Interviews with al-Ṭayyib Muḥammad al-Ṭayyib, 17 November 1986, Khartoum; ^{c}Abbās Aḥmad Muḥammad, 22 September 1987, Omdurman; al-Tijāni ^{c}Amr, 26 December 1986, Khartoum; Jīlānī Khidr ^{c}Abdallāhi, 27 September 1987, al-Qōz;

and Sharīf ᶜAbd al-Raḥmān al-Nujūmī, 18 September 1987, Omdurman. The gypsy population in Sudan were believed to come from Ḥalab (Aleppo) in Syria.

21. *General Report 1895*, 19. MAHDIA 2/11/2/125–128, 2/78/40. Rosignoli, *op.cit.*, 36. Wingate (Ohrwalder), *Ten Years' Captivity*, 96, 275. Interviews with Zakarīa Ḥannā al-Ṣarrāf, 5 December 1986, Omdurman; Abūnā Daniel, 30 October 1986, Khartoum; al-Tijānī ᶜAmr, 26 December 1986, Khartoum; al-Ṭayyib Muḥammad al-Ṭayyib, 17 November, Khartoum; and Yūsuf Bedrī, 4 November 1986, Omdurman. Bābikr Bedrī mentions an official of the *Bayt al-Māl* wearing a watch: *Memoirs*, 177. Regarding the prepared food stalls, Burckhardt noted in Shendī in 1814 that "It is an established custom not to eat in the market place, nor anywhere in public; it is even considered very indecorous for a person to be seen chewing any food beyond the threshold of his own house": *Travels*, 259.

22. Bābikr Bedrī, *Memoirs*, 158–159, 164, 181, 219. Rosignoli, *op.cit.*, 45. Wingate (Ohrwalder), *Ten Years' Captivity*, 312. Interview with Allegra Basyūnī, 8 December 1986, Khartoum. The foreign trade of the Masālma is reminiscent of Sinnār, where merchants were commissioned to conduct the royal trade in Egypt and Ethiopia: See Krump, *op.cit.*, 179, and Spaulding, "Management of exchange," 37ff.

23. Rosignoli, *op.cit.*, 39–40, 49, 61. Wingate (Ohrwalder), *Ten Years' Captivity*, 380–381, 399. O'Fahey, *State and Society*, 102. Interviews with ᶜAlī Ṣiddīq wad Ūru, 24 April 1987, Omdurman; al-Ṭayyib Muḥammad al-Ṭayyib, 17 November 1986, Khartoum. On the coinage of the Mahdīyya, see H. B. Job, "The coinage of the Mahdi and Khalifa," *S.N.R.*, 3 (1920), 161–196.

24. Yūsuf Mikhā'īl, *Memoirs*, 269. Interviews with Āmina Farajallāh Yūsuf, 1986–1987, Omdurman, and ᶜAbd al-Qādir Sharīf ᶜAbdallāhi, 21 April 1987, Omdurman.

25. Ibrāhīm Fawzī, *Al-Sūdān*, 1:234–237. *Al-Āthār al-Kāmila*, 4:635, 646. ᶜAlī Ṣāliḥ Karrār, *The Ṣūfī Brotherhoods,* 118. R. S. O'Fahey, *Enigmatic Saint: Ahmad Ibn Idris and the Idrisi Tradition* (Evanston: 1990), 73. Spaulding, "The misfortunes of some," 12. Cf. Spaulding, *The Heroic Age*, 238–272. Interviews with Isḥāq Muḥammad al-Khalīfa Sharīf, 1986, Omdurman.

26. P.F.M. McLaughlin, "Economic development and the heritage of slavery in the Sudan Republic," *Africa,* 32 (1962), 355–391. Gabriel Warburg, "Ideological and practical considerations regarding slavery in the Mahdist State and the Anglo-Egyptian Sudan," in Paul Lovejoy, ed., *The Ideology of Slavery* (Beverly Hills:

1981), 245–269. MAHDIA 2/3/2/44. Holt, *Calendar*, 59–60 no.206, 129 no.434. Wingate (Slatin), *Fire and Sword*, 506. Wingate (Ohrwalder), *Ten Years' Captivity*, 386. Rosignoli, *op.cit.*, 42–43, 50. Interviews with Muḥammad Ibrāhīm al-Nūr, 28 September 1987, Omdurman; ᶜAbbās Aḥmad Muḥammad, 22 September 1987, Omdurman; ᶜAlī Ṣiddīq wad Ūru, 24 April 1987, Omdurman; Ibrāhīm Sulaymān Mandīl, 13 April 1987, Omdurman; and Sharīf ᶜAbd al-Raḥmān al-Nujūmī, 18 September 1987, Omdurman.

27. MAHDIA 1/43, 2/3/3/21, 2/4/4/28, 2/8/1/46, 2/8/3/115, 4, 5/1/1. *S.I.R.* 60 and *I.R.E.* 41. Bābikr Bedrī, *Memoirs*, 142–143. Pallme's description of the "negro" soldiers in El Obeid in 1838 is virtually identical to the account of Omdurman given here, including his assertion that they were essentially slaves: *Travels*, 211.

28. Shuqayr, *Ta'rīkh*, 3:372. Yūsuf Mikhā'īl, *Memoirs*, 152. Cf. Holt, *Mahdist State*, 62. Interviews with Isḥāq Muḥammad al-Khalīfa Sharīf and ᶜAlī Yaᶜqūb al-Khalīfa Ḥilū, 1986–1987, Khartoum and Omdurman.

29. INTEL 2/43/359. *S.I.R.* 60, 44–54. CAIRINT 3/10/190. SAD 430/6/4. Shuqayr, *Ta'rīkh* 1:20–22, 3:553. See Robert Kramer, "The capitulation of the Omdurman notables," *Sudanic Africa*, 3 (1992), 41–55. For the "Sudanese" after the battle, see Bābikr Bedrī, *Memoirs*, 240–242. Regarding Anglo-Egyptian rule and British dealings with the former Mahdists, see M. L. Daly, *Empire on the Nile: The Anglo-Egyptian Sudan* (Cambridge: 1986). *S.I.R.* 60, 24 mentions an unpublished appendix to the report entitled "List showing the religious people who exerted powerful influence upon the people of Omdurman at the time of its capture." This is apparently lost, but likely resembles the list of religious leaders appointed to the Board of ᶜUlamā', given in INTEL 2/32/260 (1901). See also the list of Anglo-Egyptian *ᶜulamā'* contained in Mohamed Omer Beshir's *Educational Development in the Sudan* (Oxford: 1969), 47.

30. Interviews with Sharīf ᶜAbd al-Raḥmān al-Nujūmī, 25 September 1987, Omdurman; ᶜAbd al-Qādir Sharīf ᶜAbdallāhi, 21 April 1987, Omdurman; Isḥāq Muḥammad al-Khalīfa Sharīf, 17 October 1986, Omdurman; and Ṣādiq al-Mahdī, 26 September 1987, Khartoum.

31. Interviews with Sharīf ᶜAbd al-Raḥmān al-Nujūmī, 19 June and 11 July 1987, Omdurman. MAHDIA 1/43/9.

32. Interviews with Āmina Farajallāh Yūsuf, 1986–1987, Omdurman; Isḥāq Muḥammad al-Khalīfa Sharīf, 17 October 1986, Omdurman; and ᶜAlī Yaᶜqūb al-

Ḥilū, 11 November 1986, Khartoum. The Mahdī's brother ^{c}Abdallāhi never married, and all three brothers died before the fall of Khartoum. The Mahdī was also predeceased by a sister, Nūr al-Shām, before the Mahdīyya.

33. MAHDIA 1, *passim.* Interview with ^{c}Alī Ya^{c}qūb al-Ḥilū, 11 November 1986, Khartoum. Yūsuf Faḍl Ḥasan writes that "according to one genealogical tradition, there were no less than 23 families and clans which claimed Sharīfī ancestry; more names are also given by other traditions." Cf. *The Arabs and the Sudan* (Edinburgh: 1967), 171. Ashrāf have emerged in local contexts in the Sudan in response to specific conditions. ^{c}Abd al-Ghaffār Muḥammad Aḥmad writes of the Rufā^{c}a al-Hōy's adoption of Sharīfī status as a response to their incorporation of the ^{c}Arakīyīn, who were themselves regarded as Ashrāf: *Shaykhs and Followers* (Khartoum: 1974), 92. For another example of "becoming Ashrāf," see Hofheinz, "Internalising Islam," 1:256–260.

34. Shuqayr, *Ta'rīkh*, 3:608. Slatin likewise calls the *amīr* Karamallāh Kirkusāwī a relative of the Mahdī: Wingate (Slatin), *Fire and Sword*, 413. Interviews with Muḥammad Dā'ūd al-Khalīfa and the families of the Khalīfa and Amīr Ya^{c}qūb, June 1987, Omdurman. MAHDIA 2/77/163.

35. Analysis of the marriages of the Mahdīst elite derives mainly from interviews with their families, including children and grandchildren, from 1986 to1987 in Khartoum and Omdurman. Where published material was consulted, it was submitted to the families for approval of its accuracy. Shuqayr, *Ta'rīkh*, 3:363–364. *I.R.E.* 11 (1893). *S.I.R.* 60 (1898), 66–67, lists 67 women. Wingate (Ohrwalder), *Ten Years' Captivity*, 404–405. The Mahdī's family insists that the Mahdī's wives had been offered divorce before his death so they might remarry, and all but four refused: Interview with Isḥāq Muḥammad al-Khalīfa Sharīf, 13 July 1987, Omdurman. A Sudan Government report of 1909 lists the names of 19 widows who had vowed, "of their own free will," to marry no one else: INTEL 9/2/22. Layish argues that the Mahdī claimed the Prophet's privilege of "exclusivity" (*khuṣūṣiyya*), enabling him to marry over the canonical limit of four wives. The evidence for this turns on the interpretation of a few key phrases, and the claim is at odds with other aspects of the Mahdī's behavior. See Aharon Layish, "The legal methodology."

36. Ibrāhīm Fawzī, *al-Sūdān*, 1:128. Holt, *Mahdist State*, 129. For the moral debate aroused by the Mahdī's marriages, see Norman Daniel, *Islam, Europe and Empire*, 434–445.

37. Wingate (Slatin), *Fire and Sword*, 520–522. *S.I.R.* 60, 67–68. *I.R.E.* 11 (1893).

38. Holt, *Mahdist State*, 136, 200. *I.R.E.* 11 (1893).

39. Bābikr Bedrī, *Memoirs*, 40, 145, 187, 200. For marriage alliances in Sudanic practice, see Lobban, "A genealogical and historical study"; Spaulding, "Misfortunes," 10, "Evolution of the Islamic judiciary," 415; and O'Fahey and Spaulding, *Kingdoms*, 48–49, 161. An example from Darfur is provided by Browne, *Travels,* 296.

40. Zulfō, *Kararī*, 261. Bābikr Bedrī, *Memoirs*, 212. Interview with Sharīf Maḥmūd Ḥasan, 21 July 1987, al-Kawwa. Ohrwalder, *Ten Years' Captivity*, 392, 399.

41. McHugh, *Holy Men*, 190–191.

Chapter Six

1. Bābikr Bedrī, *Memoirs*, 237. G. W. Steevens, *With Kitchener to Khartum* (Edinburgh: 1898), 299–300. F. Maurice, "Omdurman," *The Nineteenth Century,* 44 (Dec.1898), 1048–54. R. W. Felkin, "The Soudan Question," *The Contemporary Review,* 74 (1898), 482–97. Ernest Bennett, "After Omdurman," *The Contemporary Review,* 75 (1899), 18–33. Maj. Gen. W. Gatacre, "After the ᶜAṭbara and Omdurman," *The Contemporary Review,* 75 (1899), 299–304. Lord Cromer, *Report on the Finances, Administration and Condition of Egypt and the Soudan, 1899* (London: 1900), 43. *The Sudan Gazette*, 1 (7 March 1899) and 3 (31 July 1899).

2. Bābikr Bedrī, *Memoirs*, 240–242. Kramer, "The capitulation." J. Kelly Giffen, *The Egyptian Sudan* (New York: 1905), third edition, 49–50, 67. Giffen also observed of Omdurman that "there was no rush for corner lots, for there were no corners. It is only the western mind that works in straight lines and angles. The savage and the Oriental follow curves." (40).

3. O'Fahey and Spaulding, *Kingdoms, passim*. Holt, *Sudan of the Three Niles*, 22, 25. Spaulding, "Precolonial trade," 61 n.90 and "Management of exchange," 37. Griselda al-Tayyib, "An illustrated record." The *taqīyya umm qarnayn* is shown worn by a Mahdist *amīr* in Wingate (Ohrwalder), *Ten Years' Captivity*, 136. The names "Mismār" and "Nayl" that occur in Mahdist circles also suggest a Funj connection.

4. Fr. Giovanni Beltrame in Toniolo and Hill, *The Opening*, 36. Karrār, *The Ṣūfī Brotherhoods*. For the interconnectedness of religious, political and economic complaints in the later Turco-Egyptian period, see Bjørkelo, *Prelude*, 143–146.

5. Bābikr Bedrī, *Memoirs*, 22. O'Fahey and Spaulding, *Kingdoms*, 29. Fr. Giovanni Beltrame in Toniolo and Hill, *The Opening*, 38. Yūsuf Mikhā'īl, *Memoirs*, 25. Rudolf Peters, "Islam and the legitimation of power: the Mahdi revolt in the Sudan," *Zeitschrift der Deutschen Morgenländischen Gesellschaft* (Berlin: 1980), 417. ᶜAlī al-Mahdī, *Daftar* (MAHDIA 8/10/70), 164. Bjørkelo (*Prelude*, 146) regards the Mahdīyya as giving rise to "cross-ethnic nationalist ideas about being 'Sudanese.'"

BIBLIOGRAPHY

Published Primary Sources

Aḥmad Ibrāhīm Abū Shouk and Anders Bjørkelo, eds. and trans. *The Public Treasury of the Muslims: Monthly Budgets of the Mahdist State in the Sudan, 1897* (Leiden: 1996).

Baker, Samuel. *The Albert N'yanza: Great Basin of the Nile* (London: 1866).

Bedrī, Bābikr. *Memoirs*, trans. Y. Bedrī and G. Scott (London: 1969).

Bennett, Ernest. "After Omdurman," *The Contemporary Review*, 75 (1899), 18–33.

Browne, W. G. *Travels in Africa, Egypt and Syria* (London: 1799).

Bruce, James. *Travels and Adventures in Abyssinia*, ed. J. M. Clingan (Edinburgh: 1860).

Burckhardt, John Lewis. *Travels in Nubia*, second edition (London: 1822).

Burleigh, Bennet. *Khartoum Campaign 1898* (London: 1899).

Churi, Joseph. *Sea Nile, the Desert and Nigritia* (London: 1853).

Cromer, Earl. *Report on the Finances, Administration, and Condition of Egypt and the Soudan, 1899* (London: 1900).

———. *Report on the Finances, Administration and Conditions of Egypt and Sudan, 1904* (London: 1905).

Felkin, R. W. "The Soudan Question," *The Contemporary Review*, 74 (1898), 482–497.

Garstin, Sir William. *Report on the Soudan*, Command Paper, Egypt n.5 (London: 1899).

Gatacre, Maj. Gen. W. "After the ᶜAṭbara and Omdurman," *The Contemporary Review*, 75 (1899), 299–304.

Giffen, J. Kelly. *The Egyptian Sudan*, third edition (New York: 1905).

Gordon, Charles G. *The Journals of Major General C .G. Gordon at Khartoum*, ed. A. E. Hake (London: 1885).

Grant, J. A. *Khartoom as I Saw It in 1863*, second edition (Edinburgh: 1885).

Great Britain (War Office). *General Military Report 1890* (London: 1891).

———. *General Military Report on the Egyptian Sudan 1891* (London: 1892).

Great Britain (Foreign Office). *General Report on the Egyptian Soudan 1895* (London: 1895).

Hillelson, S. "David Reubeni, an early visitor to Sennar," *S.N.R.*, 16 (1933), 55–66.

Holt, P. M. *The Sudan of the Three Niles: The Funj Chronicle* (Leiden: 1999).

———, ed. and trans. *Calendar of Correspondence of the Khalifa Abdullahi and Mahmud Ahmad* (Khartoum: 1950 [sic: 1956]).

Ibrāhīm Fawzī, *al-Sūdān bayna yadāy Ghurdūn wa Kitshanir* (Cairo: 1901), two volumes.

Ismāᶜīl b. ᶜAbd al-Qādir. *Kitāb saᶜādat al-mustahdī bi-sīrat al-Imām al-Mahdī*, ed. M. I. Abū Salīm (Beirut: 1982).

Kapteijns, Lidwien, and Jay Spaulding, eds. *After the Millenium: Diplomatic Correspondence from Wadai and Dar Fur on the Eve of the Colonial Conquest*, (East Lansing: 1988).

Krump, Theodor. *Hoher und fruchtbarer palm-baum des heiligen evangelij* (Augsburg: 1710), trans. Jay Spaulding at www.kean.edu/~jspauldi/krump2one.html.

Machell, Percy. "Memoirs of a Soudanese Soldier," *Cornhill Magazine*, 74/n.s.1 (1896).

Maurice, F. "Omdurman," *The Nineteenth Century*, 44 (Dec. 1898), 1048–1054.

Muḥammad Ibrāhīm Abū Salīm, ed. *al-Āthār al-kāmila li'l-Imām al-Mahdī* (Khartoum: 1990–1994), seven volumes.

Muḥammad al-Nūr b. Ḍayfallāh. *Kitāb al-ṭabaqāt fī khuṣūṣ al-awliyā' wa'l-ṣāliḥīn wa'l- ᶜulamā' wa'l-shuᶜarā' fī'l-Sūdān*, ed. Yūsuf Faḍl Ḥasan, third edition (Khartoum: 1985).

Nachtigal, Gustav. *Sahara and Sudan*, trans. A.G.B. Fisher and H. J. Fisher (Berkeley: 1971), volume four: Darfur.

Naᶜūm Shuqayr. *Ta'rīkh al-Sūdān al-qadīm wa'l-ḥadīth wa jughrāfīyatuhu* (Cairo: 1903), three volumes.

Neufeld, Charles. *A Prisoner of the Khaleefa* (London: 1899).

Pallme, Ignatius. *Travels in Kordofan* (London: 1844).

Qurashī Muḥammad Ḥasan. *Qaṣā'id min shuᶜarā' al-mahdīyya* (Khartoum: 1974).

Rosignoli, Fr. Paolo. "Omdurman during the Mahdiya," ed. and trans. F. Rehfisch, *S.N.R.*, 48 (1967), 33–61.

Steevens, G. W. *With Kitchener to Khartum* (Edinburgh: 1898).

Stevens, E. S. *My Sudan Year* (London: 1912).

Taylor, Bayard. *A Journey to Central Africa*, tenth edition (New York: 1856).

Toniolo, Elias and Richard Hill, eds. *The Opening of the Nile Basin* (New York: 1975).

ᶜUthmān ibn Fūdī (Usumān dan Fōdio). *Bayān wujūb al-hijra ᶜala'l-ᶜibād*, ed.

and trans. F. H. El Masri (Khartoum: 1978).
Wingate, F. R. (from Fr. Joseph Ohrwalder). *Ten Years' Captivity in the Mahdi's Camp*, third edition (London: 1892).
——— (from Rudolf C. Slatin). *Fire and Sword in the Sudan*, second edition (London: 1896).

Secondary Works

ᶜAbd al-Ghaffār Muḥammad Aḥmad. *Shaykhs and Followers* (Khartoum: 1974).
ᶜAbd al-Wahhāb Aḥmad ᶜAbd al-Raḥmān. *Ṭūshkī* (Khartoum: 1979).
Adams, William. *Nubia: Corridor to Africa* (Princeton: 1977).
Ahmed Uthman Ibrahim. "Some aspects of the ideology of the Mahdiya," *S.N.R.*, 60 (1979), 28–37.
ᶜAlī Ṣāliḥ Karrār. *The Sufi Brotherhoods in the Sudan* (Evanston: 1992).
Beswick, Stephanie. *Sudan's Blood Memory: The Legacy of War, Ethnicity and Slavery* (Rochester, NY: 2004).
Bjørkelo, Anders. *Prelude to the Mahdiyya: Peasants and Traders in the Shendi Region* (Cambridge: 1989).
Boyd, Jean. *The Caliph's Sister: Nana Asma'u* (London: 1989).
Crawford, O.G.S. *The Fung Kingdom of Sennar* (Gloucester: 1951).
Cunnison, Ian. "Classification by genealogy: a problem of the Baqqāra belt," in Yūsuf Faḍl Ḥasan, ed., *Sudan in Africa*, second edition (Khartoum: 1985), 186–196.
Daly, M. L. *Empire on the Nile: The Anglo-Egyptian Sudan* (Cambridge: 1986).
Daniel, Norman. *Islam, Europe and Empire* (Edinburgh: 1966).
Dekmejian, R. and M. Wyszomirski. "Charismatic leadership in Islam: The Mahdi of the Sudan," *Comparative Studies in Society and History,* 14 (1972), 193–214.
Ewald, Janet. *Soldiers, Traders and Slaves* (Madison: 1990).
Felkin, R. W. "The Soudan Question," *Contemporary Review,* 74 (1898), 482–497.
Hill, Richard. *Egypt in the Sudan* (London: 1959).
Holt, P. M. "Modernization and reaction in the 19th century Sudan," in W. Polk and R. Chambers, eds., *The Beginnings of Modernization in the Middle East* (Chicago: 1968).
———. *The Mahdist State in the Sudan*, second edition (Oxford: 1970).
Ḥusayn Sīd Aḥmad al-Muftī. *Taṭawwur niẓām al-qaḍā' fī'l-mahdīyya* (Khartoum: 1959).

ᶜIsmat Ḥasan Zulfō, *Kararī* (Khartoum: 1973).

Job, H. B. "The coinage of the Mahdi and Khalifa," *S.N.R.*, 3 (1920), 161–196.

Johnson, Douglas. "Sudanese military slavery from the eighteenth to the twentieth century," in Léonie Archer, ed., *Slavery and Other Forms of Unfree Labour* (London: 1988), 142–156.

Kapteijns, Lidwien. "The religious background of the Mahdi," *African Perspectives*, 2 (1976).

———. "Islamic rationales for the changing social roles of women in the western Sudan," in M. W. Daly, ed., *Modernization in the Sudan* (New York: 1985), 57– 72.

Kapteijns, Lidwien, and Jay Spaulding. "Precolonial trade between states in the eastern Sudan, ca. 1700–ca.1900," *African Economic History*, 11 (1982), 29–62.

Kramer, Robert. "The capitulation of the Omdurman notables," *Sudanic Africa*, 3 (1992), 41–55.

Layish, Aharon. "The legal methodology of the Mahdī in the Sudan, 1881–1885," *Sudanic Africa* 8 (1997), 37–66.

Lobban, Richard A. "A genealogical and historical study of the Maḥas of the Three Towns," *S.N.R.*, 61 (1980), 89–109.

MacMichael, H. A. *A History of the Arabs in the Sudan* (Cambridge: 1922), two volumes.

———. *The Tribes of Northern and Central Kordofan* (Cambridge: 1912).

McHugh, Neil. "Land, lords and holy men in eighteenth century Sinnār," *Bulletin Fontes Historiae Africanae*, 7/8 (1982–1983), 12–32.

———. *Holymen of the Blue Nile* (Evanston: 1994).

McLaughlin, P.F.M. "Economic development and the heritage of slavery in the Sudan Republic," *Africa*, 32 (1962), 355–391.

McLean, W. H. *The Planning of Khartoum and Omdurman* (London: 1911).

Mohamed Omer Beshir. *Educational Development in the Sudan* (Oxford: 1969).

Muḥammad ᶜAbd al-Raḥīm. *Nafathāt al-yarāᶜ fī'l-ādab wā'l-ta'rīkh wā'l-ijtimāᶜ* (Khartoum: 1931).

———. *Al-Nidā' fī dafᶜ al-iftirā'* (Cairo: 1953).

Muḥammad Ibrāhīm Abū Salīm. "*Al-Būlīs fī'l-mahdīyya*," *Majallat al-Būlīs* (July 1966).

———. *al-ᶜArḍ fī'l-mahdīyya* (Khartoum: 1970).

———. *Ta'rīkh al-Kharṭūm* (Beirut: 1979).

Muḥammad Maḥjūb Mālik. *al-Muqāwama al-dākhilīyya li-ḥarakat al-Mahdīyya* (Beirut: 1987).

Muḥammad Saᶜīd al-Qaddāl. *al-Sīyāsa al-iqtiṣādīyya li'l-dawla al-Mahdīyya*

(Khartoum: 1986).

Mūsa al-Mubārak al-Ḥasan. *Ta'rīkh Dār Fūr al-siyāsī* (Khartoum: 1970).

O'Fahey, R. S. *State and Society in Dār Fūr* (London: 1980).

———. *Enigmatic Saint: Ahmad Ibn Idris and the Idrisi Tradition* (Evanston: 1990).

———, ed. *Arabic Literature of Africa: The Arabic Writings of Eastern Sudanic Africa* (Leiden: 1997).

O'Fahey, R. S., and J. L. Spaulding. *Kingdoms of the Sudan* (London: 1974).

Peters, Rudolf. "Islam and the legitimation of power: the Mahdi revolt in the Sudan," *Zeitschrift der Deutschen Morgenländischen Gesellschaft* (Berlin: 1980).

Rehfisch, F. "A sketch of the early history of Omdurman," *S.N.R.*, 45 (1964), 35–47.

———. "An Unrecorded Population Count of Omdurman," *S.N.R*,. 46 (1965), 33–39.

El-Sayed el-Bushra. "Towns in the Sudan in the 18th and early 19th centuries," *S.N.R.*, 52 (1971), 63–70.

Spaulding, Jay. "The evolution of the Islamic judiciary in Sinnar," *The International Journal of African Historical Studies,* 10:3 (1977), 408–426.

———. "The misfortunes of some—the advantages of others: land sales by women in Sinnar," in Margaret Jean Hay and Marcia Wright, eds., *African Women and the Law* (Boston: 1982), 3–18.

———. "Slavery, land tenure and social class in the northern Turkish Sudan," *The International Journal of African Historical Studies,* 15:1 (1982), 1–20.

———. "The management of exchange in Sinnār, c.1700," in Leif Manger, ed., *Trade and Traders in the Sudan* (Bergen: 1984), 25–48.

——— "Taxation in Sinnar in about 1700," *Northeast African Studies*, 6:1–2 (1984), 127–46.

———. *The Heroic Age in Sinnār* (East Lansing: 1985).

Spaulding, Jay, and Stephanie Beswick, "Sex, bondage and the market: the emergence of prostitution in northern Sudan," *Journal of the History of Sexuality*, 5:4 (1995), 512–34.

Stevenson, R. C. "Old Khartoum, 1821–1885," *S.N.R.*, 47 (1966), 1–38.

Al-Tijānī ᶜAmr. *Darāwīsh wa firsān* (Khartoum: n.d.).

ᶜUmar ᶜAbd al-Rāziq al-Naqar. *The Pilgrimage Tradition in West Africa* (Khartoum: 1972).

———, ed. *Dirāsāt fī ta'rīkh al-Mahdīyya* (Khartoum: 1981).

Voll, John O. "The Mahdi's Concept and Use of *Hijra*," *Islamic Studies*, 26:1 (1987), 31–42.

Warburg, Gabriel. "Ideological and practical considerations regarding slavery in the Mahdist State and the Anglo-Egyptian Sudan," in Paul Lovejoy, ed., *The Ideology of Slavery* (Beverly Hills: 1981), 245–269.

Yaḥya Muḥammad Ibrāhīm. *Ta'rīkh al-ta^c^līm al-dīnī fī'l-Sūdān* (Beirut: 1987).

Yūsuf Faḍl Ḥasan. *The Arabs and the Sudan* (Edinburgh: 1967).

———, ed. *Sudan in Africa*, second edition (Khartoum: 1985).

Unpublished Theses

Deemer, James. "Umm Durman during the Mahdiyya," doctoral dissertation (Harvard University: 1987).

Hargey, Taj. "The suppression of slavery in the Sudan, 1898–1939," D.Phil. thesis (Oxford: 1981).

Hofheinz, Albrecht. "Internalising Islam: Shaykh Muḥammad Majdhūb, scriptural Islam and local context," doctoral dissertation (University of Bergen: 1996), two volumes.

Muḥammad Sayyid Dā'ūd. "*Al-Ṣirā^c^ baynā awlād al-balad wa awlād al-^c^Arab fī ^c^ahd al- Khalīfa ^c^Abdallāhi, 1885–1898*," M.A. thesis (Khartoum University: 1971).

Ṣāliḥ Muḥammad Nūr. "A critical edition of the memoirs of Yūsuf Mikhā'īl," D.Phil thesis (University of London: 1962).

Soad el-Fatih. "The teachings of Muhammad Ahmad, the Sudanese Mahdi," M.A. thesis (University of London: 1961).

Al-Tayyib, Griselda. "An illustrated record of Sudanese national costumes," M.A. thesis (Khartoum University: 1976).

INDEX

www.ingramcontent.com/pod-product-compliance
Lightning Source LLC
Chambersburg PA
CBHW020702270326
41928CB00005B/227
9781558765160